Women and Prison

Jada Hector

Editor

Women and Prison

 Springer

Editor
Jada Hector
University of Louisiana at Lafayette
Lafayette, LA, USA

ISBN 978-3-030-46171-3   ISBN 978-3-030-46172-0   (eBook)
https://doi.org/10.1007/978-3-030-46172-0

This Springer imprint is published by the registered company Springer Nature Switzerland AG
The registered company address is: Gewerbestrasse 11, 6330 Cham, Switzerland

Contents

Chapter 1
An Overview: What We Know About Incarcerated Women and Girls

Jodi Lane

1.1 An Introduction

One of the most pressing social problems in the USA in the last few decades has been mass incarceration of people who are convicted of breaking the law (Clear & Frost, 2014; Western, 2006). Despite housing around 4% of the world's population, the USA accounts for close to 20% of incarcerated people (U.S. Bureau of the Census, 2019; Walmsley, 2018). By the end of 2009, the number of people incarcerated in the USA had reached an all-time high, including more than 1.6 million Federal and state prison inmates. In recent years this number has begun to wane, but prisons still housed nearly 1.5 million by 2017. Counting all types of incarceration (e.g., juvenile facilities, jails, military institutions), the total population of incarcerated people in the USA stands at over 2.1 million people (Kaeble & Cowhig, 2018). This "grand social experiment" of mass incarceration is unique to the USA and has primarily affected men, especially young black men, but has not left women unscathed (Clear & Frost, 2014, p. 2). The number of women imprisoned in State and Federal prisons in 1980 was just over 12,000, increased by nine times to more than 113,000 by 2009 and stood at more than 111,000 in 2017 (Beck & Gilliard, 1995; Bronson & Carson, 2019; West & Sabol, 2010). Including prison inmates, and over 100,000 women in local jails (Swavola, Riley, & Subramanian, 2016) and various other facilities, there now are more than 200,000 women and girls incarcerated across the USA (Walmsley, 2017), and about 7000 women are serving life sentences (The Sentencing Project, 2019b). While incarceration is a problem throughout the world and has increased by 24% since 2000, this international rate of change approximates the general rate of population increase. In total, there are almost 11 million people incarcerated internationally, including those in the USA (Walmsley, 2018). Of these worldwide, about 714,000 are women and girls. While the USA

J. Lane (✉)
University of Florida, Gainesville, FL, USA
e-mail: jlane@ufl.edu

© Springer Nature Switzerland AG 2020   1
J. Hector (ed.), *Women and Prison*,
https://doi.org/10.1007/978-3-030-46172-0_1

incarcerates the most women and girls, the countries just behind are China, with about half as many, and the Russian Federation, with about a quarter of the US number (Walmsley, 2017, 2018).

Though women and girls constitute a small percentage of incarcerated populations (generally between 10% and 15%), they nevertheless deserve scholarly and policymaker attention (Bronson & Carson, 2019; Ehrmann, Hyland, & Puzzanchera, 2019). First, the imprisonment rate for women and girls, in the USA and internationally, has increased much faster than that for men and boys (The Sentencing Project, 2019a; Walmsley, 2016), in the USA in part due to changes in drug laws that require mandatory incarceration and to changes in law enforcement practices (National Resource Center on Justice Involved Women, 2016). Second, women and girls have unique problems and needs and consequently cannot be well-served by programs designed for men and boys. That is, even if they have similar risk factors for crime and recidivism, these risk factors may operate in different ways based on gender (Belknap & Holsinger, 1998, 2006; Chesney-Lind, 1997). Studies have shown that both staff and clients think that institutionalized women and girls are an "afterthought" and that girls in the system are "invisible" (e.g., Bloom, Owen, Deschenes, & Rosenbaum, 2002a, p. 535). Consequently, if for equity and justice reasons alone, policymakers and practitioners have an obligation to find appropriate ways to serve the needs of women and girls. Even if equity does not provide a convincing argument to those faced with limited resources and an incarcerated population primarily consisting of men and boys, meeting the needs of their incarcerated female population can serve more practical purposes of reducing incarceration and other costs if recidivism and other problems can be reduced (Welsh & Farrington, 2000).

1.2   Who Are Imprisoned Women and Girls?

Before we tackle all the issues related to incarceration, it is important to paint a demographic picture of the women and girls who are locked up. Unfortunately, one cannot talk about incarceration without discussing race and ethnicity, because historically in the USA imprisonment has disproportionately affected communities of color, no matter one's gender. Current times are no different (Roberts, 2004; Tonry, 2009). In 2017, while there were twice as many white women in prison as either African-American or Hispanics, the rate of imprisonment for black women was almost twice the rate of white women and the rate for Hispanic women was also higher than for whites. The same disproportion is evident for girls in residential placement, where African-American girls are housed at three and half times the rate of white girls and Hispanic girls are a third more likely to be there (Bronson & Carson, 2019; The Sentencing Project, 2019a). Globally, women from minority groups are also overrepresented in the prison populations of many countries other than the USA (Prais & Sheahan, 2019).

This overrepresentation of minority groups in carceral institutions cannot be uncoupled from their similar disproportionate residence in areas faced with concentrated disadvantage and crime (see Gaardner & Belknap, 2002; Jargowsky, 2015; Ulmer, Harris, & Steffensmeier, 2012). People in prison, including women in the USA and abroad, are overwhelmingly poor and from disadvantaged neighborhoods and, as detailed later, are struggling with many of the problems that come with that experience (Henriques & Manatu-Rupert, 2001; Western, 2006). As Chesney-Lind and Pasko (2013) argued, many women in the justice system face multiple marginality due to the combination of race and ethnicity, gender, and poverty. The majority of women in US prisons, no matter their race or ethnicity are in their twenties and thirties (Bronson & Carson, 2019), and they often do not have much education (Owen & Bloom, 1995).

Girls and women represent an increasing percentage of those arrested but are less likely than men to be violent. While crime has been decreasing overall in the last few decades, the proportion arrested that are women have increased by 6% since 2008 (Federal Bureau of Investigation, 2018). Interestingly, since 2000, while the incarceration *rate* for white women has increased by about 47%, and for Hispanic women has increased by more than 23%, the rate of incarceration for black women has *declined* more than 30%. According to Mauer (2013) these changes in rates are related to population changes, differential involvement in crime, and shifting policies, including changing police practices, especially related to drug enforcement.

Similarly, in 1980, girls represented less than 20% of juvenile arrests in the USA but by 2017 comprised about 30%. However, imprisoned women and girls are more likely to be institutionalized for drug and property offenses and less likely to be imprisoned for violence than men and boys are (Bronson & Carson, 2019; Ehrmann et al., 2019; The Sentencing Project, 2019a). Still, about 1 in 15 imprisoned women in the USA are serving virtual (at least 50 years) or actual life sentences, and between 2008 and 2016, the number of women imprisoned for violence increased slightly (2%) (The Sentencing Project, 2019b).

1.3 What Do We Know About Their Lives Outside Incarceration?

As noted above, imprisoned women and girls in the USA and abroad disproportionately come from backgrounds of concentrated and cumulative disadvantage (Bloom, Owen, Deschenes, & Rosenbaum, 2002b; Owen, Wells, & Pollock, 2017; Prais & Sheahan, 2019; Western, 2006), and many are struggling with the other problems that can come with economic inequality and structural disadvantage, such as substance abuse, difficult and/or abusive relationships or relationship histories, money concerns, mental and physical health problems, and sometimes participation in illegal activities primarily to support their families (Bloom, Owen, & Pollock, 2017; Henriques & Manatu-Rupert, 2001; Loucks, 2004; McDonald, 2013; Owen &

Bloom, 1995; Taylor, Williams, & Eliason, 2002). Many report troubles with under-employment or unemployment or trouble keeping jobs. Most women in prison also have children, and many women in prison were not living with a partner before incarceration and were the primary caretakers before and will be after prison. Many also get no financial support from the fathers of their children. If the children were not removed by the system, women often have to find someone to care for their children while they are incarcerated (Bloom & Steinhart, 1993; Enos, 2001; Henriques & Manatu-Rupert, 2001; Owen & Bloom, 1995; Van Voorhis, Wright, Salisbury, & Bauman, 2010; Wright, Van Voorhis, Salisbury, & Bauman, 2012).

Family problems are common among incarcerated girls and women, including conflict, lack of communication, parental stress, and having parents who were not able to parent well (Bloom et al., 2002b; Van Voorhis et al., 2010). Physical and sexual trauma in childhood and adulthood, sometimes resulting in severe injuries, is a critical factor in the lives of women and girls who are arrested and wind up in the justice system (Belknap, Holsinger, & Dunn, 1997; Bloom et al., 2002b; Chesney-Lind & Rodriguez, 1983; Gaardner & Belknap, 2002; Garcia & Lane, 2013; Henriques & Manatu-Rupert, 2001; Owen et al., 2017; Schaffner, 2006, 2007), although some studies do not show that women who are abused are more likely to offend (see Van Voorhis et al., 2010 for a summary). Still, some research shows that, similar to findings for males, there is a subset of women who are abused who become chronic offenders (Widom, 2000). Some evidence indicates that the major-ity of incarcerated women meet the diagnostic criteria for serious mental illness, post-traumatic stress disorder, and/or substance use disorder (Lynch, DeHart, Belknap, & Green, 2013). Interestingly, there is indication that the effects of abuse may vary by race. For example, one study found that for black girls it was related to violence, while for white girls it was more often connected to self-harm, such as suicide attempts and self-injury (Holsinger & Holsinger, 2005).

Some women and girls report that their crimes were attempts to stop the abuse, while others acted out as a result of victimization. Many have experienced intimate partner violence and physical, sexual, and emotional abuse as children, and scores of incarcerated women have faced multiple relationship and physical traumas throughout their lives. Some also report that when they were children, adults in their lives provided them with alcohol and/or drugs, sold their bodies for sex, and involved them in theft activities (DeHart, 2008; Wright et al., 2012). Women and girls indi-cate relationship strain as a critical factor leading them into trouble (Garcia & Lane, 2012). There is also some indication that women who are repeatedly incarcerated experience more economic insecurity, substance use, risky sexual behaviors, and victimization experiences than those who have fewer experiences in facilities (Herbst et al., 2016).

Troubled women and girls also struggle with mental health issues more than men and boys, including depression, anxiety, and self-injurious behavior. Women and girls in the system are also often struggling with substance abuse. Some research indicates more of them are struggling with drug dependence compared to men, and recent numbers show that they are more likely to be incarcerated for a drug offense than men are. It is not uncommon for girls and women to have dual diagnoses (e.g., both mental health and substance abuse problems) (Baunach, 1985; Belknap et al., 1997; Bloom et al., 2002b; Bronson & Carson, 2019; Van Voorhis et al., 2010). Girls caught up in the system also often experience trouble in school, including academic failure, truancy, discipline issues, and dropout, as well as peer problems, including friends who are in trouble and use drugs (Bloom et al., 2002b; Gaardner & Belknap, 2002; Garcia & Lane, 2013).

It is not that men and boys do not experience any of these problems that plague incarcerated women and girls, but rather that they often affect women more frequently or differently than they do men (Belknap & Holsinger, 1998; Chesney-Lind, 1997; Wright et al., 2012), which has led many to argue for gender-responsive programming for women and girls (e.g., Bloom et al., 2002a, 2002b; Bloom, Owen, & Covington, 2004; Bloom, Owen, Rosenbaum, & Deschenes, 2003; Chesney-Lind, 1997; Chesney-Lind & Pasko, 2013; Covington, 2003; Garcia & Lane, 2012, 2013; Greene, Peters, and Associates, 1998; Holsinger, 2000; Schaffner, 2006). According to Greene, Peters, and Associates' (1998), executive summary, gender-specific programming refers to "…a comprehensive approach to female delinquency rooted in the experience of girls …It bridges theory-into-practice by combining female adolescent theory with juvenile justice practices." In essence, the goal of gender-specific programming is to concentrate on the specific psychological, social, and developmental needs of women and girls. The problem is that most gender-neutral programs have actually been designed based on the needs of the most prominent group in the system—men and boys (Chesney-Lind & Shelden, 2014; Covington, 2003; Shearer, 2003).

1.4 What Is Incarceration Like for Women and Girls?

While women can report worsening or better mental health during incarceration, depending on their experiences (Harner & Riley, 2013), being locked up is generally a demeaning experience. Women also continue to experience gender, class, and race inequalities inside that exist outside the walls (Owen et al., 2017). Scholars have known for decades that incarceration is a traumatic experience due to the deprivation and degradation inherent in the experience, including loss of freedom, privacy, independence, personal relationships, sexual relationships, and sense of safety (Sykes, 1958; Toch, 1992). The loss of agency, or the ability to make daily decisions for themselves, is a major stressor for people in prison and diminishes their life skills over time. For women, the inability to choose their personal hair and clothing style, including being forced to wear recycled undergarments, are degrading, for example (Irwin & Owen, 2005; Owen et al., 2017).

Both male and female prisoners also still experience other difficult and stark living conditions, such as the subpar housing, verbally abusive or uncaring staff, sometimes physically abusive workers, inadequate food and nutrition, exposure to disease and lack of good medical care and treatment options (Owen et al., 2017; Schaffner, 2006). Irwin and Owen (2005) report, for example, that women's specific diseases, such as breast and uterine cancers, often go undiagnosed and untreated because there is no systematic plan for preventive screening such as mammograms and pap smears. In addition, pregnant women are rarely provided prenatal or postnatal care, and in some low-income countries deliver in unsanitary conditions (United Nations, 2014).

Women also face the possibility of property and personal victimization while inside (Wooldredge & Steiner, 2016). Owen et al. (2017) discuss multiple vulnerabilities that put women inside at risk of exploitation by others, including physical frailty, mental health, language barriers, and seeing oneself as a victim or acting afraid. They discuss the commonness of arguments, gossip, economic exploitation, and sometimes physical violence, including some sexual coercion by fellow inmates, although exploitation tends to be less physically violent than that often seen in men's prisons. They found that some women also experienced inappropriate sexual behavior from staff, ranging from comments, which are common, to rape, which is rare. In many places, even when nude, incarcerated women find it hard to avoid male staff visually violating their privacy, for example (Irwin & Owen, 2005). Lack of privacy in bathrooms can be especially degrading when women are menstruating. Strip searches also are not uncommon (Chesney-Lind & Shelden, 2014). Moreover, dealing with ridiculous rules, many of which are difficult to follow, lead to feelings of anger and injustice, especially when they result in disciplinary infractions. As Owen et al. (2017) argue, "Threats to safety and well-being are embedded in the world of prison" (p. 3). Together, these negative experiences can retraumatize women and girls, for example, serving as triggers for people who are already suffering from post-traumatic stress disorder (PTSD) (Covington, 2003; Owen et al., 2017).

In addition, personal loss of connection, especially to children, can be very traumatic for women, especially because many do not get to see their children while incarcerated. Prisons are often far from women's homes, and families of women prisoners frequently have limited transportation options and financial resources to allow for regular visits (Irwin & Owen, 2005; Mignon & Ransford, 2012). Some have babies in prison and have them removed within a few days (Baunach, 1985), while in some countries children can remain with their mothers for a while, often up to somewhere between 1 year old and 6 years old (United Nations, 2014). The inability to see and connect with children is a significant emotional loss for women and often the most painful part of being inside (United Nations, 2014). Many mothers in prison worry that their children will be taken from them and they will not be able to be together once they are released, and this is especially true in some states where criminal behavior and incarceration can be grounds for terminating parental rights. They also agonize about what is happening to children in their absence, and they worry about reconnecting once they are released (Baunach, 1985; Enos, 2001; Hairston, 2003). Research shows that parental incarceration is related to lower parental attachment and higher risk of criminal involvement, antisocial behavior, psychological problems, as well as lower educational achievement in children (Martin, 2017). When their children are in the foster care system rather than with family, these worries are heightened, especially when women lose track of their children's locations (Baunach, 1985). As Roberts (2012) argued, the prison system and foster care systems together can be especially punitive spaces for mothers, especially black mothers who are disproportionately struggling to navigate both systems.

1.5   What Might We Do to Help Women and Girls?

The goal should be to reduce harm overall, for the public but also for those who are managed in the system (Owen et al., 2017). First, women's basic needs for nutrition, personal hygiene, adequate medical care, personal safety, privacy, etc., must be addressed in ways that provide basic respect for their humanity. While this is true for all prisoners, women's specific needs also must be addressed, such as adequate supplies to manage their menstrual cycle and specific medical testing for their unique health issues, as well as the ability to birth and nurse children in safe, clean, and humane environments (United Nations, 2014).

More broadly, feminist scholars have argued for gender-responsive practices and programming which are specifically designed to meet the unique and multifaceted needs of girls and women (e.g., Bloom et al., 2002a, 2002b, 2003, 2004; Chesney-Lind, 1997; Chesney-Lind & Pasko, 2013; Covington, 2003; Garcia & Lane, 2012, 2013; Greene, Peters, and Associates, 1998; Holsinger, 2000; Schaffner, 2006). Because females involved in the system face struggles in multiple and interconnected areas of their lives, the need is for collaborative, comprehensive, integrated, and targeted approaches to helping them, rather than trying to serve women and girls with multiple and disparate programs (Bloom et al., 2002b; Covington, 2003).

Feminist scholars agree that these efforts need to be therapeutic rather than punitive (e.g., Van Voorhis et al., 2010). Because relationships are critically important to women and girls and many of their troubles are rooted in relationship trauma and strain, it is important that programs and practices address this part of their lives. According to The World Health Organization (2014) addressing the needs of abuse victims through trauma-informed care and cognitive-behavioral treatment has the potential to reduce the serious mental health consequences of relationship traumas. The effort to recognize and respond to trauma is especially important for incarcerated women and girls, because trauma can be worsened by the correctional experience itself. And, addressing women's needs related to their multiple traumas can help ensure that they are more receptive to the cognitive-behavioral treatment (CBT) efforts provided them (Miller & Najavits, 2012). As Mollard and Hudson (2016) argued, providing trauma-informed care can reduce stress levels of both women and staff which can increase security and help improve women's chances of successful reentry.

In addition, it is important to provide programming that allows women to remain connected to their children, because this helps the women but also the children. Options include, for example, nursery programs for newborn babies to stay with their mothers, extended visits, overnight or long term stays, and programs designed to help moms understand child development and improve parenting, as well as reading and letter writing programs, such as those provided by the Children's Literacy

Foundation (Baunach, 1985; Children's Literacy Foundation, 2020). In the USA, some programs also now exist to allow women to live with their preschool age children for extended periods of time. A 2009 report by the Women's Prison Association found that seven states allowed women to keep children with them in prison as did as Rikers Island in New York City. As of 2018, there were eight prison nurseries in the USA, including the oldest one at New York's Bedford Hills Correctional Facility which began in 1901 (Chuck, 2018), although most programs did not open until the late 1990s or early 2000s (Women's Prison Association, 2009). Other US examples include the Residential Parenting Program at the Washington Correctional Center for Women, which allows children to stay with their mothers up to 30 months and the California Community Prisoner Mother Program (CPMP), a substance abuse treatment program that allows nonviolent women to live with children under 6 years of age and works to build parenting skills and improve the likelihood of successful transition to the community (California Department of Corrections and Rehabilitation, 2020; Washington Department of Corrections, 2017). There are also evidence-based programs available, such as Parenting Inside Out (n.d.). (http://www.parentinginsideout.org/) and Strengthening Families tailored for institutional settings (Miller et al., 2014).

Scholars have provided a wide array of suggestions about other specific efforts that might work. For example, Bloom et al. (2002b, p. 52) argued for a continuum of care with graduated sanctions from prevention through aftercare, including school-based, family-focused, healthcare and substance abuse efforts as well as specialized training for justice and school system staff on gender-specific concerns such as "adolescent development, sexual exploitation, awareness of family backgrounds, trust and emotional issues, relationship needs, and strategies and techniques for working with girls and young women." When women in prison were asked what would help girls in the system, they said they wanted many of these things as well. In terms of counseling and treatment programs, they wanted them to focus on sexual abuse, parenting, independent living skills, drug treatment, grief and loss, healthy relationships, self-esteem and empowerment, and transitioning to the community. In terms of system personnel, they wanted more female staff, role models, and mentors, more caring staff, and workers and volunteers that had similar experiences to females in the system (Garcia & Lane, 2010), and girls in the system echoed these needs (Garcia & Lane, 2012). Consequently, Garcia and Lane (2013) argued that it is important to ensure that we hire women to work with women and girls (although Owen et al. (2017) recently found that some thought female staff were worse than males), ensure that the staff are willing and interested in working with this population (which can be perceived by some as more difficult to work with than men and boys), and screen all potential staff for implicit and explicit gender biases.

We know that most women returning to the community from prison are often going back to the community without many skills and to neighborhoods without adequate jobs, housing, and educational opportunities, which means women inside need help transitioning to the community. In some countries, some women cannot even leave the facility unless a "male guardian" will come and get them from prison

(United Nations, 2014). Petersilia (2003), an important reentry scholar who understood the practical limitations of the field, argued that programs and planning to transition to the community should begin as soon as someone begins a stint in incarceration. She suggested that prison administrators need to embrace successful reentry as part of their mission and that it would be prudent to create work, treatment, and education tracks in prison to better meet the variable needs of inmates. Additionally, she suggested that daily life inside should parallel life on the outside as much as possible to encourage responsibility. Moreover, she argued for more use of discretionary parole release but increased monitoring only of those who are high risk for return, so that others are able to live more normal lives on the outside. Subsequently, there have been nationally funded programs designed to improve reentry, and a number of them have shown no real effects (e.g., the Second Chance Act Demonstration Programs) (D'Amico & Kim, 2018) or only modest effects on outcomes, including for women (e.g., Serious and Violent Offender Reentry Initiative (SVORI)) (Lattimore & Visher, 2009). However, as many program evaluators know, often the lack of effects is due to implementation difficulties and not necessarily issues with the goals and objectives of programs (Gendreau, Goggin, & Smith, 1999; Lattimore & Visher, 2009; Petersilia, 1990). To make a real difference for women and girls in the system, I echo the arguments of others that there need to be evidence-based gender-responsive efforts at all levels, from prevention to reentry. These efforts also need to be reflexive, adjusting and responding to evaluation results in efforts to improve, and they must have buy-in from those involved in the implementation to at least encourage adherence to program fidelity.

References

Baunach, P. J. (1985). *Mothers in prison*. New Brunswick, NJ: Transaction Books.

Beck, A. J., & Gilliard, D. K. (1995). *Prisoners in 1994*. Washington, DC: Bureau of Justice Statistics.

Belknap, J., & Holsinger, K. (1998). An overview of delinquent girls: How theory and practice have failed and the need for innovative changes. In R. T. Sapling (Ed.), *Female offenders: Critical perspectives and effective interventions* (pp. 31–64). Gaithersburg, MD: Aspen.

Belknap, J., & Holsinger, K. (2006). The gendered nature of risk factors for delinquency. *Feminist Criminology, 1*(1), 48–71.

Belknap, J., Holsinger, K., & Dunn, M. (1997). Understanding incarcerated girls: The results of a focus group study. *Prison Journal, 77*, 381–404.

Bloom, B., Owen, B., & Covington, S. (2004). Women offenders and the gendered effects of public policy. *Review of Policy Research, 21*(1), 31–48.

Bloom, B., Owen, B., Deschenes, E. P., & Rosenbaum, J. (2002a). Improving juvenile justice for females: A statewide assessment in California. *Crime & Delinquency, 48*(4), 526–552.

Bloom, B., Owen, B., Deschenes, E., & Rosenbaum, J. (2002b). Moving toward justice for female juvenile offenders in the new millennium: Modeling gender-specific policies and programs. *Journal of Contemporary Criminal Justice, 18*, 37–56.

Bloom, B., Owen, B., Rosenbaum, J., & Deschenes, E. P. (2003). Focusing on girls and young women: A gender perspective on female delinquency. *Women & Criminal Justice, 14*, 117–136.

Bloom, B., & Steinhart, D. (1993). *Why punish the children: A reappraisal of the children of incarcerated mothers in America*. San Francisco: National Council on Crime and Delinquency.

Bronson, J., & Carson, E. A. (2019). *Prisoners in 2017*. Washington, DC: Bureau of Justice Statistics.

California Department of Corrections and Rehabilitation. (2020). *Community prisoner mother program*. Retrieved February 11, 2020, from https://www.cdcr.ca.gov/adult-operations/community-prisoner-mother-program/

Chesney-Lind, M. (1997). *The female offender: Girls, women, and crime*. Thousand Oaks, CA: Sage.

Chesney-Lind, M., & Pasko, L. (2013). *The female offender; girls, women, and crime* (3rd ed.). Thousand Oaks, CA: Sage.

Chesney-Lind, M., & Rodriguez, N. (1983). Women under lock and key: A view from the inside. *Prison Journal, 63*, 47–65.

Chesney-Lind, M., & Shelden, R. G. (2014). *Girls, delinquency, and juvenile justice* (4th ed.). Malden, MA: Wiley-Blackwell.

Children's Literacy Foundation. (2020). *Children of prison inmates*. Retrieved February 12, 2020, from https://clifonline.org/literacy-programs/children-of-prison-inmates/

Chuck, E. (2018). *Prison nurseries give incarcerated mothers a chance to raise their babies— behind bars*. Retrieved February 10, 2020, from https://www.nbcnews.com/news/us-news/prison-nurseries-give-incarcerated-mothers-chance-raise-their-babies-behind-n894171

Clear, T. R., & Frost, N. A. (2014). *The punishment imperative: The rise and failure of mass incarceration in America*. New York: New York University Press.

Covington, S. S. (2003). A woman's journey home: Challenges for female offenders. In J. Travis & M. Waul (Eds.), *Prisoners once removed: The impact of incarceration and reentry on children, families and communities* (pp. 67–103). Washington, DC: The Urban Institute Press.

D'Amico, R., & Kim, H. (2018). *Evaluation of seven second chance act adult demonstration programs: Impact findings at 30 months*. Oakland, CA: Social Policy Research Associates. Retrieved February 11, 2020, from https://www.ncjrs.gov/pdffiles1/nij/grants/251702.pdf

DeHart, D. D. (2008). Pathways to prison: Impact of victimization in the lives of incarcerated women. *Violence Against Women, 14*(12), 1362–1381.

Ehrmann, S., Hyland, N., & Puzzanchera, C. (2019). *Girls in the juvenile justice system*. Washington, DC: Office of Juvenile Justice and Delinquency Prevention. Retrieved May 21, 2019, from https://www.ojjdp.gov/pubs/251486.pdf

Enos, S. (2001). *Mothering from the inside: Parenting in a women's prison*. Albany, NY: State University of New York Press.

Federal Bureau of Investigation. (2018). *Table 33. Ten-year arrest trends by sex, 2008–2017*. Uniform Crime Report, Crime in the United States, 2017. Retrieved September 5, 2019, from https://ucr.fbi.gov/crime-in-the-u.s/2017/crime-in-the-u.s.-2017/topic-pages/tables/table-33

Gaardner, E., & Belknap, J. (2002). Tenuous borders: Girls transferred to adult court. *Criminology, 40*(3), 481–517.

Garcia, C. A., & Lane, J. (2013). What a girl wants, what a girl needs: Findings from a gender-specific focus group study. *Crime & Delinquency, 59*(4), 536–561.

Garcia, C. G., & Lane, J. (2010). Looking in the rearview mirror: What incarcerated women think girls need from the system. *Feminist Criminology, 5*(3), 227–243.

Garcia, C. G., & Lane, J. (2012). Dealing with the fall-out: Identifying and addressing the role that relationship strain plays in the lives of girls in the juvenile justice system. *Journal of Criminal Justice, 40*, 259–267.

Gendreau, P., Goggin, C., & Smith, P. (1999). The forgotten issue in correctional treatment: Program implementation. *International Journal of Offender Therapy, 43*(2), 180–187.

Greene, Peters, and Associates. (1998). *Guiding principles for promising female programming: An inventory of best practices*. Washington, DC: Office of Juvenile Justice and Delinquency Prevention. Available at: https://ojjdp.ojp.gov/sites/g/files/xyckuh176/files/pubs/principles/contents.html

Hairston, C. F. (2003). Prisoners and their families: Parenting issues during incarceration. In J. Travis & M. Waul (Eds.), *Prisoners once removed: The impact of incarceration and reentry on children, families and communities* (pp. 259–282). Washington, DC: The Urban Institute Press.

Harner, H. M., & Riley, S. (2013). The impact of incarceration on women's mental health: Responses from women in a maximum-security prison. *Qualitative Health Research, 31*(1), 26–42.

Henriques, Z. W., & Manatu-Rupert, N. (2001). Living on the outside: African American women before, during and after imprisonment. *The Prison Journal, 28*(1), 6–19.

Herbst, J. H., Branscomb-Burgess, O., Gelaude, D. J., Seth, P., Parker, S., & Fogel, C. I. (2016). Risk profiles of women experiencing initial and repeat incarcerations: Implications for prevention programs. *AIDS Education and Prevention, 28*(4), 299–311.

Holsinger, K. (2000). Feminist perspectives on female offending: Examining real girls' lives. *Women & Criminal Justice, 12*(1), 23–51.

Holsinger, K., & Holsinger, A. M. (2005). Differential pathways to violence and self-injurious behavior: African-American and white girls in the juvenile justice system. *Journal of Research in Crime and Delinquency, 42*(2), 211–242.

Irwin, J., & Owen, B. (2005). Harm and the contemporary prison. In A. Liebling & S. Maruna (Eds.), *The effects of imprisonment* (pp. 94–117). Portland, OR: Willan publishing.

Jargowsky, P. (2015). Architecture of segregation: Civil unrest, concentration of poverty, and public policy. *The Century Foundation.* Retrieved from https://tcf.org/content/report/architecture-of-segregation/

Kaeble, D., & Cowhig, M. (2018). *Correctional populations in the United States, 2016.* Washington, DC: Bureau of Justice Statistics. Retrieved May 21, 2019, from https://www.bjs.gov/content/pub/pdf/cpus16.pdf

Lattimore, P. K., & Visher, C. A. (2009). *The multi-site evaluation of SVORI: Summary and synthesis.* Research Triangle Park, NC: Research Triangle Institute International. Retrieved February 11, 2020, from https://www.ncjrs.gov/pdffiles1/nij/grants/230421.pdf

Loucks, N. (2004). Women in prison. In G. McIvor (Ed.), *Women who offend* (pp. 142–158). London: Jessica Kingsley publishers.

Lynch, S. M., DeHart, D. D., Belknap, J., & Green, B. L. (2013). *Women's pathways to jail: Examining mental health, trauma, and substance abuse.* Washington, DC: Bureau of Justice Assistance.

Martin, E. (2017). Hidden consequences: The impact of incarceration on dependent children. *NIJ Journal, 278*, 1–7. Retrieved February 3, 2020, from https://www.ncjrs.gov/pdffiles1/nij/250349.pdf

Mauer, M. (2013). *The changing racial dynamics of women's incarceration.* Washington, DC: The Sentencing Project. Retrieved from https://www.sentencingproject.org/publications/the-changing-racial-dynamics-of-womens-incarceration/

McDonald, M. (2013). Women prisoners, mental health, violence and abuse. *International Journal of Law and Psychiatry, 36*, 293–303.

Mignon, S. I., & Ransford, P. (2012). Mothers in prison: Maintaining connections with children. *Social Work in Public Health, 27*(1–2), 69–88.

Miller, A. L., Weston, L. E., Perryman, J., Horwitz, T., Franzen, S., & Cochran, S. (2014). Parenting while incarcerated: Tailoring the Strengthening Families Program for use with jailed mothers. *Children and Youth Services Review, 44*, 163–170.

Miller, N. A., & Najavits, L. M. (2012). Creating trauma-informed correctional care: A balance of goals and environment. *European Journal of Psychotraumatology, 3*, 1–8.

Mollard, E., & Hudson, D. B. (2016). Nurse-led trauma-informed correctional care for women. *Perspectives in Psychiatric Care, 52*, 224–230.

National Resource Center for Justice Involved Women. (2016). *Fact sheet on justice involved women 2016.* Retrieved May 30, 2019, from https://cjinvolvedwomen.org/wp-content/uploads/2016/06/Fact-Sheet.pdf

Owen, B., & Bloom, B. (1995). Profiling women prisoners: Findings from national surveys and a California sample. *The Prison Journal, 75*(2), 165–185.

Owen, B., Wells, J., & Pollock, J. (2017). *In search of safety: Confronting inequality in women's imprisonment*. Oakland, CA: University of California Press.

Parenting Inside Out. (n.d.). Retrieved February 20, 2020, from http://www.parentinginsideout.org/

Petersilia, J. (1990). Conditions that permit intensive supervision programs to survive. *Crime & Delinquency, 36*(1), 126–145.

Petersilia, J. (2003). *When prisoners come home: Parole and prisoner reentry*. New York: Oxford University Press.

Prais, V., & Sheahan, F. (2019). *Global prison trends, 2019*. London: Penal Reform International and Thailand Institute of Justice. Retrieved September 4, 2019, from https://cdn.penalreform. org/wp-content/uploads/2019/05/PRI-Global-prison-trends-report-2019_WEB.pdf

Roberts, D. E. (2004). The social and moral cost of mass incarceration in African American communities. *Stanford Law Review, 56*(5), 1271–1306.

Roberts, D. E. (2012). Prison, foster care, and the systemic punishment of black mothers. *UCLA Law Review, 59*, 1474–1500.

Schaffner, L. (2006). *Girls in trouble with the law*. New Brunswick, NJ: Rutgers University Press.

Schaffner, L. (2007). Violence against girls provokes girls' violence. *Violence Against Women, 13*(12), 1229–1248.

Shearer, R. A. (2003). Identifying the special needs of female offenders. *Federal Probation, 67*, 46–51.

Swavola, E., Riley, K., & Subramanian, R. (2016). *Overlooked: Women and jail in an era of reform*. New York: Vera Institute of Justice. Retrieved May 22, 2019, from http://www.safetyandjusti-cechallenge.org/wp-content/uploads/2016/08/overlooked-women-in-jails-report-web.pdf

Sykes, G. M. (1958). *The Society of Captives: A study of a maximum security prison*. Princeton, NJ: Princeton University Press.

Taylor, J. Y., Williams, R., & Eliason, M. J. (2002). Invisible, underserved, and diverse: The health of women in prison. *International Journal of Global Health, 2*(1), 28–42.

The Sentencing Project. (2019a). *Fact sheet: Incarcerated women and girls*. Washington, DC: The Sentencing Project. Retrieved September 3, 2019, from https://www.sentencingproject. org/publications/incarcerated-women-and-girls/

The Sentencing Project. (2019b). *Women and girls serving life sentences*. Washington, DC: The Sentencing Project. Retrieved September 3, 2019, from https://www.sentencingproject.org/publications/women-girls-serving-life-sentences/

Toch, H. (1992). *Living in prison: The ecology of survival*. Washington, DC: American Psychological Association.

Tonry, M. (2009). Explanations of American punishment policies. *Punishment & Society, 11*(3), 377–394.

U.S. Bureau of the Census. (2019). *U.S. and world population clock*. Retrieved May 21, 2019, from https://www.census.gov/popclock/

Ulmer, J. T., Harris, C. T., & Steffensmeier, D. (2012). Racial and ethnic disparities in structural disadvantage and crime: White, Black, and Hispanic comparisons. *Social Science Quarterly, 93*(3), 799–819.

United Nations. (2014). *Handbook on women and imprisonment* (2nd ed.). New York: United Nations.

Van Voorhis, P., Wright, E. M., Salisbury, E., & Bauman, A. (2010). Women's risk factors and their contributions to existing risk/needs assessment: The current status of a gender-responsive supplement. *Criminal Justice and Behavior, 37*(3), 261–288.

Walmsley, R. (2016). *World prison population list* (11th ed.). London: Institute for Criminal Policy Research. Retrieved May 20, 2019, from http://www.prisonstudies.org/sites/default/files/resources/downloads/world_prison_population_list_11th_edition_0.pdf

Walmsley, R. (2017). *World female imprisonment list* (4th ed.). London: Institute for Criminal Policy Research. Retrieved May 20, 2019, from http://www.prisonstudies.org/sites/default/files/resources/downloads/world_female_prison_4th_edn_v4_web.pdf

Walmsley, R. (2018). *World prison population list* (12th ed.). London: Institute for Criminal Policy Research. Retrieved May 20, 2019, from http://www.prisonstudies.org/sites/default/files/resources/downloads/wppl_12.pdf

Washington Department of Corrections. (2017, May). Residential parenting program: Teaching parenting, infant-child bonding to incarcerated mothers. *Fact Sheet*. Retrieved February 10, 2020, from https://doc.wa.gov/docs/publications/fact-sheets/400-FS003.pdf

Welsh, B. C., & Farrington, D. P. (2000). Correctional intervention programs and cost-benefit analysis. *Criminal Justice and Behavior, 27*(1), 115–133.

West, H. C., & Sabol, W. J. (2010). *Prisoners in 2009*. Washington, DC: Bureau of Justice Statistics.

Western, B. (2006). *Punishment and inequality in America*. New York: Russell Sage.

Widom, C. S. (2000). Childhood victimization and the derailment of girls and women to the criminal justice system. In *Research on women and girls in the justice system: Plenary papers of the 1999 conference on criminal justice research and evaluation—Enhancing policy and practice through research* (Vol. 3, pp. 27–36). Washington, DC: National Institute of Justice.

Women's Prison Association. (2009). *Mothers, infants and imprisonment: A national look at prison nurseries and community-based alternatives*. New York: Women's Prison Association. Retrieved February 10, 2020, from http://www.wpaonline.org/wpaassets/Mothers_Infants_and_Imprisonment_2009.pdf

Wooldredge, J., & Steiner, B. (2016). Assessing the need for gender-specific explanations of prisoner victimization. *Justice Quarterly, 33*(2), 209–238.

World Health Organization. (2014). *Global status report on violence prevention*. Geneva: World Health Organization. Retrieved February 10, 2020, from https://www.who.int/violence_injury_prevention/publications/violence/en/

Wright, E. M., Van Voorhis, P., Salisbury, E. J., & Bauman, A. (2012). Gender-responsive lessons learned and policy implications for women in prison: A review. *Criminal Justice and Behavior, 39*(12), 1612–1632.

Chapter 2
Pop Culture and Perception

Karen Smith

2.1 Introduction

True crime is not a new fad. It has been around since newsboys shouted "Extra! Extra!" from street corners, plying passersby with the latest, salacious headlines about a murder, mobsters or some other attention-grabbing story. Sir Arthur Conan Doyle's fictional character Sherlock Holmes became a household name in the late 1800s and his stories continue to fascinate laypersons with an interest in criminal investigations and over a century later, still serves as inspiration to practitioners well-heeled in the arena of criminal casework. In the early twentieth century, dime store books and "nickel weeklies" such as Secret Service and American Detective Series captured the imaginations of the public and began a spin on criminal activity that placed the reader into the story, allowing them an insider's view of fictional heroic detectives from the comfort of their living room.

Two decades later, the golden age of radio ushered in a new and almost glamorous twist to crime reporting. Programs such as "Suspense!", startled millions of listeners with weekly fictional thrillers, using a star-studded cast including Orson Welles, Lucille Ball, Judy Garland, and Kirk Douglas. Imagine a new weekly television series that recreates current headlines like the Casey Anthony, Chris Watts, and Aaron Hernandez murder trials or the attempted murder of Payton Leutner and the Slenderman saga, starring today's luminaries like Emilia Clarke, Idris Elba, Jennifer Lawrence, Keanu Reeves, and Eddie Redmayne. Who could resist tuning in?

Television was still in its infancy during the late 1940s and early 1950s and most people still tuned in to their living room Wurlitzer™ radio for the latest and greatest news. During the summer hiatus of radio's Suspense! in 1950, another program took its place that would change the way the media covered crime stories forever. Titled "Somebody Knows" which aired on CBS radio, this program flipped the script from

K. Smith (✉)
University of Florida, Los Angeles, CA, USA

© Springer Nature Switzerland AG 2020   15
J. Hector (ed.), *Women and Prison*,
https://doi.org/10.1007/978-3-030-46172-0_2

fictional situations to real news headlines that had already captured the nation's attention. In a smoky voice, the broadcast announcer opened the show with these words:

> You out there. You, who think you have committed the perfect crime…that there are no clues, no witnesses… listen. Somebody knows.

With the hopes of reaching listeners who may hold valid information leading to an arrest, or even the possibility of speaking directly to the perpetrator over the airwaves, CBS Radio producers offered a $5000.00 reward (about $50,000 today) for information that lead to solving the case. It was the first incarnation of America's Most Wanted, which began airing over 30 years later. Case in point, in January of 1947, the horrendous murder of Elizabeth Short, also known in popular culture as The Black Dahlia, overtook the nation's newspaper headlines for months on-end and became the focus of two back-to-back episodes of Somebody Knows that exploded over the airwaves. Millions were riveted by the salacious details and followed the broadcast that included sound effects, police radios, and 911 calls. It was the very first true crime podcast! The suspect was certainly following the newspaper headlines because what he did next shocked everyone, including the detectives.

Straight out of a Hollywood drama, the murder suspect mailed a letter along with an envelope filled with Elizabeth Short's personal belongings directly to editor James H. Richardson of *The Los Angeles Examiner* newspaper. Following leads, Examiner reporters set out on a quest to find Elizabeth's suitcase and trunk, which had been misplaced on her journey to Los Angeles. The suitcase and trunk were alleged to contain photographs, letters, and other personal effects that might break the case wide open. When they were found by the hungry reporters about a week after her murder, *Examiner* editor Richardson called lead homicide detective Captain Jack Donohoe to make a bargain. Richardson would tell Donohoe where the trunk and suitcase were located in exchange for an exclusive on the contents. Donohoe had no choice but to acquiesce to Richardson's demand and Richardson got his photographs and exclusive story for the following morning's newspaper (Richardson, 1954).

The Black Dahlia case is just one example of how the media can end-run an investigation and influence viewers and readers into a subjective whirlwind of speculation, and that was 70 years ago. Today, the internet serves as the go-to source for most individuals to find up-to-the-minute news on breaking stories, the latest updates and conjecture by subject-matter experts and man-on-the-street sound bites. A recent Pew Research poll (Perrin & Anderson, 2019) found that more than half (55%) of adults in the USA get their news from social media sites rather than television news or other sources. Go to any coffee shop and look around. Everyone has their faces buried in their phone, looking up information, reading news feeds, posting selfies, finding out what their ex is doing, and checking the number of "likes" on their latest post. Add satellite radio, podcasts, Twitter©, Facebook©, Instagram©, YouTube©, and other social media platforms to this instant gratification inferno and it is no wonder people become overwhelmed with skewed information. Our drive to work or school can now be filled with "true crime" podcasts instead of music, enough to binge through the maddening traffic on the L.A. 405 freeway or I-495 loop in Washington, D.C. There is no end to the amount of crime-related media one can ingest. In her book Prison Life in Popular Culture, Dawn K. Cecil observes, "One could live off of a diet of crime-related media. While engrossed in these images, some viewers become armchair criminologists; by ingesting all of the information fed via the mass media, they become "experts" on the inner workings of the criminal justice system and the causes of criminal behavior" (p. 2).

The true crime genre does not stop there. New additions, such as multi-day live conferences at huge venues across the nation harken to people who live and breathe criminal behavior and want answers to questions about why crimes occur and what they, as "armchair detectives," can do about it. The largest of these, called Crime Con™, has presented numerous case studies and other forensic and investigative content to thousands of attendees from across the world. Presenters have included famous attorneys, forensic professionals, Crime Scene Investigators (CSIs), crime victims, family members, television journalists, and subject-matter experts. It is a new forum that allows people from all walks of life to mingle with those "in-the-know" and get the inside scoop on some of the nation's most harrowing criminal acts. Crime Con's latest iteration, called CrowdSolve, brought 300 lay attendees from as far away as Australia and Holland to Seattle, Washington for a 3-day intensive study of two cold case homicides with the hope of bringing new evidence to light for the investigators. True crime fascination has now crossed the Rubicon into actual casework.

This multi-media onslaught is just the tip of the iceberg. Television networks still hold the brass ring when it comes to availability of true crime content and binge-watching has become the new norm. "Netflix™ and chill" is a phrase that has been coined with underlying sexual innuendo, but it has also taken on a literal meaning. On Friday and Saturday nights in America, more and more people are choosing to stay home, switch on the cable box and tune in to their guilty pleasure of true crime and takeout. In 2009, television viewing peaked in the American household, with an average of almost 9 h a day. Even with the advent of all of the clickbait available on the internet, people are still devouring almost 8 h of television every 24 h (Madrigal, 2018), a concept that is difficult to fathom in today's hustle and bustle world. Simply flipping through the number of available cable channels and true crime content is enough to make a person's head spin. A few of these streaming documentary programs have taken on a life of their own and actually made headway into the original investigations: Making a Murderer, The Keepers, Abducted in Plain Sight, The Central Park Five, The Staircase, Amanda Knox; the list goes on and on and on. Blog sites dedicated to these crimes have thousands of contributors ranging from retired detectives to librarians, all bent on bringing new ideas, evidence and in some cases, conspiracy theories, forward to solve the case. In an example of how true crime programming can spin off into new entertainment, look no further than the arrest of alleged Golden State Killer, Joseph James DeAngelo. Retired detective Paul Holes worked for over 20 years on the case files and finally cracked DeAngelo as the apparent killer through ancestral DNA links. As a result, Detective Holes has now inked a deal to star in his own television program which will highlight other true crime cases. Combine all of these programs with scripted series dramas and dramedies depicting prison life that have become nouveau such as Orange is the New Black, Wentworth, Bad Girls, Lockup, 60 Days In, and Girls Incarcerated, and the public's view of women in prison can morph into a popular culture meme rather than reality. Where is the line between true crime, prison life, and dramatic spin?

Do we really buy into this dramedy-fantasy of women in prison? Do these shows authentically portray any facts about the real prison system? How do we remain objective in the face of all of this sensationalism and how does this influx of Hollywood drama influence our perception about imprisonment?

2.2   Prison Life in the Media

The USA leads the world in rates of incarceration. According to the Bureau of Justice Statistics, nearly 2.2 million men and women are imprisoned, meaning out of every 100,000 people, about 650 are incarcerated (BJS, 2018). This statistic supersedes the prison populations of Russia, China, India, and the Philippines. Women comprise about 8% of the total population (BJS, 2016) and this creates a wide swath for true crime programming as well as dramatic scripts to showcase different representations of female incarceration, which in turn can influence the general public perception. The tableaus created by television showrunners and producers has effectively distanced any social translation between prison realities and entertainment, and instead has generated a softened and often overblown dichotomy between the two. As pointed out by Dawn K. Cecil, "Another aspect is spectacle, and nothing describes modern popular prison imagery more appropriately" (p. 182).

What is this spectacle of which Cecil speaks? What is the reality of women in prison versus what has been portrayed in shows such as Orange Is The New Black and Wentworth? To break those specifics down would take a dissertation-length, data-driven sociological study, however, we can scratch the surface and begin to understand some of the breaks between authenticity and drama within this chapter, first by dissecting these popular culture dramas and dramadies.

First, ask yourself how these dramatic prison life shows are designed to make you, the viewer, feel. Empathetic? Disgusted? Fearful? It is not by accident that show creators frame each plot as a way to capture the viewer's emotions. The protagonist, the main character, is scripted to bring the audience inside their world, to experience their view of prison. Combine that exclusive view with stereotypically cruel guards, empathetic counselors, inmate foes, racial divides, drug abuse, the fight for justice within the court system and within the prison walls and the formula writes itself—and it is a formula. Nothing in television or film is done without using one. Scripted series writers follow a carefully plotted outline that is used for every episode along new and differing storylines. The next time you watch an episode of any of the Law and Order ™ series genres, watch carefully to see the way each one follows its formula for success. The first half is based on a criminal investigation and apprehension of a suspect. The second half encompasses the district attorney's office and adjudication of the individual, an almost perfect depiction of criminal activity as an individual choice and Beccaria and Bentham's deterrence theory in practice. We are shown the consequences of crime week-to-week and left to believe that incarceration is the correct remedy, which is in line with the majority of the population's convictions. "Viewers will enjoy a show only when the idea of justice matches up with their own moral beliefs" (Cecil, 2015, p. 51). Many of the dénouements finish in the courtroom at the time of sentencing with the Judge banging a gavel and leaves viewers to assume that the perpetrator will end up in prison, providing a type of fictional catharsis. "He/She got what they deserved" is the universal lesson, and it works. Law and Order SVU™ is now into its twenty-first season, breaking the record for longest-running scripted drama. The fail-safe use of these script formulas is nothing new, but when viewers are fed a continual diet of pre-ordained beginnings, middles, and ends, how does that portray anything remotely close to an objective view of the criminal justice system and incarceration? As Tim Dant states in his book, Television and the Moral Imaginary: Society Through the Small Screen, "Television does not socialize its viewers into the changing moral order through instruction but through showing new possibilities and engaging attention and interest" (p. 144). There is no doubt that these shows have captured our interest. The question remains, how have they slanted our views? Let us take a look at two of the most popular exclusively prison-based shows as examples.

2.2.1 Oz

In pop culture dramas, characters are often one-dimensional and incarcerated because they are simply beyond redemption. Viewers are not given any backstory or explanation regarding why they were imprisoned in the first place, giving way to immediate dismissal of any empathy or understanding about individual circumstances that led to a "life of crime." Viewers are not interested in excuses. We want justice, whether that is from imprisonment or from "street justice" and a manhunt. For example, in the HBO series *Oz* (1997–2003), prison life is shown as a series of violent deadly fights, inter-inmate battles over territory and the drug trade, crooked guards on the take and very little, if any, possibility of redemption or rehabilitation for anyone involved. No backstories are provided, giving the audience no platform for context about why these men ended up in prison in the first place. The public's interest lies in their fate, not in the reasons or excuses for their criminal behavior that landed them in the notorious "Emerald City." As Brian Jarvis (2006) summarizes, prison life is mostly about passing the time and assuaging boredom, which is not very compelling for viewership. The violent scenes in every episode led many people to believe that the depiction of "Emerald City" prison life in the fictional *Oz* was reality. "As a public pedagogy the main lesson taught in Emerald City was fear" (Jarvis, 2006). Historically, prison dramas are largely based on the male experience and the use of violence for their main plotlines. The depiction of women's prisons tend to lead with sexuality first, violence second (Cecil, 2015).

2.2.2 *Orange Is the New Black*

Fast-forward 10 years to the Netflix™ hit Orange Is The New Black (2013–2019), loosely based on the true story of Piper Kerman from her book, Orange Is The New Black: My Year in a Women's Prison (Kerman, 2010). Viewers are taken into Piper's world both on the outside and inside the prison walls. We come to understand her mistakes, fallibilities, and subsequent choices as well as changes to her personality as the result of incarceration. Each character in the series, as we get to know them, is given a complete backstory and foundation as to why they ended up at "Litchfield," a fictitious prison complex. Inside this women's prison, viewers are taken along Piper's journey and the adjacent character arcs, which is again filled with stereotypes of the prison industrial complex, including corruption, misogyny, racial and ethnic cliques, drug addiction, mental illness, LGBTQ subtext, scapegoating, and self-serving alliances. While some of the stories are mundane, such as a fight between two characters over an ice cream sandwich, others involve a full bore takeover of the prison by the inmates after the murder of "Poussey," a character well on her way to rehabilitation and release. As a result of the riot, one of the main characters, "Taystee," faces a false murder charge for the death of a prison guard. These storylines are compelling and weave the inmate's humdrum everyday commissary problems into the very serious issues of sexual assault and white-collar corruption. Believe it or not, these plots are nothing new or innovative.

For some perspective, let us go back in time to 1950 and the prison film *Caged*, directed by John Cromwell and starring Eleanor Parker and Agnes Moorehead. Dubbed one of many "babes-behind-bars" films of the era, Caged follows the story of Marie Allen, a naïve widow who is sent to prison for accessory to robbery and is forever changed when she faces sadistic guards and other hardened female inmates. Let us now embed the previously discussed Hollywood formula and interweave Caged from 1950 into the present *Orange is the New Black* in Table 2.1.

There are many more similarities, but the idea is apparent and while the stories, dialog, and weaving of characters have become much more complex over the years, the basic ideas remain the same. This shows nearly seven decades of the formula at work, with the same plot lines told with different characters. "Even if viewers have not realized it, they have been seeing similar representations of women in prison repeated time and again on television" (Cecil, 2015, p. 128). The one change that *Orange is the New Black* did create for the viewer is the idea that inmates have the capacity to change, to rehabilitate, and to have introspection into the reasons why they ended up in prison in the first place, even if the catalyst was out of their direct control and especially if they are simply just flawed human beings who got caught. The show also brings to light some of the negative issues inherent in the criminal justice system, by showcasing false allegations and adjudications based on bad evidence and perjured testimony. The Hollywood formula is evolving, but still relies on many of the same tried and true methods to garner viewership.

Table 2.1 Comparison of two eras of prison dramas

Character/plot	Caged	OITNB
Protagonist	Marie Allen, charged with accessory to robbery	Piper Chapman, charged with drug trafficking
Antagonist authority figure	Matron Evelyn Harper, who beats and chides Marie, shaves her head	Guard George "Pornstache" Mendez, who sexually and physically assaults the inmates
Sympathetic authority figure	Superintendent Ruth Benton, who assigns Marie to light duty because Marie is pregnant	Counselor Sam Healy, who has issues of his own, but acts in a fair manner most of the time
Plot Line 1	An inmate is berated and pushed to the breaking point and commits suicide	"Pennsatucky" overdoses after thinking she did not pass the GED, when in reality she did
Plot Line 2	Marie ends up in solitary confinement and loses herself	"Red" ends up in the Secure Housing Unit and returns with dementia
Plot Line 3	Matron Harper is stabbed to death with a fork by the inmates	Sadistic guard Piscatella is shot to death
Plot Line 4	A riot breaks out	A riot breaks out
Plot Line 5	Marie is granted parole, but leaves a hardened, cynical woman and joins a gang	Parolees go right back to their previous life of crime after being left with no choices

2.3   Celebrities in Prison

Nothing generates tabloid fodder more quickly than a celebrity being caught for committing a crime. The public tends to forget that people in the spotlight are still people, flaws and all. When their mugshots are published on the internet and on the front pages of supermarket checkout magazines, the sweeping condemnation is sometimes hypocritical, sometimes deserved depending on the type of criminal activity alleged to have been committed. The charges and allegations vary between DUI and minor drug offenses to sexual assault (Harvey Weinstein), white-collar crime, and child trafficking (Jeffrey Epstein). The sexual assault charges by over 100 women against Harvey Weinstein have been adjudicated in court and Weinstein received 23 years in prison. Many of the women on the long list of Weinstein's victims include A-List celebrities. The dozens of reported victims of Jeffrey Epstein, who were minors at the time of the assaults, will never have their day in criminal court since he died in prison in July of 2019. These two cases were a catalyst for the *#MeToo* movement that empowered many victims of sexual assault and harassment to come forward, even after years of silence.

Some will argue that if you choose the spotlight, it shines brightly and with that money and adulation comes the additional responsibility to act in a manner that will always be respectable and above-board. On the flipside of that coin, minor offenses do happen because humans are fallible and life is not always perfect, even for our favorite movie, music, and television stars.

Table 2.2 Celebrity arrests and results

Celebrity	Charge	Plea	Sentence	Fine	Date
Bruno Mars	Possession of cocaine	Guilty	200 h of community service, 8 h of counseling	$2000.00	2010
Justin Bieber	DUI, resisting an officer	Guilty to lesser misdemeanor	Anger management	$50,000.00 to a charitable cause and court fines	2014
Khloe Kardashian	Probation violation from DUI	–	30 days in jail, served 3 h due to overcrowding	–	2008
Blac Chyna	DUI, drug possession	Charges dropped	Counseling	–	2016
John Stamos	DUI	Guilty	3 years of probation, counseling	–	2015
Michael Phelps	DUI	Guilty	Suspended sentence, probation	–	2014
Shia LaBoeuf	Public drunkenness, disorderly conduct	Guilty	Probation, counseling, anger management, 100 h of community service	$2680.00	2016
Michelle Rodriguez	DUI	Guilty	5 days in jail, probation	$500.00	2005
	Violation of probation	Guilty	180 days in jail, served only 18 days due to overcrowding		2007
Wiz Khalifa	Marijuana possession	Guilty	–	$500.00	2014

In the past 15 years alone, there have been hundreds of stories about celebs-behind-bars and some of those stories highlight how the criminal justice system may treat some of them differently than the average citizen. Table 2.2 lists just a few of the more minor offenses, with the charges and resulting adjudication.

Most celebrities can afford to hire high-powered attorneys to argue their cases and get sentences reduced or even dismissed, depending on the charges and evidence. The most famous of these cases is that of O.J. Simpson, who was acquitted in criminal court for the 1994 murders of Nicole Brown and Ronald Goldman after a trial that spanned 11 months and was dubbed "The Trial of the Century." In a twist on the criminal acquittal, the Goldman and Brown families sued in civil court and Simpson was found guilty, with compensatory damages of $8.5 million and punitive damages of $25 million. The verdict by the civil jury was a pointed contradiction to the criminal case and jurors on the civil case made it clear to the media that their verdict was not difficult. "Finding O. J. Simpson liable of the murders and acting with oppression and malice was one of the easiest decisions I have ever had to make," said Juror No. 11 (Ayres, 1997).

The Simpson case is the most widely known and hotly debated celebrity criminal case, but there are plenty of others and many female celebs have found themselves in very hot water because of bad decisions.

2.3.1   Martha Stewart

Martha Stewart, the famed homemaker with a flair for perfection, was indicted in 2003 for securities fraud, obstruction, and making false statements relating to an illegal stock trade. Stewart was found guilty and sentenced to 5 months in prison followed by 5 months of house arrest, 2 years of probation, and a $30,000 fine. She spent her 5 month prison sentence at the Alderson Federal Prison Camp in West Virginia. Reports from inside said that Stewart took her sentence in stride and used her time to become a liaison between the inmates and authorities. She did not ask for special favors and spent her sentence as the other inmates did, eating the same food and following the rules. While there is no doubt that her celebrity status provided her a bit of insulation regarding any negative actions against her by the other prisoners or staff, she did say that the experience was horrible all around:

> It's not a good experience and it doesn't make you stronger. I was a strong person to start with and thank heavens I was. And I can still hold my head up high and know that I'm fine. (NBC, 2017)

Upon her release, she posed for photos wearing a crocheted poncho created for her by one of the inmates. Stewart's career did not take much of a hit and she has reinvented herself in the years since, starring in her own show after partnering with rapper Snoop Dog called *Martha and Snoop's Pot Luck Party Challenge*. It was a network hit. The unlikely pair created on-screen magic and traded jokes about mashed potatoes and the inclusion of a "secret" ingredient in the brownies. Clearly, Stewart bounced right back and even found a way to bring herself into the hearts of millennials.

2.3.2   Winona Ryder

In December 2001, Winona Ryder was arrested for stealing nearly $6000.00 worth of clothing from a Saks Fifth Avenue store in Beverly Hills. Prosecutors stated that Ryder brought a pair of scissors with her into the store and cut the security tags out of numerous items and attempted to walk out of the store without paying when she was stopped by security. As an actress pulling in $6 million per film, the public was left shaking their collective heads and wondering what in the world pushed Ryder to do such a thing. Ryder's excuses flowed in, including the assertion that she was rehearsing for a role and needed to shoplift as research, another that she thought she had left her credit account open with a clerk earlier in the day, and yet another saying her new director told her to do it for her role in the upcoming film. Nobody, including the jury, bought it. After a 6-day trial and 5-h deliberation, they found Ryder guilty of two charges of grand theft and vandalism. Interestingly, one of the jurors was Peter Guber, a Hollywood executive who had previously worked with Ryder on several projects.

She avoided prison and was sentenced to 3 years of probation, 480 h of community service, $3700.00 in fines, counseling for "aberrant behavior," and restitution to Saks Fifth Avenue. Ryder took a 4-year hiatus from Hollywood following the conviction, but has since resurrected her career and most recently starred in the hit program *Stranger Things* and in movies with previous co-stars Christian Slater and Keanu Reeves.

2.3.3 Felicity Huffman and Lori Laughlin

More recent headlines have catapulted both Felicity Huffman and Lori Laughlin into a whirlwind of corruption and white-collar crime that involves bribes, falsifying exam scores, athletic scholarship scams, and multi-level payoffs in order to get their children into exclusive Universities. "The scam required dozens of bribes of test administrators and relied on colleges' different standards for student-athletes. William Rick Singer, the person at the center of the scam, described it more succinctly: "What we do is help the wealthiest families in the U.S. get their kids into school" (Quintana, 2019). Naturally, the public was aghast at the notion that multimillionaires could use their prestige and money to end-run what should have been a fair and balanced system based on hard work and merit, at least for average students who diligently worked their way into the schools in question, which included Stanford University, University of California Los Angeles, Wake Forest University, Georgetown University, and University of Southern California. The charged defendants included not only the actresses, but also other wealthy parents, college coaches, and administrators. In total, 50 defendants were charged in the scam. What did they do?

Huffman, Laughlin, and 30 other parents are alleged to have paid exorbitant sums of money, ranging from $200,000.00 to $6.5 million to a "consultant" in order to guarantee their children's admission. The "consultant" then changed the children's status to "recruited athletes" to boost their standing in the admissions process with the assistance of the University coaches and administrators. Photoshopped images and profiles were created to make the students look like elite high school athletes, but it was all a ruse. The "consultants" also had other people take the SAT and ACT exams for the students seeking enrollment at the behest of and after payment from the parents. It was a very far-reaching and impactful case since so many students and parents with lower incomes legitimately pay for exam tutors and those prospective students spend much time and energy on not only scholastic achievement, but also on community service and extracurricular activities with the hope of being rightfully admitted to these elite schools. For every student admitted under this scam, another who was genuinely deserving of acceptance got shut out, simply due to these parents' ability to pay-for-play.

Felicity Huffman's case has been adjudicated after she pleaded guilty to conspiracy to commit mail fraud and honest services mail fraud by paying a $15,000.00 bribe to cheat on her daughter's SAT scores. She served 11 days out of a 14-day sentence in jail and will be on probation for 1 year, pay a $30,000.00 fine, and serve 250 h of community service. Huffman made a statement about her actions in a letter to the court:

> In my desperation to be a good mother I talked myself into believing that all I was doing was giving my daughter a fair shot, "Huffman said in the three-page letter." I see the irony in that statement now because what I have done is the opposite of fair. I have broken the law, deceived the educational community, betrayed my daughter and failed my family. (Levenson, 2019)

Lori Laughlin's case is more complicated and involves quite a bit more money. The *Full House* (1987–1995) star spent years portraying a character named "Aunt Becky," the go-to for advice and level-headedness on the show. Laughlin's current situation could not be further from her "Aunt Becky" persona. At the time of this writing, her case is still pending adjudication, but the charges have been filed and an indictment has been handed down for fraud, conspiracy, and money laundering. Laughlin and her husband, Mossimo Guiannuli, have pleaded not guilty to all counts. Prosecutors are currently pressing Laughlin and her husband to change that plea to guilty and are considering adding charges to include their two daughters, who were fraudulently accepted to the University of Southern California after a half-million dollar payment to the previously mentioned "consultants." The allegations of bribery and money laundering stem from that payment and falsifying athletic records to show that both daughters were recruits of the USC crew team, even though neither had ever participated in the sport. The bribery charges against Laughlin and her husband carry a maximum sentence of 5 years in prison and a $250,000.00 fine, but when combined with the charges of money laundering and conspiracy, that total increases to a maximum of 40 years in prison if convicted on all of them. In a recent article, an unnamed source said that Laughlin maintains her innocence and continued:

> Does she regret not taking the deal? Of course she does, because it would have been easier," says the source. "But taking the deal would have admitted guilt, and she believes she was duped by unscrupulous people who enriched themselves off of her. It is her position that she was not some sort of criminal mastermind. (Helling, 2019)

Time will tell whether or not prosecutors will get their way and if Laughlin and her husband change their plea from not guilty to guilty.

2.4 Conclusion and *The CSI Effect*

The "Hollywood Machine" certainly has a way of spinning its own version of reality, which can influence the general public's view of certain areas of our criminal justice system. A prime example is the well-cited "CSI Effect" that has plagued forensic science and juries since the television show of the same name gave lay persons incorrect and often outlandish expectations about evidential possibilities in criminal cases. Jurors came to expect the "smoking gun" that is often absent and ignored other compelling evidence that could have resulted in a guilty verdict and worse, ignored exculpatory evidence for those wrongly charged for crimes they did not commit. "In recent years, concerns about a new threat to jury trials have emerged. This threat, termed the 'CSI Effect,' centers on alleged changes in the way juries have come to view forensic evidence presented at trial and is based upon a questionable understanding derived from television crime dramas," (Podlas, 2005). The 'CSI Effect' and a scathing 2009 report by the National Academy of Sciences (NAS) has also forced the forensic science community to take account of outdated mandates, training, education, and other requirements and amend obsolete standards to adhere to new technological innovations that are rapidly changing the way criminal investigations are conducted (NAS, 2009).

Perhaps these changes would have occurred without the influence of a popular television show, but it is clear that the incorrect perceptions by jurors and issues within the forensic science realm were in need of resolution regardless of the platform that brought it forward. Have the programs that focus on imprisonment done the same thing? After all, "Viewers are spectators who gaze at imagery that stimulates their minds and emotions" (Dant, 2012). If the programs about forensic science can create true change within the system, is it within the realm of possibility that sweeping changes will take effect within the prison system? Do we care about what happens to people who have been found guilty of crimes, or do we turn a blind eye and simply watch these shows for their entertainment value? As Cecil pointedly asserts, "As viewers observe the inner workings of the US prison system presented in this imagery, many of the stories invoke fear and disgust instead of empathy and concern" (p. 183). Of course, there is a difference between fictional representations of prison life, such as in *Oz* and *Orange is the New Black*, however, even the arena of prison documentary films and television programs are presented with a bias toward entertainment. Nothing that viewers watch, not even the most rudimentary documentary about prison life, is presented in a perfect light. "Something of 'reality' is always lost, and something is always added by the intervention of human action" (Dant, 2012). Dawn K. Cecil summarizes this issue best by stating, "This nonfiction imagery is not actuality, it is a representation. The prison world is reflected through a fun house mirror or sorts since it is impossible to transfer the physical world to a visual image" (p. 191).

Our pop culture world presents so many options for the public to immerse itself into the fictional and sensationalized world of true crime and the entire criminal justice system that the truth often gets lost in the ether. For women in prison, this is equally true. Yellow journalism continues to sexualize aspects of imprisonment, giving the public a completely altered sense of reality about the harsh life that women face behind bars. It is incumbent upon each individual to remember that their personal perception of these television shows, films, podcasts, social media posts, and news feeds should be filtered through a fine sieve and recall that formulas rarely, if ever, equal fact.

References

Ayres, D. (1997, February 11). *Jury decides Simpson must pay $25 million in punitive award.* Retrieved from https://www.nytimes.com/1997/02/11/us/jury-decides-simpson-must-pay-25-million-in-punitive-award.html

Bureau of Justice Statistics. (2016). Retrieved November 1, 2019, from https://www.bjs.gov/content/pub/pdf/cpus16.pdf

Bureau of Justice Statistics. (2018). Retrieved November 1, 2019, from: https://www.bjs.gov/content/pub/pdf/cpus16.pdf

Cecil, D. K. (2015). *Prison life in popular culture: From the big house to Orange is the new black.* Boulder, CO: Lynne Rienner Publishers, Inc.

Dant, T. (2012). *Television and the moral imaginary: Society through the small screen.* Basingstoke: Palgrave Macmillan.

Helling, S. (2019, October 30). *Lori Loughlin is 'about to break' in the wake of additional federal charges: Source.* Retrieved from https://people.com/tv/lori-loughlin-about-to-break-in-wake-additional-federal-charges-family-chaos/

Jarvis, B. (2006). The violence of images: Inside the prison TV drama Oz. In P. Mason (Ed.), *Captured by the media: Prison discourse in popular culture.* Portland, OR: Willan.

Kerman, P. (2010). *Orange is the new black: My year in a women's prison.* New York: Spiegel & Grau Trade Paperbacks.

Levenson, E. (2019, October 19). *Felicity Huffman reports to prison to start two-week sentence for college admissions scam.* Retrieved November 1, 2019, from https://www.cnn.com/2019/10/15/us/felicity-huffman-prison/index.html

Madrigal, A. (2018, May 20). When did TV watching peak? *The Atlantic.* https://www.theatlantic.com/technology/archive/2018/05/when-did-tv-watching-peak/561464/

National Academy of Sciences. (2009). *Strengthening forensic science in the United States: A path forward.* Committee on Identifying the Needs of the Forensic Sciences Community, National Research Council.

NBC. (2017, October 6). *Martha Stewart opens up about 'horrifying' prison stay: 'Nothing is good about it'.* New York: Today Show.

Perrin, A., & Anderson, M. (2019, April 10). *Share of U.S. adults using social media, including Facebook, is mostly unchanged since 2018.* Retrieved from https://www.pewresearch.org/fact-tank/2019/04/10/share-of-u-s-adults-using-social-media-including-facebook-is-mostly-unchanged-since-2018/

Podlas, K. (2005). "The CSI effect": Exposing the media myth. *Fordham Intellectual Property, Media and Entertainment Law Journal, 16*, 429. Available at https://ir.lawnet.fordham.edu/iplj/vol16/iss2/2

Quintana, C. (2019, March 13). *Fake disabilities, photoshopped faces: How feds say celebrities, coaches and scammers got kids into elite colleges.* Retrieved from https://www.usatoday.com/story/news/education/2019/03/12/felicity-huffman-lori-laughlin-how-college-admissions-scam-worked/3142160002/

Richardson, J. H. (1954). *For the life of me: Memoirs of a city editor.* Self-publication.

Chapter 3
Female Perpetrators: Risks, Needs, and Pathways to Offending

Michelle N. Jeanis and Sarah A. Smith

3.1 Introduction

As of 2016, nearly 219,000 women were under some form of incarceration in the USA (Kajstura, 2018). The majority of women incarcerated are housed in prisons (nearly 99,000) and jails (nearly 89,000), with the remainder housed in juvenile detention centers and federal or tribal prisons (Kajstura, 2018). Although this number is large, women only make up 7% of the incarceration population in the USA (Bronson & Carson, 2019). In addition, incarceration trends are very different for women than men. In particular, the number of women in prison has grown at a troubling pace, at least twice that of men (Sawyer, 2019). Furthermore, women are far more likely to be held in jails than prisons (compared to men), which means that most women may not receive the programming and services typically allocated to prison populations (Gray, Mays, & Stohr, 1995; Kajstura, 2018; Sawyer, 2019).

The majority of women (60%) held in jail are awaiting trial and have not yet been convicted of a crime (Kajstura, 2018). Women held in jails are most frequently charged with crimes related to property level offenses and drug related crimes, which is similar to male offending (Kajstura, 2018). Women are far more likely to commit non-violent offenses, and thus are less likely to be arrested or convicted for a violent crime, compared to men (Greenfeld & Snell, 2000). When examining types of violent crime, women are most likely to be arrested for crimes related to simple assault (Kajstura, 2018) and account for approximately 8% of all officially reported (i.e. reported to the police) homicides (UCR, 2018). In regard to sexual offending, women are significantly less likely to be arrested for a sexually based offense, as they make up only 2% of adult sexual offenders; however, it is important to note that women account for 10% of all juvenile offenders, suggesting that age

M. N. Jeanis (✉) · S. A. Smith
University of Louisiana at Lafayette, Lafayette, LA, USA
e-mail: michelle.jeanis@louisiana.edu

© Springer Nature Switzerland AG 2020
J. Hector (ed.), *Women and Prison*,
https://doi.org/10.1007/978-3-030-46172-0_3

may be a factor in the reporting of female sexual offenders (Terry, 2013). Taken together, these statistics suggest that women offend (and are incarcerated) in distinctly different ways than men. This difference may be due to the unique risk factors, societal interactions, and behavioral patterns that women encounter throughout their lives (Smart, 1977).

3.2   Risk Factors and Pathways to Female Offending

The factors associated with the causes of criminal behavior have been studied copiously; however, much of the research has focused only on the characteristics and factors of adult male offending (Cauffman, 2008). It is only within the last few decades that research has begun to shift focus on female offending (Cauffman, 2008; Cauffman, Farruggia, & Goldweber, 2008; Daly, 1992; Leve & Chamberlain, 2004; Simpson, Yahner, & Dugan, 2008). There have been significant findings regarding the factors that may influence an individual to pursue a particular pathway of criminal behavior, whether limited or life-long offending, and research suggests that many of these risk factors are distinct for women and men (Daly, 1992; Hart, O'Toole, Price-Sharps, & Shaffer, 2007; Johansson & Kempf-Leonard, 2009; Pflugradt & Allen, 2010; Reisig, Holtfreter, & Morash, 2006). There are many studies that support the etiology of deviant behavior stemming from dysfunctional families, personal relationships, mental health problems, and physical or sexual abuse, to name a few (Belknap & Holsinger, 2006; Cauffman, 2008; Cauffman et al., 2008; Daly, 1992; Herrera & McCloskey, 2001; Herrera, Wiersma, & Cleveland, 2010; Leve & Chamberlain, 2004; Pflugradt & Allen, 2010; Reisig et al., 2006). Unfortunately, most of these studies center on the experiences of men, who are referenced as the norm (Belknap & Holsinger, 2006). Factors associated with gendered conditions and societal aspects are infrequently considered for women who offend (Belknap & Holsinger, 2006). Many of these empirically relevant risk factors may be applied to both male and female offenders; however, the research regarding strictly female risk factors for delinquency is quite scarce (Belknap & Holsinger, 2006; Chesney-Lind & Shelden, 2013; Daly, 1992).

Risk factors such as familial dysfunction, physical, and/or sexual victimization have been examined to determine their role in the pathways of offending for women (Belknap & Holsinger, 2006; Daly, 1992; Johansson & Kempf-Leonard, 2009; Leve & Chamberlain, 2004). Most often, this early victimization manifests into status offending for girls, beginning the pathway to offending for some women (Belknap & Holsinger, 2006; Johansson & Kempf-Leonard, 2009). This pathway is a common finding, as girls are more likely to enter the juvenile justice system with status offenses (such as running away, truancy, or alcohol/tobacco possession) compared to boys (Herrera et al., 2010; Reisig et al., 2006; Simpson et al., 2008). In addition, familial dysfunction and the runaway experience are the most common preceding factor for girls with delinquency patterns (Belknap & Holsinger, 2006). Running away is frequently linked with abuse and victimization in the home, suggesting girls arrested for running away are only doing so to escape abuse in the home (Belknap & Holsinger, 2006; Cauffman, 2008; Cauffman et al., 2008; Hart et al., 2007; Herrera & McCloskey, 2001). Unfortunately, this escape attempt often leads to unsafe environments and coping skills, resulting in substance use/abuse, unhealthy relationships, delinquency, and reliance on deviant subsistence strategies such as prostitution (Belknap & Holsinger, 2006; Whitbeck & Hoyt, 1999).

Victimization experiences are also reported to shape adult female offending patterns as well (Cauffman, 2008; Herrera & McCloskey, 2001). For example, Herrera and McCloskey (2001) looked at factors between incarcerated women who had childhood victimization and those who did not and found that women who had been physically abused during childhood were seven times more likely to commit a violent offense compared to non-abused women. It has been supported empirically that women and girls who have a history of abuse or victimization develop self-preservation tactics that may be maladaptive in nature (Cauffman, 2008; Farr, 2000; Herrera & McCloskey, 2001; Simpson et al., 2008). Furthermore, women who have been charged with violent crimes often report to have done so specifically in response to physical, sexual, or emotional abuse (Cauffman, 2008; Farr, 2000; Reisig et al., 2006; Simpson et al., 2008). Farr (2000) conducted a meta-analysis over several different studies that examined risk factors for female offenders and prevention programs in response to those factors. Farr (2000) found that rates of child sexual abuse and domestic violence were notably higher in female inmates, compared with male inmates and even nonincarcerated women. Chesney-Lind and Shelden (2013) have also summarized female pathways to prison and find that early abuse and neglect (especially sexual in nature) often foreshadow maladaptive externalizing behaviors during adulthood. This finding reflects the gender-specific abuse patterns and behavioral responses that shape life course offending for women (Chesney-Lind & Shelden, 2013).

Multiple studies suggest that some vulnerable women are coerced into crime through negative male partnerships (Belknap & Holsinger, 2006; Cauffman, 2008; Herrera et al., 2010; Simpson et al., 2008). Simpson et al. (2008) propose that in low income neighborhoods, older men are more inclined to enlist the help of younger females to commit criminal acts for them, which results in juvenile and young adult offending for girls and women. In addition, researchers have identified unhealthy intimate partner relationships as a risk factor for offending in women (Belknap & Holsinger, 2006; Cauffman, 2008; Herrera et al., 2010). Women who experience this type of violence often will hit a "breaking point" and react in physically violent ways, sometimes referred to as "defensive violence" (Muftic, Finn, & Marsh, 2015). In addition, women are more likely to victimize an intimate partner, a friend, or a relative than a stranger, suggesting that close relationships experienced by women greatly shape the ways in which they offend (Hickey, 2016).

3.2.1 Pathways to Offending

As previously mentioned, the majority of research on what causes criminal behavior typically references male offenders as the norm, and insinuates that female offenders are generally the same (Fagan, Van Horn, Hawkins, & Arthur, 2007). One of the main focal points for female pathways into crime is the context of adverse family influences; for example, child abuse or neglect (Cauffman et al., 2008), physical or sexual victimization (Cauffman, 2008; Reisig et al., 2006), and even parents' criminality (Fagan et al., 2007; Leve & Chamberlain, 2004).

The literature on women's pathways to crime generally reflects on three main pathways that are relatively broad in scope, but focus on psychological risks and needs differ from men (Belknap & Holsinger, 2006; Cauffman, 2008; Cauffman et al., 2008; Daly, 1992; Hart et al., 2007; Herrera & McCloskey, 2001; Reisig et al., 2006; Simpson et al., 2008). The general literature has concluded that women enter criminal deviance through: (1) childhood victimization linked with maladaptive psychological processes or behaviors (Daly, 1992; Reisig et al., 2006); (2) homelessness and/or extreme poverty (Daly, 1992; Leve & Chamberlain, 2004); and (3) dysfunctional intimate relations (Muftic et al., 2015). It is hypothesized that boys and girls may experience these things equally; however, it is speculated that the culmination of these factors has a more negative impact on girls (Johansson & Kempf-Leonard, 2009).

One of the most groundbreaking studies on the pathways to offending for women was conducted by Kathleen Daly (1992), who outlined five distinct pathways in which women fall into deviance/crime: (1) *Street Women*, (2) *Drug-Connected Women*, (3) *Harmed and Harming Women*, (4) *Battered Women*, and (5) *Other*. The *Street Women* pathway suggests females fled abusive homes, became addicts, and used criminal means (i.e. prostitution, drug dealing, property theft) to survive on the streets (Daly, 1992). The *Drug-Connected* pathway includes women involved in the use, manufacture, or distribution of drugs and often experiences substance addiction as their primary risk factor (Daly, 1992). *Harmed and Harming* refers to women who grew up victimized throughout life and are now reversing the roles and victimizing someone else (Daly, 1992). *Battered Women* have abuse histories and are confined to relationships with violent intimate partners and their main motivations of offending are fear-based (Daly, 1992; Simpson et al., 2008). The *Other* category refers to women who lack any notable abuse history, were not violent themselves, and did not seem to have any identifiable substance abuse problem, but exhibit offending in adulthood and seem to be motivated by material success (Daly, 1992). Some researchers have found that the risk factors associated with this pathway are not necessarily gender specific and are seen in pathways for both men and women (Reisig et al., 2006).

Although Daly's pathways are relatively specific, there are still crimes committed by women that would not fit into any of these categories. Like most of the literature on female offenders, there is lack of research pertaining to the risk factors associated with female sexual offenders (Freeman & Sandler, 2008; Pflugradt &

Allen, 2010) and female serial offenders (Harrison, Hughes, & Gott, 2019; Harrison, Murphy, Ho, Bowers, & Flaherty, 2015). This, in part, may be due to society's general impression of how women should behave and conform to gender norms (Center for Sex Offender Management, 2007; Freeman & Sandler, 2008; Harrison et al., 2019; Pflugradt & Allen, 2010).

3.2.2 Offense-Specific Risk Factors

The little research that has been conducted on female sex offenders has found that these women are significantly different from their male counterparts (Freeman & Sandler, 2008). Researchers have examined risk factors related to dysfunctional socialization processes, mental health problems, and abusive family histories for many women who commit sex crimes (Center for Sex Offender Management, 2007; Freeman & Sandler, 2008; Pflugradt & Allen, 2010; Vick, McRoy, & Matthews, 2002). For example, Vick et al. (2002) found that female sex offenders are more likely to have previously been sexually victimized, have higher rates of mental health problems, and have higher histories of a dysfunctional home life, compared to men. Furthermore, these risk factors, along with difficulties in intimate relationships, were supported in varied samples of female sexual offenders (Freeman & Sandler, 2008; Pflugradt & Allen, 2010).

Previous research and national statistics agree that women are less likely to commit (and be arrested for) violent crimes, compared to men (Belknap & Holsinger, 2006; Cauffman, 2008; UCR, 2018). Some studies suggest that women incarcerated for violent crimes typically act as an accessory to the crime, or act in perceived self-defense (Hart et al., 2007; Reisig et al., 2006). An overwhelmingly number of female offenders have a history of abuse and victimization, and research suggests that those with higher rates of victimization are associated with higher risk of violent offending (Farr, 2000; Herrera & McCloskey, 2001). Of all serious and violent criminal acts, murder is considered as one of the rarest (Hickey, 2016; Holmes & De Burger, 1988), and even more so for women (Harrison et al., 2015, 2019). Women who commit murder most often do so in what is referred to as "crimes of passion" and can involve intimate partner violence as a precursor (Harrison et al., 2015; Reisig et al., 2006). In addition, women are most often one-time offenders when it comes to serious violent crimes (Cauffman, 2008). However, a very small portion of violent female offenders are convicted of serial crimes, such as serial homicide. Specifically, women account for roughly 8% of all serial murders (Harrison et al., 2015, 2019; Hickey, 2016). Hickey (2016) conducted one of the most in-depth studies of female serial killers by examining the history and crimes committed of 64 female serial killers in the USA and concluded that female serial killers are typically motivated by financial gain or revenge (Harrison et al., 2015, 2019; Hickey, 2016). Hickey (2016) found an overwhelming history of child abuse throughout his sample of female serial killers, as well as broken homes, poverty, and other psychological problems; interestingly, these are often at higher rates than male serial offenders. In summation, even when women exhibit extreme violence, research suggests distinct risk factors, experiences, and histories than their male counterparts (Harrison et al., 2015, 2019; Hickey, 2016).

Taken together, research suggests that women who offend have distinct pathways to offending (Daly, 1992; Johansson & Kempf-Leonard, 2009; Leve & Chamberlain, 2004; Reisig et al., 2006). In addition, studies that examine general risk for delinquency and offending of women find that they are often shaped by their early life experiences, many of which center on abuse and victimization (Belknap & Holsinger, 2006; Daly, 1992; Johansson & Kempf-Leonard, 2009; Leve & Chamberlain, 2004). These findings suggest that a victim-offender focus may be needed in order to better understand the ways in which women become offenders.

3.3   The Role of the Victim-Offender Overlap

There is an empirically well-established relationship between victimization and offending (Flexon, Meldrum, & Piquero, 2016; Gottfredson, 1981; Jennings, Piquero, & Reingle, 2012); however, examination of how this relationship shapes the offender behavior of women has received less focus. Researchers have examined the overlap between victimization and offending for a variety of criminal behaviors including sexual abuse, property crimes, and violent offending (Flexon et al., 2016; Gottfredson, 1981; Jennings et al., 2012). Although many researchers have examined the presence of a victim/offender overlap, less is known about the casual mechanism that shapes this co-occurrence, especially for female offenders (Flexon et al., 2016).

Flexon et al. (2016) examined the relationship between low self-control and the victim/offender overlap for both men and women and found that low self-control accounted for a significant proportion of the victim-offender overlap for men, but not for women. This finding supports previous studies that suggest traditional theories of offending may do little to explain the motivations of offending behavior in female offenders. In a similar vein, Farrell (2017) examined the role of neighborhood disadvantage in the victim-offender overlap for women by utilizing the National Longitudinal Study of Adolescent Health (Add Health) data. Results indicate that women in disadvantaged neighborhoods are more likely to exhibit violent criminal behavior after a with-force sexual assault experience than those in more economically prosperous communities (Farrell, 2017). This finding suggests not just gender specific offending responses to victimization, but also social class/economic effects that shape the victim/offender relationship.

More commonly, the victim/offender overlap in female samples is typically examined with offense-specific focus. For example, the victim-offender overlap has been examined for those who experience intimate partner violence, or IVP (Muftic et al., 2015; Tillyer & Wright, 2014). Tillyer and Wright (2014) used the fourth wave of the Add Health data to examine the victim/offender overlap for IVP and found the presence of a victim/offender overlap for both men and women, with women exhibiting nearly the same amount of violence as men. In addition, women were significantly more likely to be victims of IPV, as opposed to victim-offenders; however, when they are both victims and offenders, women share similar risk factors as men, including substance abuse problems and feelings of isolation (Tillyer & Wright, 2014). Muftic et al. (2015) also examined the victim-offender overlap for women who experience IVP by utilizing official police records to follow 1256 individuals over a 30-month period. Results indicate that women, whether they were victims only or victim/offenders were significantly more likely to be arrested for a crime prior to the initial IVP experience, suggesting a persistent risky lifestyle (Muftic et al., 2015). In addition, when examining the temporal order of the victim/offender overlap in IVP, women were more likely to begin as victims, but during the 30-month follow-up period, become offenders at some point (Muftic et al., 2015). These findings suggest distinct patters in the victim/offender overlap experience for women, compared to men. Muftic et al.' (2015) findings also suggest that a complex relationship exists in the experience of offending and victimization for women, where although they are likely to start out as IVP victims and become IVP offenders, their life histories indicate police contact prior to the start of this victim-offender IVP manifestation.

The victim-offender overlap has also been examined in regard to women who participate in the sex industry. Muftic et al. (2015) examined the victim/offender relationship in a small sample of sex workers and found distinct characteristics for those who experienced both victimization and offending, compared to women with no victimization experiences. Specifically, women who have both victim and offender histories are more likely to have substance abuse problems, suffer physical injuries, and remain in the sex work industry longer, compared to non-victim sex workers (Muftic et al., 2015). This finding suggests that women who experience victimization either before or during their time participating in sex work are more likely to struggle with other types of offending, as well as having a more difficult time in transitioning out of the sex industry Muftic et al. (2015).

3.4 Theoretical Perspectives to Female Offenders

Many researchers have attempted to assess the utility of traditional criminology theories in their ability to explain the causes and correlates of female offenders (Alarid, Burton, & Cullen, 2000; Broidy & Agnew, 1997; Flexon et al., 2016; Steffensmeier & Allen, 1996). For example, Broidy and Agnew (1997) assessed general strain theory's ability to explain both the higher rate of male offending as well as the motivations of female offenders. Results of the study suggest that men and women may experience and cope with strains and their related negative emotions differently, which in turn shapes offending rates for men and women (Broidy & Agnew, 1997). Broidy and Agnew (1997) also suggest that many women experience an additional level of societal oppression, which shapes opportunity to commit certain types of crimes, which likely has an effect on the rate of female offending.

This study suggests that general theories of offending may work to explain female offending, if accompanied by a perspective that incorporates how women experience the world around them.

In addition, Alarid et al. (2000) tested the utility of social control and differential association theory in a gendered sample of individuals convicted of felonies. Results of the study suggest both general and gender-specific findings (Alarid et al., 2000). Full sample analyses suggest that differential association and social control variables work to explain offending patterns; however, when examined by gender, distinct gendered patterns emerge (Alarid et al., 2000). Differential association variables are not significantly associated with female offending but are strongly related to male offending (Alarid et al., 2000). In addition, marital or parental attachment proved to be strongly related to female offending and not male offending (Alarid et al., 2000). Furthermore, men appear to be more strongly influenced by peer attachment than women, in regard to offending behavior (Alarid et al., 2000). The findings of this study suggest unique gender-specific relationships between traditional criminology theories and offending behavior. A similar pattern was found in Flexon et al. (2016) study that examined Gottfredson and Hirshi's self-control theory, where this "general" theory of crime failed to shape the offending behavior of women.

Considering the very limited evidence that traditional general theories of criminal behavior work to consistently explain female offending, many researchers have moved to examine the utility of gender-specific theories (Burgess-Proctor, 2006; Chesney-Lind, 1986; Chesney-Lind & Shelden, 2013). Feminist criminology, the dominant gender-based theory, was created due to the neglect of women in traditional criminology theories and the inability of these theories to adequately explain female offending (Chesney-Lind & Shelden, 2013). There are various forms of feminist criminology (see Chesney-Lind and Shelden (2013) for an in-depth review); however, all sub-theories aim to identify both individual and macrolevel factors that shape female offending behavior (Chesney-Lind & Shelden, 2013). Generally speaking, feminist criminology focuses on examining how socialized gender roles and structural conditions of a patriarchal society are related to the ways in which women commit crimes in the USA, as well as other nations that value traditional masculine traits over traditional feminine traits (Belknap & Holsinger, 2006; Chesney-Lind, 1986).

Assessments of feminist criminology theory have found that, as it relates to the causes of offending, women and men often differ in meaningful ways. For example, Salisbury and Van Voorhis (2009) found that victimization is a key causal mechanism for offending in women, but this relationship is not as strongly represented in male samples. In addition, dysfunctional intimate and reduced social capital are strongly related to female offending (Salisbury & Van Voorhis, 2009). Although some similarities exist between the causes of criminal behavior for men and women, in-depth examinations of women who offend highlight causal mechanisms that are often missed by gender aggregated studies (Chesney-Lind & Shelden, 2013; Jones, Brown, Wanamaker, & Greiner, 2014; Salisbury & Van Voorhis, 2009). For example, using the Add Health data, Jones et al. (2014) identified a traditional combination of antisocial beliefs and high impulsivity leading to offending for both men and women; however, a subsample of women were motivated to offend due to victimization, financial constraints, and mental health difficulties. Again, results suggest that traditional theories often miss the varied cause of many female offenders when gender-based perspectives are not considered. Taken together, a growing body of literature suggests that women experience and interact with society in ways that are distinct from men, which in turn shape their frequency and type of offending (Chesney-Lind & Shelden, 2013).

3.5 Recidivism of Female Offenders

A growing body of research aims to identify the factors that shape reoffending among women. Unfortunately, the research on factors that shape recidivism and related risk/needs assessments for female offenders is greatly underdeveloped (Bonta, Pang, & Wallace-Capretta, 1995). In addition, risk/needs assessments often overclassify female offenders, often placing them in higher risk levels than needed and restricting them from needed programming and intervention (Burke & Adams, 1991; Freeman & Sandler, 2008; Van Voorhis & Presser, 2001).

Most risk/needs assessments are created based on the histories and behaviors of men who offend, and research suggests that many of these assessments do not function well to assess the specific risks and needs of women (Bonta et al., 1995; Smart, 1977). However, one assessment that shows promise for female offenders is the Level of Service/Case Management Inventory (LS/CMI), which generates an overall general risk score (Rettingler & Andwers, 2010). The LS/CMI assesses criminal histories, antisocial peers, antisocial cognitions, and antisocial patterns and findings suggest strong correlations with recidivism risk for both men and women (Rettingler & Andwers, 2010).

Unfortunately, assessments of the predecessor of the LS/CMI, the Level of Supervision Inventory-Revised (LSI-R), which is a commonly applied risk/needs assessment (based on social learning theory principles), suggest mixed support in its ability to predict the risk and needs of female offenders (Lowenkamp, Holsinger, & Latessa, 2001; Reisig et al., 2006; Rettingler & Andwers, 2010). For example, Reisig et al. (2006) found that the LSI-R was only predictive of offending for women who were economically motivated to offend, and utility was not found for other types of female offenders. Research also suggests that risk/needs assessments, like the LSI-R, may work best (or only) for female offenders who have antisocial or violent histories, whose behaviors most resemble that of men who offend (Reisig et al., 2006; Rettingler & Andwers, 2010). This suggests that some risk/needs assessments may only be functioning successfully for certain type of female offenders (Reisig et al., 2006; Rettingler & Andwers, 2010).

Research suggests that risk of recidivism for women may be strongly shaped by personal distress via circumstance or mental state, and that this factor may be a stronger predictor of offending than childhood abuse (Rettingler & Andwers, 2010).

Lowenkamp et al. (2001) also found that the inclusion of prior abuse in a risk/needs assessment was not a significant predictor of female reoffending. This may be contradictory to traditional gender-based pathways to offending studies, in that childhood abuse is said to be a significant factor that leads to life course offending (Lowenkamp et al., 2001); however, additional research is needed in order to fully understand the relationship between abuse and offending for women. Taken together, it is apparent that much is needed in the study of female reoffending, as successfulness of risk/needs assessments in their ability to predict reoffending, as well as appropriate risk classification, is greatly needed.

Taken together, research on recidivism of female offenders suggests that researchers have only begun to understand (and subsequently predict) the factors that shape repetitive offending of women. In addition, it appears that insufficient attention has been paid to the academic study of recidivism of women, as many aspects of risk and protective factors remain unexplored (Lowenkamp et al., 2001; Reisig et al., 2006; Rettingler & Andwers, 2010). Fortunately, a growing body of literature suggests that gender-based assessments are being created and tested in their utility to explain female offending and recidivism.

References

Alarid, L., Burton, V., & Cullen, F. (2000). Gender and crime among felony offenders: Assessing the generality of social control and differential association theories. *Journal of Research in Crime and Delinquency, 37*(2), 171–199.

Belknap, J., & Holsinger, K. (2006). The gendered nature of risk factors for delinquency. *Feminist Criminology, 1*(1), 48–71.

Bonta, J., Pang, B., & Wallace-Capretta, S. (1995). Predictors of recidivism among incarcerated female offenders. *The Prison Journal, 75*(3), 277–294.

Broidy, L., & Agnew, R. (1997). Gender and crime: A general strain theory perspective. *Journal of Research in Crime and Delinquency, 34*(3), 275–306.

Bronson, J., & Carson, A. (2019). *Prisoners in 2017* (US Department of Justice, Office of Justice Programs, Bureau of Justice Statistics, NCJ 252156). Washington, DC: US Department of Justice.

Burgess-Proctor, A. (2006). Intersections of race, class, gender, and crime: Future directions for feminist criminology. *Feminist Criminology, 1*(1), 27–47.

Burke, P., & Adams, L. (1991). *Classification of women offenders in state correctional facilities: A handbook for practitioners.* Washington, DC: COSMOS Corporation.

Cauffman, E. (2008). Understanding the female offender. *The Future of Children, 18*(2), 119–142.

Cauffman, E., Farruggia, S. P., & Goldweber, A. (2008). Bad boys or poor parents: Relations to female juvenile delinquency. *Journal of Research on Adolescence, 18*(4), 699–712.

Center for Sex Offender Management. (2007). *Female sex offenders* [PDF file]. Retrieved from https://www.csom.org/pubs/female_sex_offenders_brief.pdf

Chesney-Lind, M. (1986). Women and crime: The female offender. *Signs: Journal of Women in Culture and Society, 12*(1), 78–96.

Chesney-Lind, M., & Shelden, R. G. (2013). *Girls, delinquency, and juvenile justice.* New York: Wiley.

Daly, K. (1992). Women's pathways to felony court: Feminist theories of lawbreaking and problems of representation. *Southern California Review of Law and Women's Studies, 2*(11), 11–52.

Fagan, A. A., Van Horn, M. L., Hawkins, J. D., & Arthur, M. W. (2007). Gender similarities and differences in the association between risk and protective factors and self-reported serious delinquency. *Society for Prevention Research, 8*(2), 115–124.

Farr, K. A. (2000). Classification for female inmates: Moving forward. *Crime & Delinquency, 46*(1), 3–17.

Farrell, C. (2017). Exploring the overlap between sexual victimization and offending among young women across neighborhoods: Does the type of force and type of offending matter? *Journal of Interpersonal Violence, 35*(3–4), 571–599. https://doi.org/10.1177/0886260516689778

Flexon, J., Meldrum, R., & Piquero, A. (2016). Low self-control and the victim-offender overlap: A gendered analysis. *Journal of Interpersonal Violence, 31*(11), 2052–2076.

Freeman, N., & Sandler, J. (2008). Female and male sex offenders: A comparison of recidivism patterns and risk factors. *Journal of Interpersonal Violence, 23*(10), 1394–1413.

Gottfredson, M. (1981). On the etiology of criminal victimization. *Journal of Criminal Law and Criminology, 72*(2), 714–726.

Gray, T., Mays, L., & Stohr, M. (1995). Inmate needs and programming in exclusively women's jails. *The Prison Journal, 75*(2), 123–131.

Greenfeld, L., & Snell, T. (2000). *Women offenders* (US Department of Justice, Office of Justice Programs, Bureau of Justice Statistics, NCJ 175688). Washington, DC: US Department of Justice.

Harrison, M. A., Hughes, S. M., & Gott, A. J. (2019). Sex differences in serial killers. *Evolutionary Behavioral Sciences, 13*(4), 295–310.

Harrison, M. A., Murphy, E. A., Ho, L. Y., Bowers, T. G., & Flaherty, C. V. (2015). Female serial killers in the United States: Means, motives, and makings. *The Journal of Forensic Psychiatry & Psychology, 26*(3), 383–406.

Hart, J. L., O'Toole, S. K., Price-Sharps, J. L., & Shaffer, T. W. (2007). The risk and protective factors of violent juvenile offending: An examination of gender differences. *Youth Violence and Juvenile Justice, 5*(4), 367–384.

Herrera, V. M., & McCloskey, L. A. (2001). Gender differences in the risk for delinquency among youth exposed to family violence. *Child Abuse & Neglect, 25*(8), 1037–1051.

Herrera, V. M., Wiersma, J. D., & Cleveland, H. H. (2010). Romantic partners' contribution to the continuity of male and female delinquent and violent behavior. *Journal of Research on Adolescence, 21*(3), 608–618.

Hickey, E. W. (2016). *Serial murderers and their victims.* Belmont, CA: Wadsworth, Cengage Learning.

Holmes, R. M., & De Burger, J. (1988). *Serial Murder.* Thousand Oaks, CA: Sage.

Jennings, W., Piquero, A., & Reingle, J. (2012). On the overlap between victimization and offending: A review of the literature. *Aggression and Violent Behavior, 17*(1), 16–26.

Johansson, P., & Kempf-Leonard, K. (2009). A gender-specific pathway to serious, violent, and chronic offending? Exploring Howell's risk factors for serious delinquency. *Crime & Delinquency, 55*(2), 216–240.

Jones, N. J., Brown, S. L., Wanamaker, K. A., & Greiner, L. E. (2014). A quantitative exploration of gendered pathways to crime in a sample of male and female juvenile offenders. *Feminist Criminology, 9*(2), 113–136.

Kajstura, A. (2018). *Women's mass incarceration: The whole pie 2018.* Retrieved from https://www.prisonpolicy.org/reports/pie2018women.html

Leve, L. D., & Chamberlain, P. (2004). Female juvenile offenders: Defining an early-onset pathway for delinquency. *Journal of Child and Family Studies, 13*(4), 439–452.

Lowenkamp, C., Holsinger, A., & Latessa, E. (2001). Risk/need assessment, offender classification, and the role of child abuse. *Criminal Justice and Behavior, 28*(5), 542–563.

Muftic, L., Finn, M., & Marsh, E. (2015). The victim-offender overlap, intimate partner violence, and sex: Assessing differences among victims, offenders, and victim-offenders. *Crime & Delinquency, 61*(7), 899–926.

Pflugradt, D. M., & Allen, B. P. (2010). An exploratory analysis of executive functioning for female sexual offenders: A comparison of characteristics across offense typologies. *Journal of Child Sexual Abuse, 19*(4), 434–449.

Reisig, M., Holtfreter, K., & Morash, M. (2006). Assessing recidivism risk across female pathways to crime. *Justice Quarterly, 23*(3), 384–405.

Rettinger, L., & Andwers, D. (2010). General risk and need, gender specificity, and the recidivism of female offenders. *Criminal Justice and Behavior, 37*(1), 29–46.

Salisbury, E. J., & Van Voorhis, P. (2009). Gendered pathways: A quantitative investigation of women probationers' paths to incarceration. *Criminal Justice and Behavior, 36*(6), 541–566.

Sawyer, W. (2019). *The gender divide: Tracking women's state prison growth*. Retrieved from https://www.prisonpolicy.org/reports/women_overtime.html

Simpson, S. S., Yahner, J. L., & Dugan, L. (2008). Understanding women's pathways to jail: Analysing the lives of incarcerated women. *The Australian and New Zealand Journal of Criminology, 41*(1), 84–108.

Smart, C. (1977). *Women, crime, and criminology: A feminist critique*. New York: Routledge Publishing.

Steffensmeier, D., & Allen, E. (1996). Gender and crime: Toward a gendered theory of female offending. *Annual Review of Sociology, 22*(1), 459–487.

Terry, K. (2013). *Sexual offenses and offenders: Theory, practice, and policy*. Belmont, CA: Cengage Publishing.

Tillyer, M., & Wright, E. (2014). Intimate partner violence and the victim offender overlap. *Journal of Research in Crime and Delinquency, 51*(1), 29–55.

Uniform Crime Report (UCR). (2018). *2018 Crime in the United States* (Criminal Justice Information Service Division). Washington, DC: US.

Van Voorhis, P., & Presser, L. (2001). *Classification of women offenders: A national assessment of current practices*. Washington, DC: National Institute of Corrections.

Vick, J., McRoy, R., & Matthews, B. M. (2002). Young female sex offenders: Assessment and treatment issues. *Journal of Child Sexual Abuse, 11*(2), 1–23.

Whitbeck, L. B., & Hoyt, D. R. (1999). *Nowhere to grow*. Hawthorne, NY: Walter de Gruyter.

Chapter 4
Criminal Justice Processing and Procedure, Generally and for Justice-Involved Women

Kathleen Murphy

4.1 The Backstory

Amber D. Lee loved Johnny Bentley. Maurice's Pawn Shop, where they worked together, was the conduit for the downfall. The con occurred at the pawn shop when a plan was devised to rob a local bank. Although Amber Dawn and Johnny Bentley remind you of someone, the couple is fictional and drawn solely from this author's fictional database.

While planning the bank robbery, Johnny Bentley made side income selling methamphetamines to the people who eventually learned of their hotspot, the pawn shop. Traffic was steady in the pawn shop and all types were in and out. It was Johnny and Amber because was Maurice was old and frail—they had complete control over the shop.

On the day of the robbery, Friday, March 13th, they each cleared over $50,000.00 and Amber cried when she learned that Johnny and she would share this money equally. Their drug scores with the money from the robbery made Amber's dream come true—she was going to buy a home and she and Johnny Bentley were to live happily ever after. No more drugs, no more crime. Johnny was romantic and told Amber Dawn that he was going to be "the man" and they drank a beer.

On Monday following the robbery, the police visited Maurice's Pawn Shop in an effort to track down cameras and witnesses. Amber Dawn, nervous, nauseated and in no way ready for this interview, told the officers not to tell Johnny but she knew he went to the bank on Friday. She drove him there and she saw money. After further investigation, a warrant was issued to search the shop.

The $50,000.00 was located in the safe and Johnny and Amber were arrested. During the arrest, the police discovered the operation of a drug syndicate where Amber Lee and Johnny Bentley were selling and distributing drugs.

K. Murphy (✉)
Law Offices of Kathleen Murphy, Raleigh, NC, USA
e-mail: kathleenmurphy@ncdomesticlaw.com

© Springer Nature Switzerland AG 2020   41
J. Hector (ed.), *Women and Prison*,
https://doi.org/10.1007/978-3-030-46172-0_4

4.2 Moving Through the System Post-arrest

Johnny Bentley was taken to county jail and Amber Dawn was housed in the female section of the same jail.

Amber Dawn and Johnny Bentley were both facing prison yet at the jail stage, prior to conviction, intake varied greatly from state to state but the first step is always identification.

Amber Dawn was identified with photographs, fingerprints and had a medical evaluation. It was discovered she was pregnant. No special arrangements were made for her at this time.

Monday was a good day to be arrested because the next day was the *First Appearance* court date. At this time, both Amber D and Johnny were before a judge. If they were arrested on a Friday, they would spend all weekend in jail.

On Monday night, Amber was processed for identification by being photographed and fingerprinted. She was housed in a group cell and the next day she had her first appearance.

In identifying the post-arrest system, there are different stages in each individual jurisdiction but generally speaking, all post-arrests systems are similar in the following steps.

- Processing and Intake
- Advisement Hearing
- Arraignment
- Bond or Pre-Trial Release programs
- Pre-Trial Diversion
- Plea Bargaining
- Trial
- Sentencing

Each topic covered in this chapter will be that general information on what happens to the female detainee whether she is in state court or federal court, whether she is "misdemeanored" or charged with a felony and whether she is arrested or convicted.

4.2.1 Advisement Hearing

In Big Town, Amber's first appearance was her advisement hearing. An advisement hearing in Big Town criminal court is the first time the accused appears in a courtroom and learns the accusations against her. On April 6th, the Judge told Amber she is being accused of possession of and distributing a Schedule II controlled substance and felony bank robbery, the same charges against Johnny and bond were set for each party at $100,000.00.

Amber's mom and sister were in court and heard the amount of the bond. At this time there was no money to pay for a bail bondsman so Amber was returned to the county jail.

While sitting in jail, Amber waited for weeks to hear from her court appointed attorney. She told him of the extreme control Johnny had over her—he was a drug addict and an alpha male and she was afraid of him. Her PD (public defender) took notes and went from there to talk to the prosecutor. The prosecutor in this case was Debbie Bryson, a woman who was older and went to law school later in life. She had escaped an abusive spouse and now was using her office to prosecute abusers.

Amber called her mother and asked her to help gather evidence. There were two restraining orders she had taken out against Johnny. She was 24 and they met in high school. She also told her mom to get Johnny's criminal record. He had a prior DUI and misdemeanor assault on female. Johnny also was presently charged with shoplifting.

Amber Dawn told her lawyer in her first meeting that she had never stepped into the bank. She was told to drive Johnny to the bank to "make a deposit" for the shop. She had no idea he was planning to rob the bank. When she saw the money he stole, she did not call the police because of the prior assaults. She was afraid he would kill her and claim it was a shop robbery. Amber also told her PD to have her drug tested immediately as she had no drugs in her system. The PD would try to arrange this test while she was in jail.

On July 17th, a second advisement hearing was held and it was at this time that Amber Dawn learned she was actually just charged with conspiracy to commit bank robbery (Class 5 Felony) and the meth was a Schedule II controlled substance which means possession or manufacturing is a Class 2 drug *felony* punishable by up to 8 years in jail, 2 additional years of parole, and fines up to $750,000.00.

Her attorney advised $_{old}$ her if an individual is charged with selling or transferring methamphetamine or possessing it for sale, it is a Big Town felony drug offense. The punishment for selling methamphetamine or possessing it for sale varies from 6 months in jail to 32 years in prison depending on the quantity of methamphetamine and whether the individual sold the drug (or intended to sell) to a minor at least 2 years younger than the accused.

Amber Dawn did not enter a plea at this time and was returned to jail. Before she was returned to jail, she asked for a bond reduction. A bond reduction was granted and her bond was lowered to $10,000.00. A 10% fee would be affordable and her mother was again in the courtroom. No plea was entered at this stage.

As she was released from jail, Amber went to live with her mother.

4.2.2   Arraignment

After an accused is advised, the next court appearance would typically be the arraignment. During the arraignment in open court, Amber was informed of the offense for which she was charged and she was required to enter a plea to the charge at this time. Amber knew that she had special circumstances and she wanted to present these circumstances to the Court. Amber had a plan.

Prior to arraignment, Amber Dawn learned that Johnny Bentley was in jail and was not talking, not even to his family. Her attorney told her that Johnny Bentley was not going to plead guilty and he could not make bond.

On September 11th and during the arraignment, Judge Settler announced the formal charges against her and Amber Dawn plead "not guilty."

4.2.3   Pre-trial Sentencing and Prosecution Diversion

Amber asked if she could take any steps to avoid a criminal record (see Ulrich, 2002). She was pregnant and leaving an abusive relationship and had a clean record. Was there any program that would help her avoid penalty to maintain her clean record?

A common prosecution diversion program involves drug court where individuals are offered substance abuse education, monitoring, and other rehabilitation services as an alternative to conviction. Usually, upon successful completion of the agreed upon prosecution diversion program (within 18 months as a general time frame), charges are dismissed. Some pre-trial (before conviction) programs result in dismissals prior to charges being formalized.

According to a study published by Denno, forty-four (44%) percent of the individuals who were diverted from prosecution and received for pre-trial diversion supervision during the 5-year period were female. This was much higher proportionally than in pre-trial services cases activated overall, for which, during the same period, only 16% of defendants were female. Several factors appear to account for this difference. Female defendants, as a group, are less likely to have prior offenses and are more often charged with offenses for which pre-trial diversion is frequently used (Denno, 1994).

For example, during the study period, across all pre-trial services cases activated, fraud was the most serious offense charged for 21% of women, compared to 13% of men. Larceny/theft was the most serious offense for 8% of women, and 3% of men; embezzlement was the offense for 7% of women, 1% of men (Denno, 1994).

Amber had some choices because she had no record and a common prosecution diversion program was for drug charges. She had that robbery charge and now she focused on a prosecution drug diversion program with comorbid mental health care.

Amber called her mom again because when she was in school, she had an Individualized Education Plan (IEP) for her attention deficit hyperactivity disorder. Special adaptive services were always made. As part of her having an IEP, she was also diagnosed as having a personality disorder. Could she get this documentation to her lawyer and argue for a diversion?

Diversion can occur at many different levels of the criminal justice process. The process can be prior to: first appearance or bail hearing, after initial arraignment, after preliminary hearing or probable cause hearings, after a guilty plea but before sentencing or after conviction and sentencing with sentencing suspended pending treatment completion (Center for Substance Abuse Treatment, 2005).

In crafting her plea, Amber asked her attorney to let the District Attorney know her circumstances. She had no drug test now to prove she was clean so she would use the system to ask for drug help. She had a learning disability and she had a mental health personality disorder diagnosis. She was also pregnant. She argued to her lawyer that she knew nothing about the robbery. Amber was smart enough and cried with her visitors about her innocence.

4.2.4   Pre-trial Hearings

After pleading not guilty, Amber Dawn was scheduled for another court date—the pre-trial conference and it was set for October 30th. After her court date was set, the arraignment process concluded.

Prior to the pre-trial hearing, Amber Dawn again met with her PD and learned that Johnny was not talking. The chemical report was reviewed and she learned that no cameras outside caught the bank robbery. The police report outlined that the robber was covered completely, and had an automatic weapon. No witness would be able to make an identification and the surveillance footage was grainy.

Amber, at this time, realized her plan. She told her PD about life at the pawn shop, how Johnny ran the show and how she never owned a gun in her life.

The PD met again with the DA and discussion was made about Amber Dawn's hard life.

Johnny was charged with aggravated robbery, a Class 3 felony. Big Town's Criminal Code Section covers bank robbery charges. Generally speaking, a bank robbery would be classed as an aggravated robbery, which is a Class 3 felony.

4.2.5   Going to Prison

Amber negotiated a plea. It was determined by the District Attorney that there was not enough evidence to convict Amber of the bank robbery charges. Johnny Bentley would not testify or talk and Amber had portrayed her status a victim of domestic violence. There was clear evidence that Johnny was controlling and abusive.

Amber was sentenced to prosecutorial diversion programs for the drug charges and if she successfully completed the programs, her record would be clean.

Johnny had a trial and was convicted of Felony Bank Robbery and possession of drugs. Johnny never had a bond reduction and remained in jail until the trial. He was not offered pre-trial diversion due to his prior convictions and the severity of the charges against him.

As a result, Johnny was convicted and transferred to the intake facility in prison.

Amber had 18 months to complete her diversion program. During this time, the police continued to investigate the bank robbery. Only half of the money was located during the initial search at the pawn shop and the police decided to visit Johnny Bentley in jail. He was serving 10 years for the robbery charges concurrent with the drug charges. There were no pending charges against him and thus he no longer had the need for court appointed lawyers.

The police learned that Amber kept her share of the robbery and she was subsequently arrested. She not only drove the getaway car, Johnny was able to show the police evidence of her planning the robbery. She was also significantly involved in the procurement and distribution of the methamphetamines.

Amber, with her prosecutorial diversion program completed, was arrested and convicted after trial. She was never bonded pre-trial and she was convicted, just like Johnny, of bank robbery with a sentence of 10 years.

4.2.6   Intake

First, upon conviction of a specific period of time, a prisoner is transferred to an intake facility. It is there you will be evaluated for what prison you will be housed and that process also determines your risk level.

There are functions in every intake facility that comprise what is known as the intake process.

The intake system can be exhaustive and in the State of Colorado it is a 14-day process of various intake tasks (Hardyman, Austin, & Peyton, 2004).

The intake process in every system is different but the first function of this process is to identify the prisoner. The identification involves fingerprinting and photographing the prisoner. A method of tagging is created and the prisoner is thereafter set to be screened for medical needs and mental health needs.

Amber had been fingerprinted and photographed in jail but now she was at the intake facility prior to headed to women's prison.

Amber was no longer pregnant and there were no drug charges. She was now going through a system of evaluation to determine where she was housed, how she was housed, what services would be offered, and what were her risks to the general prison population.

The intake process times vary with each facility but at some point, in a large prison system, there is a security threat analysis to determine if the prisoner is to be segregated. There are blood tests, academic testing, substance abuse assessments, mental health evaluations, DNA testing, dental exams, and historical data such as criminal background checks and social objective history intake. In the larger systems, the intake process will include classifying the prisoner's needs after the assessments and then rate areas to determine if the prisoner is a high needs prisoner or low needs prisoner.

Amber was assigned a prison identification number and her ID card was issued. At the beginning of her intake, she was issued toiletries including deodorant, toothpaste, and some soap. The intake process had begun. At the end of the intake process, a committee makes a final determination as to the classification level of each prisoner. The Committee considers many elements when classifying the prisoner such as potential for escape, the prisoner's past incarceration history, and whether the prisoner has known issues or enemies to be segregated from while in prison.

Amber was attending the Orientation Program where she received information on rules and regulations, disciplinary processes, education on prohibited behaviors, how to report violations of rules and available treatment and counseling options.

After her orientation, staff conducted a health screening and appraisal for each prisoner who arrives for intake, including dental and optometric exams. All newly committed prisoners are also given a TB test and a physical, including a blood test for venereal disease, hepatitis C (HCV), and the human immunodeficiency virus (HIV). However, testing is not required if the prisoner has a documented prior positive test result. HIV and HCV education and counseling will be provided to prisoners upon intake and physical. The test results will be provided confidentially to the prisoner along with any recommended follow-up medical care and treatment (Michigan Department of Corrections, 2020).

Amber was assessed by a psychologist. She told them she had ADD and had a diagnosed personality disorder. She was administered psychological testing and it was recommended that she receives mental health services.

Because Amber did not have a high school diploma, her transcript would be secured so that she could complete her GED or obtain her high school diploma.

The final stage of intake was DNA testing.

On an arrest and not post-conviction incarceration, in some states, the intake process is simplified. In North Carolina, the North Carolina Department of Corrections conducts intake on any prisoner with a 90 day or longer sentence—whether it is a misdemeanor or felony. A sentenced prisoner in North Carolina is required to be transferred from the county jail within 5 days of notification that the prisoner is awaiting transfer.

The intake facility has a classification committee which approves and reviews all the data to determine the facility placement.

Because Amber was placed at low risk of escape, no history of violence, and no known enemies, she was in a low-level security prison. This placement allowed her to receive visits from her minor child.

4.3   How Is Sentencing Handled for Women

In a 2015 study from the University of Michigan Law School, sentences for men were on average 63% longer than sentences for women (Starr, 2015). The exhaustive and well analyzed study in this publication demonstrates that when examining sentencing disparities, the study should include all aspects of the post-arrest processing steps.

Early criminal justice decisions can constrain later ones (Starr, 2015). To consider carte blanche that there are disparities in sentencing based on the actual convictions is a trite conclusion. The study that evaluated and decompensated the factors in post-arrest is as follows:

- Initial Charging/Offense Severity
- Sentencing Fact Finding

    - Drug quantity
    - Role in the criminal act

- Final Sentencing

In Amber's original case, her sentencing was handled by a prosecutorial diversion program. After her arrest for bank robbery, Amber's final sentencing was, in large part, handled by sentencing guidelines.

In 2006, the federal sentencing guidelines were watered down when the United States Supreme Court decided *United States v. Booker*. In *Booker*, the Court decided that the guidelines violated the Sixth Amendment of the United States Constitution by requiring a judge to enhance a defendant's sentence based on facts that were neither found by a jury nor admitted by the defendant (Acosta, 2015). In determining the guidelines violated the Constitution, the Court decided to make the guidelines advisory so that judges may be able to adjust a defendant's sentence based on the facts of each case. The Court did not clarify or explain what it meant to treat the guidelines as advisory, thus judges did not change their sentencing practices because they were unsure how to deviate from the sentencing range. The Court's vague holding did not mend the problems caused by the guidelines.

The guidelines and sentences demonstrate a disparity in gender.

Sentences Relative to the Guideline Range

- For each of the past 5 years, female offenders were sentenced within the guideline range in less than half of all cases (49.7% in fiscal year 2009 and 40.2% in fiscal year 2013), compared to 55.3% and 49.8% for male offenders.
- The rate of government sponsored below range sentences increased from 28.0% in fiscal year 2009 to 32.9% in fiscal year 2013, compared to 26.3% and 28.7% for male offenders.

    - Substantial assistance departures were granted in 20.9% of cases involving female offenders in fiscal year 2013. This represents 63.6% of all government sponsored below range sentences for female offenders.
    - Early Disposition Program (EDP) departures were granted in 18.9% of cases involving female offenders.
    - Other government sponsored below range sentences were granted in 17.6% of cases involving female offenders.

- The percentage of female offenders that received a non-government sponsored below range sentence increased over the last 5 years (from 21.1% of cases in fiscal year 2009 to 25.8% in fiscal year 2013), compared to 16.3% and 19.2% for male offenders.

- The average guideline minimum for female offenders has increased over the last 5 years from 36 months in fiscal year 2009 to 41 months in fiscal year 2013.
- The average sentence imposed slightly increased over the last 5 years, from 25 months in fiscal year 2009 to 27 months in fiscal year 2013 (United States Sentencing Commission, 2020).

Amber knew that every early stage of the process, she was out of chances. She had manipulated the system such that no charges were levied with regard to the bank robbery and she had prosecutorial diversion for the drug charges.

What happened to the money not in the safe—the other half, the fifty thousand ($50,000.00) dollars? Amber bought her little house and had her baby and continued manipulating Maurice at the pawn shop. As she went back into the system for the bank robbery, no District Attorney gave her a break at the early stages and her conviction stood.

4.3.1 Different Elements/Components of Sentencing

There are societal factors that play a role and factor into the offenses charged. Culpability in the crime itself is a sentencing fact-finding element. The prosecutors who consider the charges may determine that the women are less culpable as she is a minor player (Raeder, 2006). This thought process is sometimes referred to as the "Girlfriend" Theory—the preconceived notions that a woman is along for the ride and was somehow caught up on the crime as led by the male counterpart (Starr, 2015).

Another leading theory of why there are gender gaps and as explained in a 2006 report from Ann Martin Stacey and Cassia Spohn (2006) is that women received disparity in sentencing with less time because of "family responsibilities, offender characteristics and other variables."

Sentencing guidelines are in place and as such, once the conviction is entered, the guidelines control with little room to deviate by the judge. The true test of gender disparity is prior to the conviction—the charge, the plea, the ultimate determination of what the individual is facing before they enter their plea or before the trial.

4.3.2 Are Women More Likely to Be Sentenced Easier or Harsh

Professor Starr's recent paper, "Estimating Gender Disparities in Federal Criminal Cases," looks closely at a large dataset of federal cases, and reveals some significant findings. After controlling for the arrest offense, criminal history, and other prior characteristics, "men receive 63% longer sentences on average than women do," and "[w]omen are…twice as likely to avoid incarceration if convicted." This gender gap is so significant that it is easy to conclude that women are sentenced easier.

When Professor Starr conducted the in-depth study referenced above, she was approaching her study in a way that had never been analyzed before. She looks at every stage of post-arrest process—and at each stage, there are clear chances where factors come into play in the final conviction, the final sentence.

4.4 A Trending Exception

In a now outdated prior set of data cited by the ACLU, it was suggested that the average prison sentence for men who kill their female partners is two to 6 years. By contrast women, who kill their partners are sentenced on average 5 to 15 years (American Civil Liberties Union, 2020). Yes, men receive sentences sixty three (63%) percent less than women but in an intimate partner violence case, that same woman has much longer sentences. No studies cited have examined this disparity.

In the case study of Catina Curley, the woman is a victim of domestic violence and was granted a new trial after appeal (Rice, 2018). The movement to treat survivors of domestic violence as victims versus perpetrators is the focus of efforts by many organizations.

In an article that reviews the increase in conviction rates of women who kill intimate partners, it has been found that a wider gender gap exists in sentencing (Chalabi, 2019).

References

Acosta, J. (2015). Mandatory sentencing guidelines disparately affect female offenders. *FIU Law Review*. Retrieved March 2, 2020, from https://law.fiu.edu/2015/04/20/mandatory-sentencing-guidelines/

American Civil Liberties Union. (2020). *Words from prison – Did you know?* Retrieved March 2, 2020, from https://www.aclu.org/other/words-prison-did-you-know?redirect=words-prison-did-you-know

Center for Substance Abuse Treatment. (2005). *Substance abuse treatment for adults in the criminal justice system: Treatment Improvement Protocol (TIP) series 44* (DHHS Publication No. SMA 05–4056). Rockville, MD: Substance Abuse and Mental Health Services Administration.

Chalabi, M. (2019). *Are women punished more harshly for killing an intimate partner?* Retrieved March 2, 2020, from https://www.theguardian.com/news/datablog/2019/jan/12/intimate-partner-violence-gender-gap-cyntoia-brown

Denno, D. W. (1994). Gender, crime, and the criminal law defenses. *Journal of Criminal Law and Criminology, 85*, 80.

Hardyman, P. L., Austin, J., & Peyton, J. (2004). *Prisoner intake systems: Assessing needs and classifying prisoners*. Washington, DC: US Department of Justice, National Institute of Corrections.

Michigan Department of Corrections. (2020). *Reception center processing – New prisoners*. Retrieved March 2, 2020, from https://www.michigan.gov/corrections/0,4551,7-119-68854_68856_63694-292545%2D%2D,00.html

Raeder, M. S. (2006). Gender-related issues in a Post-Booker federal guidelines world. *McGeorge Law Review, 37*, 691.

Rice, J. D. (2018). *New Orleans woman sentenced to life in prison for killing abusive husband is granted new trial*. Retrieved March 2, 2020, from https://theappeal.org/new-orleans-woman-sentenced-to-life-in-prison-for-killing-abusive-husband-granted-new-trial/

Stacey, A. M., & Spohn, C. (2006). Gender and the Social Costs of Sentencing: An Analysis of Sentences Imposed on Male and Female Offenders in Three U.S. District Courts. *Berkeley Journal of Criminal Law, 11*, 43.

Starr, S. B. (2015). Estimating gender disparities in federal criminal cases. *American Law and Economics Review, 17*(1), 127–159.

Ulrich, T. E. (2002). Pretrial diversion in the federal court system. *Federal Probation, 66*, 30.

United States Sentencing Commission. (2020). *Quick facts: Women in the federal offender population*. Retrieved March 2, 2020, from https://www.ussc.gov/sites/default/files/pdf/research-and-publications/quick-facts/Quick_Facts_Female_Offenders.pdf

Chapter 5
The Female Prison Experience

Haley R. Zettler

5.1 Introduction

Historically, females have largely been neglected by the policies and procedures used in managing correctional institutions and in the research examining the prison experience (Pollock & Pollock-Byrne, 2002). As the number of women incarcerated has increased over the past two decades, more recent scholarly efforts have considered the experiences of incarcerated women (Belknap, 2007; Bloom, Owen, & Covington, 2003; Bronson & Carson, 2019; Calhoun, Messina, Cartier, & Torres, 2010; Greenfield & Snell, 2000; Sabol, Couture, & Harrison, 2007). Incarcerated women face many "pains" of incarceration including stigma, anxiety about their children, physical and emotional problems that occur from withdrawal, abuse by staff and other inmates, and cognitive dissonance (Faith, 1993, pp. 151–153). Females also bring specific challenges with them to prison including substance abuse, mental health, and victimization histories (Goodstein & Wright, 1989; Gover, Perez, & Jennings, 2008). As a result of these differences, research has explored whether a distinct subculture guides the female prison experience.

A number of ethnographic studies of female prisons have found that the prison social environment and role adaptations among females are different than those observed in male prisons (Carroll, 1974; Irwin, 2005; Owen, 1998; Sykes, 1958). The first researchers to study female subcultures in prison identified the presence of "pseudofamilies" or family networks that reflect roles such as mother, daughter, father, cousin, and grandmother (Giallombardo, 1966; Ward & Kassebaum, 1965). Females tend to recreate these familial relationships for closeness and support, whereas men are likely to seek out gang membership for protection (Pollock-Byrne, 1990). Researchers have historically focused on the structure of male prison gangs in terms of their predatory and exploitative nature as compared to the supportive

H. R. Zettler (✉)
University of North Texas, Denton, TX, USA
e-mail: haley.zettler@unt.edu

© Springer Nature Switzerland AG 2020
J. Hector (ed.), *Women and Prison*,
https://doi.org/10.1007/978-3-030-46172-0_5

nature of female pseudofamilies (Forsyth & Evans, 2003). Further research on female subcultures has found that incarcerated females are more likely prioritize their needs of comfort and control through the formation of relationships; whereas males are more likely to prioritize status, safety, and passing their time (Irwin, 2005; Kruttschnitt & Gartner, 2003). Research on prison environments has found that female prisons are generally less violent, have less gang activity, and do not have as much racial tension as compared to male prisons (Greer, 2000). Potentially influenced by the dramatic increase in the number of women incarcerated, there is evidence that interpersonal relationships may be less stable and familial as compared to the past; with a number of women expressing that they had not formed close bonds with other inmates (Greer, 2005). Overall, there is evidence that both the background factors and relationships formed in female prisons are different than male institutions, thus it is important to consider whether these factors influence the adjustment and needs of females during their incarceration. An examination of how these gender-specific risk factors and needs impact behavioral misconduct and social support during incarceration warrants further investigation.

5.2   Behavioral Misconduct in Female Prisons

There have been several studies looking at behavioral misconduct in female prisons; however, a large number of these studies were conducted more than a decade ago. Although disciplinary problems occur in female prisons, research has found that majority of females either do not commit any infractions or engage in very minor, nonviolent infractions during their sentences (Casey-Acevedo & Bakken, 2003). In their study of 222 females released from a maximum-security facility, a very small group of females were responsible for the vast majority of serious and/or violent infractions (Casey-Acevedo & Bakken, 2003). More recently, a study explored the trajectories of female inmate misconduct over three years and found that over half of their women had no serious disciplinary infractions (Reidy, Cihan, & Sorensen, 2017). The authors found that the largest group of rule violators were those who maintained a steady, but infrequent pattern of serious rule violations. Overall, the research suggests that serious or violent misconduct by females is a rare occurrence during incarceration.

Additionally, research has examined which factors predict misconduct among females. In a study of 123 females who had documented rule violations, Casey-Acevedo and Bakken (2001) found that those incarcerated for long sentences more frequently engaged in rule violations than those incarcerated for less than 18 months. Further, the authors found that the most common rule violation by short-term individuals were considered minor, whereas the most common rule violation among long-term individuals were violent. Thompson and Loper (2005) found that females with long- and medium-length sentences had a higher number of behavioral infractions. These findings suggest that the length of incarceration and prior criminal history might be a salient predictor of adjustment, as females who are isolated from their families and children may be more likely to act out during their incarceration.

Other factors surrounding women's behavioral adjustment tie back to the challenges that females bring in with them to the institution. For instance, victimization as a child or adolescent has been linked to behavioral misconduct during incarceration (Salisbury, Van Voorhis, & Spiropoulos, 2009; Warren, Hurt, Booker Loper, & Chauhan, 2004). Wright, Salisbury, and Van Voorhis (2007) explored how gender-responsive needs were related to prison misconduct among 272 incarcerated women in Missouri and found that experiencing childhood abuse, having depression or anxiety, psychosis, and having unsupportive relationships were related to both the prevalence and frequency of behavioral incidences. Gender-responsive scholars contend that justice-involved females are inherently very different than males, as demonstrated by their pathways to offending, the offenses they commit, their lower rates of violence, and their needs surrounding victimization, substance use, mental health, self-concept, child care, and relationships (Bloom et al., 2003; Covington, 2000). Exploring mental health as a risk factor of misconduct, Houser, Belenko, and Brennan (2012) found that females with a major mental health disorder or co-occurring disorders were significantly more likely to engage in both minor and serious behavioral infractions. Similarly, Houser and Welsh (2014) found that rates of misconduct among female inmates were highest for those with mental health disorders (34.1%), followed by those with co-occurring disorders (32.9%), inmates with substance use disorders (26.7%), and inmates with no disorder (17%). These authors found that the odds of any behavioral infractions were 2.2 times higher for inmates with mental health disorders and 2.4 times higher for inmates with co-occurring disorders (Houser & Welsh, 2014). Research has not only shown that co-occurring disorders may be predictive of female misconduct, but also that the odds of receiving severe disciplinary responses to minor infractions are significantly higher for those who suffer from co-occurring disorders (Houser & Belenko, 2015). In sum, there is strong evidence that women's unique histories of victimization, mental health, and substance abuse histories are predictive of behavioral misconduct during incarceration.

Another predictor of female misconduct is related to the strained familial relationships that affect many women during incarceration. In a study of 158 incarcerated mothers, more than half of the women with young children did not receive any visits from them (Casey-Acevedo, Bakken, & Karle, 2004). Interestingly, the study found that mothers who received visits from their children were more likely to engage in both serious and in violent misconduct than mothers who did not receive visits from their children (Casey-Acevedo et al., 2004). The authors surmise that this finding might be due to the fact that the emotional difficulty surrounding continued visitation and separation may make adjustment to prison life more difficult.

5.2.1   Gender Differences and Misconduct

Prior research has found mixed support for gender differences in the prevalence of prison misconduct. Several studies have found that females are more likely to commit minor infractions and less likely to commit serious or violent infractions than males, similar to the findings that females are less likely to engage in violence in the general population (Houser & Belenko, 2015; Jiang, 2005; Marcum, Hillinski-Rosick, & Freiburger, 2014). For instance, data from the 1997 survey of inmates in State and Federal Correctional Facilities illustrated that female facilities had higher rates of violations including abusive language, horseplay, and hygiene (Jiang, 2005). Additionally, the study found higher rates of serious violations in male facilities including possession of weapons, assaults, and escapes. In a recent nationally representative dataset of prisoners, Celinska and Sung (2014) reported that females had fewer overall rule violations, and that being a female reduced the likelihood of infractions by 24.8%. In contrast, Steiner and Wooldredge (2014) examined 46 facilities in Ohio and Kentucky and found no significant gender differences in the prevalence and incidence of both nonviolent and violent misconduct.

There is also mixed evidence as to whether predictors of misconduct vary by gender. In a sample of federal prisoners, Camp, Gaes, Langan, and Saylor (2003) found no gender differences in environmental and individual predictors of misconduct. Gover et al. (2008) found that women with prior incarcerations were less likely to commit rule violations, whereas men with incarceration histories were more likely to engage in misconduct. Further, these authors found that length of incarceration was only predictive of misconduct for females, suggesting that women may have more stressors to face upon incarceration (e.g., abuse histories, mental health problems, separation from children). In a sample of 1005 inmates, the authors found that both male and females who had prior disciplinary infractions from a prior incarceration were more likely to have both nonviolent and nonviolent infractions during subsequent incarceration periods (Drury & DeLisi, 2010). These conflicting findings illustrate the need to conduct more research examining gender differences with regard to institutional misconduct.

One investigation of inmates' participation in rehabilitative programming found that both males and females who had a work assignment were less likely to commit an assault during their incarceration (Solinas-Saunders & Stacer, 2012). For both males and females, Jiang (2005) demonstrated that misconduct was more common among individuals that were younger, had substance abuse histories, and more extensive criminal backgrounds. Similarly, Steiner and Wooldredge (2014) found that background factors such as age, and incarceration experiences (such as involvement in rehabilitative programming) were related to misconduct for both males and females. Overall, the findings suggest that male and female risk factors for behavioral misconduct are largely similar.

In addition to gender differences in the prevalence and predictors of misconduct, several studies have evaluated whether or not disciplinary practices for misconduct vary by gender. McClellan (1994) reported that among Texas inmates, women were cited more frequently for rule violations, experienced higher surveillance, and were punished more severely than males. In a sample of incarcerated females, Freeman (2003) concluded that officers, regardless of race or gender, who preferred adopting a personal, informal, surveillance relationship were less likely to file minor rule violation reports, indicating that connecting on a personal level encourages officers to ignore or handle rule violations informally. More research is necessary to understand how institutional disciplinary policies vary by gender.

5.3   Social Support and the Prison Experience

Unlike in many aspects of research on women in prison, there is a wealth of research assessing the impact of social support on both behavioral adjustment and post-release success for incarcerated females. Although there are a large number of parents incarcerated, females are more likely to be parents and be the sole caregiver to their children prior to their incarceration (Booker-Loper, Carlson, Levitt, & Scheffel, 2009; Bureau of Justice Statistics, 2000). Mothers are more likely to have daily interactions with their children than males and the more frequent single-parent status of mothers prior to incarceration increases the likelihood that children are placed in foster care than children of incarcerated fathers (Glaze & Maruschak, 2008). Thus, incarcerating females is more likely to disrupt a family unit than incarcerating a male (Pollock, 2002). Moreover, incarcerated mothers often express that their children provide motivation for change both during and after incarceration (Casey-Acevedo & Bakken, 2002).

One challenge to social support is the location of women's prisons, as many are located in areas far from their city of residence prior to incarceration. Since there are fewer female facilities (many states have only one), incarcerated women may experience more profound deprivations due to the inability to transfer to another facility for programming needs, problems within the facility, or to be closer to family (MacKenzie, Robinson, & Campbell, 1989). For instance, one study found that the average distance between female institutions and city of residence was 122.67 miles (Bedard & Helland, 2004). The physical distance can make visitation between family members and children difficult for incarcerated women. An examination of the Bureau of Justice Statistics' 2004 Survey of Inmates in State Correctional Facilities found that 49.6% of incarcerated people in a facility less than 50 miles from their home reported visitation in the past month as compared to 25.9% of persons in a facility more than 100 miles from their home (Rabuy & Kopf, 2015). In a sample of 158 incarcerated mothers, Casey-Acevedo et al. (2004) reported that women who were incarcerated outside of their metropolitan area were much less likely to receive visits from their children. Similarly, Bedard and Helland (2004) found that 47% of women whose city of residence was less than 50 miles from the institution saw their children at least once a month; compared to 24% of women whose city of residence was 50 miles or more from the institution. Lack of visitation not only impacts the mother, but also the relationship with her children. While phone and mail contact significantly predict post-release attachment between parents and children, face-to-face visits have the greatest positive impact on parent-child relationships post-release (La Vigne, Naser, Brooks, & Castro, 2005).

Receiving visits, phone calls, mail, and money for commissary are ways that support networks provide support during a loved one's incarceration. Research has shown that separation from loved ones during incarceration can cause feelings of shame or guilt during incarceration that may impede successful reentry, and how ongoing family contact enhances emotional survival (Dodge & Pogrebin, 2001). Although family support is important for both males and females, there is evidence that maintaining relationships with loved ones may be more salient for incarcerated female, and these relationships may serve as a stronger protective factor against behavioral misconduct (Mumola, 2000; Wright, DeHart, Koons-Witt, & Crittenden, 2013).

Prior research has illustrated that females may experience social support during their incarceration in distinct ways. Pollock (2002) notes that "visitation rooms in women's prisons are mostly filled with family members and children, visitation rooms in men's prisons are usually filled with wives and girlfriends" (p. 111). In general, women who are incarcerated report more frequent contact with their children than incarcerated men (Booker-Loper et al., 2009). For instance, a national sample of male and female prisons found that females received more calls (52% vs. 36%), received more mail (62% vs. 43%), and had more visits by children (33% vs. 25%) than males (Jiang & Winfree, 2006). Regarding financial support, Smoyer (2015) found that money for commissary was one of the central ways that women received support, from loved ones during their incarceration.

Additionally, there are gender differences regarding institutional visitation policies and procedures. In a survey of 193 facilities, Hoffman, Dickinson, and Dunn (2007) found that women's facilities had more visits each month, more open visitation policies, were more likely to allow physical contact with visitors, less likely to require a correctional officer during a visit, and were allowed more telephone calls than male facilities. Monroe (2012) found that significantly more visitors were approved in female facilities as compared to male facilities.

Prior studies report mixed findings as to how social support (e.g. phone calls, mail, and visits with friends and family) is related to misconduct and emotional well-being during incarceration. Several studies have found that visitation, and more frequent visitation, is associated with less behavioral misconduct for both males and females (Cochran, 2012; Jiang & Winfree, 2006). However, other studies have provided results differentiated by gender. For instance, Celinska and Sung (2014) found that the number of visits from family and friends in the past month decreased the likelihood of rule violations for females by 6%, but did not have an effect on males. In contrast, a study of 6000 incarcerated parents reported that both males and females who received visits from their children, and females who received mail from their children were more likely to be written up and/or found guilty of behavioral infractions (Benning & Lahm, 2016). These mixed findings may be attributed to the complex emotional stress generated by parental incarceration that may lead to misconduct (Booker-Loper et al., 2009; Wright, Van Voorhis, Salisbury, & Bauman, 2012). Overall, more research is needed to understand the nuanced findings surrounding the impact of social support specific to the female prison experience.

The distinctive challenges that influence females' behavior during incarceration may also shape their post-release success. Not only is social support linked to institutional adjustment, but a growing body of literature consistently finds that social support is a strong predictor of successful reentry for females (Cobbina, Huebner, & Berg, 2012; Dowden & Andrew, 1999; Leverentz, 2006; Simons, Steward, Gordon, Conger, & Elder Jr., 2002; Slaght, 1999; Van Voorhis, Salisbury, Wright, & Ashley, 2008). Formerly incarcerated women report that one of the most negative aspects of being incarcerated is being separated from their children and families (Bui & Morash, 2010), and that family support is a crucial aspect to fostering successful reintegration to the community (Cobbina, 2010). Just as social support such as visitation is associated with behavior during incarceration, a meta-analysis by Mitchell, Spooner, Jia, and Zhang (2016) found that visitation resulted in an average 26% decrease in recidivism post-release. Overall, there is strong support that female institutions should implement policies and programs that foster social support during incarceration.

5.4   How to Address the Impact of Incarceration for Females

Historically, most examinations on the effects of incarceration on prisoners have focused on male offenders. More recently, research has begun to consider the perceptions and experiences of incarcerated females (Greer, 2005). As men and women adapt to incarceration in different ways, it is necessary to understand the unique experiences of incarcerated women. The prison experience is often described as more painful for women due to the emphasis placed on the importance of family and loved ones, especially children (Collica, 2010; Ward & Kassebaum, 1965). Many women express reuniting with their children as their primary motivation during their incarceration (Belknap, 2007; Jiang & Winfree, 2006). Maintaining contact with family members, especially children, can help strengthen social bonds (Howser & MacDonald, 1982), alleviate the pains of imprisonment (Gordon, 1999), decrease the effects of prisonization (Zingraff, 1980), reduce behavioral misconduct (Celinska & Sung, 2014), and improve the odds of successful reentry (Mitchell et al., 2016). As the supportive "pseudofamily" subculture seems to be diminishing in female institutions (Greer, 2005), correctional programming is another way that women may experience conventional support during their incarceration (Koons, Burrow, Morash, & Bynum, 1997; Severance, 2005).

As research has illustrated how social support shapes the female prison experience, correctional institutions should implement programming that focuses on maintaining and strengthening bonds to family members, especially children. Table 5.1 provides an overview of three prison-based programs designed to improve familial bonds and communication with children during incarceration. Although empirical investigations have established benefits of such programming, studies of prison visitation find that less than half of incarcerated persons receive support thorough in-person visits (Derkzen, Gobeil, & Gileno, 2009; Duwe & Clark, 2013; Mears, Cochran, Siennick, & Bales, 2012), thus it is important that programming is available to increase social bonds with family and children. One example of a

Table 5.1 Programs designed to strengthen bonds/increase visitation for incarcerated mothers

Program name	Description of program
Partners in Parenting (PIP)	Skills-based program focusing on strengthening family relationships and promoting positive behaviors. Program increases parental knowledge regarding risks, resiliency factors, and developmental assets. A focus on reintegration issues include: establishing positive support networks, the school system, and high-risk behavior in children
Girl Scouts Beyond Bars (GSBB)	Institutional-based enhanced visiting program for incarcerated mothers and their daughters. Addresses the needs of both daughters and mothers through regular meetings with a Girl Scouts facilitator. A focus on issues include building self-esteem, prosocial decision-making, and other life skills
Reading Family Ties: Face-to-Face	Weekly family visits using videoconferencing technology. Incarcerated mothers keep a weekly journal to overcome their hesitancy to use the equipment. The class improves literacy levels, encourages letter-writing, and quality of long-distance visits

program designed to strengthen familial bonds is the Partners in Parenting (PIP) program at women's correctional facilities in Colorado. An evaluation of the PIP program found that women who participated in the program reported feeling more confident in their parenting abilities and stronger bonds with their children, and as a result, felt more motivated to avoid incarceration upon release (Gonzalez, Romero, & Cerbana, 2007).

Several evaluations of visitation programs have also provided promising results for incarcerated women. For instance, parent-child visitation programs such as Girl Scouts Beyond Bars (GSBB) have been shown to improve relationships and communication between incarcerated mothers and their daughters (Block & Potthast, 2017). As many family members express difficulty physically visiting their incarcerated loved ones (Christian, 2005), it is important that prisons consider other ways that social support may be facilitated (Hoffman, Byrd, & Kightlinger, 2010). For example, the use of technology such as videoconferencing may be one way that incarcerated mothers may maintain contact with their children. In Florida, the "Reading Family Ties: Face to Face" program allows mothers to have weekly virtual visits with their children (Bartlett, 2000). As the use of technology to facilitate social support becomes more commonplace, evaluations of these types of programs should be employed to examine how they impact the experience of incarcerated women.

5.5   Policy Recommendations and Future Research Directions

Overall, the extant research highlights how women experience incarceration in distinctive ways. Females bring with them background characteristics such as substance abuse, mental health, and trauma histories that must be considered during their incarceration (Gover et al., 2008). The use of trauma-informed programs, such as Seeking Safety, that simultaneously address both trauma-symptoms and substance use disorders may be especially important for incarcerated females (Najavits, Gallop, & Weiss, 2006). There is evidence that stressors evoked during incarceration, especially surrounding separation from their children, are especially salient for women (Wright et al., 2012). As social support is an important predictor of successful reintegration, institutions should provide programs that help to maintain and strengthen familial bonds. Further, due to the fact that facilities are often located far away from incarcerated females' families, the use of technology such as video conferencing should be provided to maintain family contact.

While there has been more attention to incarcerated females in the past, less is known about the long-term impact of female incarceration as compared to males. Multidisciplinary research from the fields of criminology, psychology, and social work might provide fruitful results for correctional policy in female institutions. Future research should assess the impact of gender-responsive programming for incarcerated females. Existing evaluations of programs in female institutions have largely focused on their effectiveness during incarceration. Therefore, future research should assess these programs' impact on successful reintegration. More research is necessary to identify which programming is most effective in mitigating the negative experiences of incarceration for females and promoting desistance.

References

Bartlett, R. (2000). Helping inmate moms keep in touch—Prison programs encourage ties with children. *Corrections Today, 62*(7), 102–104.

Bedard, K., & Helland, E. (2004). The location of women's prisons and the deterrence effect of "harder" time. *International Review of Law and Economics, 24*, 147–167.

Belknap, J. (2007). *The invisible woman: Gender, crime, and justice.* Belmont, CA: Wadsworth.

Benning, C. L., & Lahm, K. F. (2016). Effects of parent-child relationships on inmate behavior: A comparison of male and female inmates. *International Journal of Offender Therapy and Comparative Criminology, 60*(2), 189–207.

Block, K. J., & Potthast, M. J. (2017). Girl scouts beyond bars: Facilitating parent-child contact in 5 correctional settings. In *Children with Parents in Prison* (pp. 93–110). London: Routledge.

Bloom, B., Owen, B., & Covington, S. (2003). *Gender-responsive strategies: Research, practice, and guiding principles for women offenders.* Washington, DC: National Institute of Corrections.

Booker-Loper, A., Carlson, L., Levitt, L., & Scheffel, K. (2009). Parenting stress, alliance, child contact, and adjustment of imprisoned mothers and fathers. *Journal of Offender Rehabilitation, 48*, 483–503.

Bronson, J., & Carson, E. A. (2019). *Prisoners in 2017.* Bureau of Justice Statistics: Washington, DC.

Bui, H. N., & Morash, M. (2010). The impact of network relationships, prison experiences, and internal transformation on women's success after prison release. *Journal of Offender Rehabilitation, 49*, 1–22.

Bureau of Justice Statistics. (2000). *Incarcerated parents and their children.* Washington, DC: U.S. Department of Justice.

Calhoun, S., Messina, N., Cartier, J., & Torres, S. (2010). Implementing gender-responsive treatment for women in prison: Client and staff perspectives. *Federal Probation, 74*(3), 27–33.

Camp, S. D., Gaes, G. G., Langan, N. P., & Saylor, W. G. (2003). The influence of prisons on inmate misconduct: A multilevel investigation. *Justice Quarterly, 20,* 501–533.

Carroll, L. (1974). *Hacks, Blacks, and cons: Race relations in a maximum security prison.* Lexington, MA: Lexington Books.

Casey-Acevedo, K., & Bakken, T. (2001). The effect of time on the disciplinary adjustment of women in prison. *International Journal of Offender Therapy and Comparative Criminology, 45*(4), 489–497.

Casey-Acevedo, K., & Bakken, T. (2002). Visiting women in prison: Who visits and who cares? *Journal of Offender Rehabilitation, 34,* 67–83.

Casey-Acevedo, K., & Bakken, T. (2003). Women adjusting to prison: Disciplinary behavior and the characteristics of adjustment. *Journal of Health & Social Policy, 17*(4), 37–60.

Casey-Acevedo, K., Bakken, T., & Karle, A. (2004). Children visiting mothers in prison: The effects on mothers' behavior and disciplinary adjustment. *The Australian and New Zealand Journal of Criminology, 37*(3), 418–430.

Celinska, K., & Sung, H. E. (2014). Gender differences in the determinants of prison rule violations. *The Prison Journal, 94*(2), 220–241.

Christian, J. (2005). Riding the bus: Barriers to prison visitation and family management strategies. *Journal of Contemporary Criminal Justice, 21,* 31–48.

Cobbina, J. E. (2010). Reintegration success and failure: Factors impacting reintegration and formerly incarcerated women. *Journal of Offender Rehabilitation, 49,* 210–232.

Cobbina, J. E., Huebner, B. M., & Berg, M. T. (2012). Men, women, and postrelease offending: An examination of the nature of the link between relational ties and recidivism. *Crime & Delinquency, 58,* 331–361.

Cochran, J. C. (2012). The ties that bind or the ties that break: Examining the relationship between visitation and prisoner misconduct. *Journal of Criminal Justice, 40,* 433–440.

Collica, K. (2010). Surviving incarceration: Two prison-based peer programs build communities of support for female offenders. *Deviant Behavior, 31,* 314–347.

Covington, S. (2000). Helping women to recover: Creating gender-specific treatment for substance-abusing women and girls in community corrections. In M. McMahon (Ed.), *Assessment to assistance: Programs for women in community corrections* (pp. 171–233). Lanham, MD: American Correctional Association.

Derkzen, D. M., Gobeil, R., & Gileno, J. (2009). *Visitation and post-release outcome among federally-sentenced offenders.* Correctional Service of Canada. Retrieved from http://www.csc.scc.gc.ca/text/rsrch/reports/r205/r205-eng.pdf

Dodge, M., & Pogrebin, M. R. (2001). Collateral costs of imprisonment for women: Complications for reintegration. *The Prison Journal, 81*(1), 42–54.

Dowden, C., & Andrew, D. (1999). What works for female offenders: A meta-analysis review. *Crime & Delinquency, 45,* 438–452.

Drury, A. J., & DeLisi, M. (2010). The past is prologue: Prior adjustment to prison and institutional misconduct. *The Prison Journal, 90*(3), 331–352.

Duwe, G., & Clark, V. (2013). Blessed be the social tie that binds: The effects of prison visitation on offender recidivism. *Criminal Justice Policy Review, 24*(3), 271–296.

Faith, K. (1993). *Unruly women: The politics of confinement and resistance.* Vancouver: Press Gang.

Forsyth, C. J., & Evans, R. D. (2003). Reconsidering the pseudo-family/gang gender distinction in prison research. *Journal of Police and Criminal Psychology, 18*(1), 15–23.

Freeman, R. M. (2003). Social distance and discretionary rule enforcement in a women's prison. *The Prison Journal, 83*(2), 191–205.

Giallombardo, R. (1966). *Society of women: A study of women's prison.* New York: John Wiley.

Glaze, L., & Maruschak, L. (2008). *Parents in prison and their minor children* (U.S. Department of Justice Bureau of Justice Statistics Special Report). pp. 1–25.

Gonzalez, P., Romero, T., & Cerbana, C. (2007). Parent education program for incarcerated mothers in Colorado. *Journal of Correctional Education, 58,* 357–373.

Goodstein, L., & Wright, K. N. (1989). Inmate adjustment to prison. In L. Goodstein & D. L. Mackenzie (Eds.), *The American prison: Issues in research and policy* (pp. 229–251). New York, NY: Plenum.

Gordon, J. (1999). Are conjugal and familial visitation effective rehabilitative concepts? *The Prison Journal, 79*, 119–124.

Gover, A., Perez, D., & Jennings, W. (2008). Gender differences in factors contributing to institutional misconduct. *The Prison Journal, 88*, 378–403.

Greenfield, L. A., & Snell, T. L. (2000). *Women offenders*. Washington, DC: Bureau of Justice Statistics.

Greer, K. R. (2000). The changing nature of interpersonal relationships in a women's prison. *The Prison Journal, 80*(4), 442–468.

Greer, K. R. (2005). The changing nature of interpersonal relationships in a women's prison. *The Prison Journal, 80*(4), 442–468.

Hoffman, H. C., Byrd, A. L., & Kightlinger, A. M. (2010). Prison programs and services for incarcerated parents and their underage children: Results from a national survey of correctional facilities. *The Prison Journal, 90*(4), 397–416.

Hoffman, H. C., Dickinson, G. E., & Dunn, C. L. (2007). State facilities for women and men: A comparison of communication and visitation policies. *Corrections Compendium, 32*(1), 1–5.

Houser, K., & Belenko, S. (2015). Disciplinary responses to misconduct among female prison inmates with mental illness, substance use disorders, and co-occurring disorders. *Psychiatric Rehabilitation Journal, 38*(1), 24–34.

Houser, K., Belenko, S., & Brennan, P. (2012). The effects of mental health and substance use disorders on institutional misconduct among female inmates. *Justice Quarterly, 29*, 799–828.

Houser, K. A., & Welsh, W. (2014). Examining the association between co-occurring disorders and seriousness of misconduct by female prison inmates. *Criminal Justice and Behavior, 41*(5), 650–666.

Howser, J., & MacDonald, D. (1982). Maintaining family ties. *Corrections Today, 44*, 96–98.

Irwin, J. (2005). *The warehouse prison: Disposal of the new dangerous class*. Los Angeles, CA: Roxbury.

Jiang, S. (2005). Impact of drug use on inmate misconduct: A test of the deprivation, importation, and situational models. *The Prison Journal, 82*, 335–358.

Jiang, S., & Winfree Jr., L. T. (2006). Social support, gender, and inmate adjustment to prison life: Insights from a national sample. *The Prison Journal, 86*(1), 32–55.

Koons, B., Burrow, J., Morash, M., & Bynum, T. (1997). Expert and offender perceptions of program elements linked to successful for incarcerated women. *Crime & Delinquency, 43*(4), 512–532.

Kruttschnitt, C., & Gartner, R. (2003). Women's imprisonment. In M. Tonry (Ed.), *Crime and justice: A review of research* (Vol. 30, pp. 1–81). Chicago, IL: The University of Chicago Press.

La Vigne, N. G., Naser, R. L., Brooks, L. E., & Castro, J. L. (2005). Examining the effect of incarceration and in-prison family contact on prisoners' family relationships. *Journal of Contemporary Criminal Justice, 21*(4), 314–335.

Leverentz, A. (2006). *People, places, and things: The social process of reentry for female offenders*. Washington, DC: National Criminal Justice Reference Service.

MacKenzie, D. L., Robinson, J., & Campbell, C. (1989). Long-term incarceration of female offenders. *Criminal Justice and Behavior, 16*(2), 223–238.

Marcum, C. D., Hillinski-Rosick, C. M., & Freiburger, T. L. (2014). Examining the correlates of male and female inmate misconduct. *Security Journal, 27*(3), 284–303.

McClellan, D. (1994). Disparity in the discipline of male and female inmates in Texas prisons. *Women & Criminal Justice, 5*, 71–97.

Mears, D. P., Cochran, J. C., Siennick, S. E., & Bales, W. D. (2012). Prison visitation and recidivism. *Justice Quarterly, 29*(6), 888–918.

Mitchell, M. M., Spooner, K., Jia, D., & Zhang, Y. (2016). The effect of prison visitation on reentry success: A meta-analysis. *Journal of Criminal Justice, 47*, 74–83.

Monroe, A. (2012). Effects of prisoner location on visitation patterns. *McNair Scholars Research Journal, 8*(1), 41–52.

Mumola, C. J. (2000). *Incarcerated parents and their children* (Bureau of Justice Statistics Special Report).

Najavits, L. M., Gallop, R. J., & Weiss, R. D. (2006). Seeking Safety therapy for adolescent girls with PTSD and substance use disorder: A randomized controlled trial. *The Journal of Behavioral Health Services & Research, 33*(4), 453–463.

Owen, B. (1998). *In the mix: Struggle and survival in a women's prison*. Albany, NY: State University of New York Press.

Pollock, J. M. (2002). *Women, crime, and prison*. Belmont, CA: Wadsworth.

Pollock, J. M., & Pollock-Byrne, J. M. (2002). *Women, prison, & crime*. Belmont, CA: Wadsworth Thomson Learning.

Pollock-Byrne, J. (1990). *Women, Prison & Crime*. Pacific Grove, CA: Brooks/Cole Publishing.

Rabuy, B., & Kopf, D. (2015). Separation by bars and miles: Visitation in state prisons. *Prison Policy Initiative, 20.*

Reidy, T. J., Cihan, A., & Sorensen, J. R. (2017). Women in prison: Investigating trajectories of institutional female misconduct. *Journal of Criminal Justice, 52*, 49–56.

Sabol, W. J., Couture, H., & Harrison, P. M. (2007). *Prisoners in 2006*. Washington, DC: Bureau of Justice Statistics.

Salisbury, E. J., Van Voorhis, P., & Spiropoulos, G. V. (2009). The predictive validity of a gender-responsive needs assessment: An exploratory study. *Crime & Delinquency, 55*(4), 550–585.

Severance, T. (2005). You know who you can go to: Cooperation and exchange between incarcerated women. *The Prison Journal, 85*(3), 343–367.

Simons, R. L., Steward, E., Gordon, L. C., Conger, R. D., & Elder Jr., G. H. (2002). A test of life-course explanations for stability and change in antisocial behavior from adolescence to young adulthood. *Criminology, 40*, 401–434.

Slaght, E. (1999). Family and offender treatment focusing on the family in the treatment of substance abusing criminal offenders. *Journal of Drug Education, 19*(1), 53–62.

Smoyer, A. B. (2015). Feeding relationships: Foodways and social networks in a women's prison. *Affilia: Journal of Women and Social Work, 30*(1), 26–39.

Solinas-Saunders, M., & Stacer, M. J. (2012). Prison resources and physical/verbal assault in prison: A comparison of male and female inmates. *Victims and Offenders, 7*, 279–311.

Steiner, B., & Wooldredge, J. (2014). Sex differences in the predictors of prisoner misconduct. *Criminal Justice and Behavior, 41*(4), 433–452.

Sykes, G. (1958). *The society of captives*. Princeton, NJ: Princeton University of Press.

Thompson, C., & Loper, A. B. (2005). Adjustment patterns in incarcerated women: An analysis of differences based on sentence length. *Criminal Justice and Behavior, 32*, 714–732.

Van Voorhis, P., Salisbury, E., Wright, E., & Ashley, B. (2008). *Achieving accurate pictures of risk and identifying gender responsive needs: Two new assessments for women offenders*. Washington DC: University of Cincinnati Center for Criminal Justice Research, National Institute of Corrections.

Ward, D. A., & Kassebaum, G. G. (1965). *Women's prisons: Sex and social structure*. Chicago: Aldine.

Warren, J. I., Hurt, S., Booker Loper, A., & Chauhan, P. (2004). Exploring prison adjustment among female inmates: Issues of measurement and prediction. *Criminal Justice and Behavior, 31*(5), 624–645.

Wright, E. M., DeHart, D. D., Koons-Witt, B. A., & Crittenden, C. A. (2013). 'Buffers' against crime? Exploring the roles and limitations of positive relationships among women in prison. *Punishment & Society, 15*(1), 71–95.

Wright, E. M., Salisbury, E. J., & Van Voorhis, P. (2007). Predicting the prison misconducts of women offenders: The importance of gender-responsive needs. *Journal of Contemporary Criminal Justice, 23*(4), 310–340.

Wright, E. M., Van Voorhis, P., Salisbury, E. J., & Bauman, A. (2012). Gender-responsive lessons learned and policy implications for women in prison: A review. *Criminal Justice and Behavior, 39*(12), 1612–1632.

Zingraff, M. T. (1980). Inmate assimilation: A comparison of male and female delinquents. *Criminal Justice and Behavior, 7*, 275–292.

Chapter 6
Justice-Involved Girls and Women, Health and Pregnancy, Mental Health, and Substance Abuse Concerns

Jada Hector and Kristy D. Fusilier

6.1 Introduction

According to the National Alliance on Mental Illness (NAMI), it is estimated that one in every five adults in the USA experiences mental illness—one in every 25 will experience a serious mental illness (NAMI, 2020). As mentioned throughout this text, society's ills tend to be concentrated in our jails and prisons. The latest Bureau of Justice Statistics report estimates that one in seven state and federal prisoners and one in four jail inmates indicated at least a baseline level of *serious* psychological distress in the last 30 days via an array of self-report survey responses (Bronson & Berzofsky, 2017). Moreover, this report reveals that 37% of prisoners and 44% of jail inmates have been diagnosed with a mental health disorder by a professional (also indicated by self-report), with females in prison (20%) and jail (32%) far exceeding males in prison (14%) and jail (26%) having indications of at least a baseline level of serious psychological distress in the past 30 days. In other words, one in every three women that enter American jails recently experience severe psychological distress.

Generally speaking, females tend to seek mental health (including substance use) treatment at rates that far exceed males. Current data among American adults with any mental illness indicate the following treatment-seeking rates by demographic (NAMI, 2020):

- Male: 34.9%
- Female: 48.6%
- Lesbian, gay, or bisexual: 48.6%
- Non-Hispanic Asian: 24.9%
- Non-Hispanic white: 49.1%
- Non-Hispanic black or African-American: 30.6%

J. Hector (✉) · K. D. Fusilier
University of Louisiana at Lafayette, Lafayette, LA, USA

- Non-Hispanic mixed or multiracial: 31.8%
- Hispanic or Latinx: 32.9%

It should be noted, that generally, women are more likely to be officially diagnosed with a mental illness due to the candid nature and willingness to share their thoughts and feelings. Given this and the revelation of the data above, it should not be surprising that the Bureau of Justice Statistics report reveals that female prisoners self-report a history of a mental health problem at *nearly double* the rate than male prisoners do (65.8% versus 34.8%); American jail inmates show a similar pattern (67.9% versus 40.8%; Bronson & Berzofsky, 2017). Yet, the gendered differences in serious psychological stress in the last 30 days are revealing—measuring mental health in this manner partially circumvents the differences in treatment seeking and official diagnosis. The totality of evidence in the literature suggests that girls and women with traumatic histories and severe psychological distress are overrepresented in the criminal justice system.

Considering the overrepresentation of justice-involved individuals with mental illness, both inside and out of jails and prisons, the need for treatment becomes a central focus. Women especially have specific needs that also must often include working with families and children, treatment for previous trauma and abuse, as well as substance use. When looking at the needs of girls and women in jails and prison, one must also consider the female environment both inside and out of the jail or prison walls. Treatment programs and resources are a necessity while a woman is incarcerated. Additionally, roughly 81,000 women are released from state prisons each year, while about 1.8 million girls and women leave American jails each year at last count (Sawyer, 2019):

> Given the dramatic growth of women's incarceration in recent years, it's concerning how little attention and how few resources have been directed to meeting the reentry needs of justice-involved women. After all, we know that women have different pathways to incarceration than men, and distinct needs, including the treatment of past trauma and substance use disorders, and more broadly, escaping poverty and meeting the needs of their children and families…. A handful of programs have sprung up in communities around the country to meet the needs of women returning home: some founded by formerly incarcerated women themselves, some running on shoestring budgets for years, and all underscoring the need for greater capacity to meet the demand…. While many people are released from jail within a day or so and may not need reentry support, jail releases can't be overlooked, especially for women, who are more likely than men to be incarcerated in jails as opposed to prisons. (Moreover, jails typically provide fewer programs and services than prisons, so individuals released from jails are even less likely to have received necessary treatment or services while incarcerated than those in prison.)

As with many issues endemic to both the mental health and criminal justice systems, robust and consistent funding for programing and resources is often problematic and under stress—resulting in a sheer lack of options. Luckily, there have been more recent movements to offer care, treatment, and resources specifically for women and even their children. In addition, both the Office of Justice Programs (embedded in the U.S. Department of Justice) and the Substance Abuse and Mental Health Services Administration have recently been offering Federal grants for gender-responsive treatment programming for justice-involved women and girls.

In addition to the above mental health concerns, substance use disorder is a commonplace diagnosis for many people in the system; a person with a mental illness is generally more likely to also be diagnosed with substance use disorder. In fact, it is estimated that 36% of individuals with a personality disorder, 23% with bipolar disorder, 22% with schizophrenia, 16% with anxiety disorder, adjustment disorder, or depressive disorders, and 10% with attention deficit disorders are also diagnosed with a substance use disorder compared to only 2% of individuals without any other history of mental health disorders (SAMHSA, 2018). A person with a diagnosis of mental illness and substance use disorder is considered to have a co-occurring disorder (COD) as defined by the DSM-V (Diagnostic and Statistics Manual)—the book used by mental health and medical professionals for diagnosis. A person with COD will need additional resources to aid in their overall success both inside and out of prison. Additionally, as previously noted many times within this book, incarcerated women are often previous victims of trauma, which radically increases the likelihood of psychological distress and substance use disorder. There is little doubt that the needs of incarcerated women in girls vastly exceed that of their male counterparts (Garcia & Ritter, 2012).

Importantly, none of the above considers the uniquely female concern of pregnancy, justice-involvement, and incarceration. It is estimated that nearly three in four incarcerated women are in their childbearing years (in this case, defined as being between 18 and 44 years old), two in three are already mothers and *primary* caregivers to their children, and more than four in five have been previously pregnant (Sufrin, Beal, Clarke, Jones, & Mosher, 2019). Considering, again, that vast majority of these women will be released back into society and to their families, ensuring the positive wellness of these women is critical. Studies show that children of incarcerated parents are far more likely to also be incarcerated in their adult futures. Therefore, rehabilitation and wellness of incarcerated mothers can additionally impact future generations to exponentially reduce incarceration and subsequent recidivism.

This chapter explores the most current literature on girl- and woman-responsive treatment and care for substance use disorder, mental health concerns, and pregnancy, both domestically and abroad. While incomplete as many innovations are currently emerging and being developed, the following provides a glimpse into the activity that is ongoing to resolve the overwhelming need justice-involved girls and women face on a day-to-day basis.

6.2 Substance Use Disorder

Throughout this text, it is revealed that girls and women are the fastest-growing portion of the prison population (Begun, Rose, Lebel, & Teske-Young, 2009; Drug Policy Alliance, 2018; Lucente, Fals-Stewart, Richards, & Goscha, 2001). More than a quarter of those women incarcerated in state prison in 2015 were for drug offenses. When looking at Federal prisons, approximately 61% of females incarcerated are for drug offenses. The Jail Inmates in 2017 report by the Bureau of Justice Statistics indicates that Americans are jailed at a rate of 229 inmates per 100,000 citizens; females are jailed at a rate of 69 per 100,000 citizens. Yet, the proportion of girls and women going to jail has increased from 2005 to 2017—the jail incarceration rate for females increased 10% over the last 10 years, while men saw their rate decline by 12% (Zeng, 2019). More women than men are currently incarcerated for drug offenses. Additionally, Caucasian individuals make up almost half of the population. The average jail time is 26 days.

Female prisoners have specific needs. They are more likely to have a drug related offense, more likely to have a substance abuse disorder, and lack overall social support (Andersen, 2018). Often, they experience intimate partner violence (Lucente et al., 2001). When looking at female substance use, research shows that lack of parental supervision often contributes to use (Bowles, DeHart, & Webb, 2012). Additionally, history of adverse childhood experiences (abuse, neglect, rape, etc.) often results in substance use being utilized as a means to cope (Bowles et al., 2012). Any of these can lead to substance use, depression, post-traumatic stress disorder, and/or criminal activity (NIDA, 2014).

Female offenders more likely have history of maltreatment, witnessing violence and growing up with absent, addicted, and/or mentally ill caregivers. Substance use can be from a need to cope with these adversities as well as a means of self-medicating (Bowles et al., 2012). In addition, women and girls are more likely to have substance abuse histories, co-occurring mental disorders, prior treatment for both, more physical health problems, histories of physical and/or sexual abuse, victims of domestic violence (NIDA, 2014).

6.2.1   Available Substance Use Programming

There are several types of programs available to incarcerated individuals. Availability of such programs is dependent upon variables such as location, size of facility, funding, and overall resources. The Federal Bureau of Prisons (2020) takes a comprehensive treatment strategy incorporating effective evidence-based practices, literature findings as well as population needs. This strategy often becomes a model for states to emulate; however, a handful of states have offered such model strategies on their own, as well.

When programs are well-designed and implemented appropriately, the benefits are enormous and can greatly impact physical and mental health. Relationships with inmates as well as general populations have shown improvement. Additional benefits include reducing relapse, criminal behavior, and therefore, recidivism. Role in society can be increased, thus resulting in overall safety and economic benefits to self and community (FBOP, 2020). Not only is effective treatment necessary for recovery, follow-up management is also important. Outcomes are improved with monitoring and continued treatment participation (NIDA, 2014). Untreated upon release leads to continued use, relapses, and subsequent criminal behaviors (Begun et al., 2009).

Treatment based on level of use and personal problems that may impact use/ sobriety. Thorough assessment of the situation is necessary. Difficult in prisons and inmates may not be incarcerated long enough for appropriate level of treatment. Needs of the incarcerated individual should be taken into consideration in order to tailor services to have the best chance of success. Treatment should also include the criminal behavior. For women with custodial children, treatment should also look at long term parenting rights. Coordinated care with outside treatment providers if in house treatment is not readily available/accessible (NIDA, 2014).

According to the Federal Bureau of Prisons (2020), programs offered may include drug abuse education, nonresidential drug abuse treatment, residential drug abuse programs (RDAP), and community treatment services (CTS).

6.2.1.1 Drug Abuse Education

In addition to standard substance abuse and its effects, education should also focus on issues specific to women: Prenatal substance exposure, breastfeeding, and substance use, as well as effects on children residing in the household both during use and while incarcerated. Part of the substance education should involve how use, abuse, and addiction can affect one's behavior (NIDA, 2014).

6.2.1.2 Nonresidential Drug Abuse Treatment

These types of programs are geared toward individuals who may only be incarcerated for shorter periods of time or as a transitional program prior to release into the community. Similar to an Intensive Outpatient Program in the community, these programs can include both individual and group counseling, AA and NA programming, and reintegration into their communities/society as a whole.

6.2.1.3 Residential Drug Abuse Program (RDAP)

Similar to inpatient treatment, these programs are more intensive in nature and have a set timeline for completion. There is usually a separate wing for those "inpatient" and they work their programs while incarcerated. Upon completion of the program, individuals are usually placed in the nonresidential treatment program or community depending upon timeline to reintegration into society. Yet, it should be noted that many RDAP programs across the country vary in quality, with many offering bare-bones offerings with low fidelity to evidence-based practices and services. At the time of this writing, it is still very unclear just how variable these offerings can be; yet, all indications suggest that it is highly likely that offerings for girls and women tend to be less rigorous and robust than their male counterparts.

6.2.1.4   Community Treatment Services (CTS)

Formerly referred to as Transitional Drug Treatment, the CTS is a reentry program that allows for continued care upon release. Improved outcomes can be expected by monitoring use and obstacles (FBOP 2020). In order to be successful, these programs need to anticipate barriers to continued treatment once released.

Rose, Lebel, Begun, and Fuhrmann (2014) referred to these barriers as internal vs external. External refers to long waiting lists, lack of consistent therapists, strict abstinence requirements, family responsibilities, lack of childcare, social disapproval, lack of support from friends/family. Conversely, internal barriers refers to inability to pay for treatment, lack of health insurance to, belief need to use to deal with stress, fear of admitting/getting help will take children away.

Treatment needs should be gender specific as much as possible, but especially when trauma is involved (NIDA, 2014). Females need medical and mental health services, childcare, assistance with housing and employment; need to account for parental responsibilities, regaining/retaining custody of children; and should also offer childcare and parenting classes (NIDA, 2014).

6.3   Available Mental Health Programming

The first step of ensuring the referral connection to individualized services throughout justice-involvement currently revolves around the screening and assessment tools used by criminal justice practitioners (Taxman, 2016). Only in the last few years has the American criminal justice system seen a movement to refine these tools to be "gender-responsive" and take the science behind girls' and women's risk of criminality and victimization into mind (Salisbury, Boppre, & Kelly, 2016). Feminist criminological literature suggests four broad orientations that highlight different aspects of psychological needs and life history pathways for girls and women who become victims and offenders: traumatic theory, relational theory, holistic addiction theory, and social capital theory (Salisbury et al., 2016; Salisbury & Van Voorhis, 2009). Each of these orientations suggests a tailored therapeutic approach to be taken by mental health professionals to disrupt criminal and victimization pathways.

Traumatic events and adverse life experiences can have long lasting impact on anyone's level of functioning, including their mental, physical, social, and emotional well-being. Trauma-informed care is becoming commonplace to serve individuals with these needs. Relational theory details the research that shows that relative to men, women's psychological and cognitive development tends to be more dependent on their relationships and the care for others. Thus, harmful relationships tend to impact women very differently than their male counterparts. Therapy often addresses relationships; female-centered therapy can address these issues uniquely. Holistic addiction therapy acknowledges the distinction that girls and women tend to use substances as a coping mechanism to deal with traumatic life experiences much more than their male counterparts do. It should not be surprising that "(f)emale substance abusers also tend to have co-occurring mental disorders, lower self-esteem, histories of sexual abuse, additions to multiple substances and more acute drug histories than their male counterparts" (Salisbury et al., 2016, p. 223). Again, trauma-informed care tends to be the remedy for these girls and women. Last, social capital theory acknowledges that social and human capital distributed unevenly in society, impacting women differently than their male counterparts by often isolating them from access to prosocial support structures. Thus, therapies designed to increase access to human capital such as education and vocational training, self-efficacy trainings, and self-esteem work should be tailored to the female experience.

Each of these approaches is being explored by mental health clinicians working with justice-involved girls and women across the USA and beyond. Many of these experiences go on in everyday individualized therapy casework, as has been the case for many years. Yet, the collective approach is changing given the emerging development of best practices among girl and women offenders. The passages below highlight some emerging experiences and approaches recently hitting the scene from around the world.

6.3.1 England and Wales Studies

In England and Wales, researchers studied women in a mental health assessment unit between the years of 2008 and 2010. This study was launched in response to increases both in population of women in prison, but also to a perceived (and actualized) increase of need as indicated by higher rates of mental health diagnoses, self-harm, and suicide attempts. By partnering with the National Health Service, the researchers noted that the overall improvements to the quality of prison healthcare had been documented. Yet, the inreach services that were provided across the country were under-evaluated.

In 2008, Hales, Somers, Reeves, and Bartlett (2016) set out to evaluate all women transferred to one targeted mental health assessment unit embedded in a prison in South East England to better describe what was happening "on the ground" over the course of almost 2 years. These researchers were specifically exploring the mental health needs of the women placed in this acute/triage unit with 24-h "round the clock" staffing. Further, they hypothesized that this unit was fulfilling the role of assessing and managing women with serious mental illness prior to inpatient hospitalization or attending to acute mental health crises that presented significant risk of harm to one's self.

The South East England mental health assessment unit featured 14 individual beds per cell with an overall capacity of 501. The unit was staffed with two part-time psychiatrists with two nurses, two to three activity coordinators, and six "line" correctional officers for security during the day; one nurse and one "line" correctional officer at night. By the study's end, Hales and her colleagues determined that their hypothesis was not substantiated by the evidence collected. This unit was not uniquely being utilized other than "its strict remit." Specifically, only less than a third of the unit's women were being transferred to an outside hospital. The majority of women (52%), some overlapping with this hospitalized group, were being treated under suicide or serious self-harm risk protocols. Only roughly 20% of women were released or returned to prison as they did not meet criteria to be served by the unit. Importantly, four out of every five women seen were previously "known" to external mental health services, with 30% presenting to prison staff as being so unwell that they were directly transferred to the unit for prompt assessment. Last, and most critically, over a third of all admissions of women were re-admitted to the unit over the course of the entire study, particularly after these women were released back into the community.

Even with a strong continuum of care, it appears that much more needs to be discovered about the epidemiology of these women's needs as they pass through each phase of treatment. In this case, the researchers were not comfortable enough to claim that this inreach approach was sufficient to address suicidality and self-harm, particularly in the long term.

In a different study in the UK, researchers conducted a qualitative study on self-harm among the female incarcerated population. "In the UK, non-fatal suicidal behavior is defined as 'an act of intention self-poisoning or injury irrespective of the apparent purpose of the act'" (National Health Service Center for Reviews and Dissemination, 1998). In this study, Kenning et al. (2010) set out to better understand the high rates of self-harm among the women in prisons across the UK as this behavior is strongly linked to suicidality. The approach that they took was unique— the team of researchers interviewed both female prisoners and the prison staff responsible for their care to examine the effects of their attitudes on the inmate/staff relationship. Revealing these attitudes may just influence the provision of services and, perhaps, the development of new care to address previously unidentified barriers to treatment.

As such, these researchers conducted a revealing survey of women in prison in Northwest England (Manchester). In this study, that took place between 2006 and 2009, a randomized controlled sample of women who engaged in self-harming behaviors were given a survey embedded in treatment. In order to better identify the women for the study, a risk assessment was used—only women who had committed an act of self-harm within the 2 weeks prior to the study were included. The urgency of their study was revealed in their review of the literature:

> Self-harm is one of the strongest predictors of subsequent suicide and therefore, an important target for suicide prevention. The National Suicide Prevention Strategy for England identified prisoners as a population at particularly high risk of suicide, supported by several studies with rates of 9% and 10% among pre-trial and sentenced women, respectively. There was a 37% increase in incidence of self-harm in UK prisons between 2003 and 2007, with a 48% increase in women prisoners. A number of previous studies have explored attitudes of medical staff towards patients who self-harm and present to hospitals. Nearly all of the studies report evidence of negative staff attitudes, stereotyping self-harmers…. One study [by Patterson and his colleagues] reported that professionals, including mental health nurses, general nurses and social workers, may build negative emotional responses along

with hostile cognitions and rejecting behavior. It is suggested that antipathy in professional carers (sic) may act to increase the risk of future self-harm in patients, negatively influencing help-seeking behaviour and interfering with a person's willingness to engage with services. There is also evidence that those who may be initially empathic can develop negative attitudes when faced with repeated episodes and little improvement in the people with whom they are working with.

Perhaps not surprisingly, Kenning et al. (2010) discovered a steep divide among the attitudes of staff and inmates. Prison staff tended to perceive self-harming behaviors as manipulative and attention-seeking, while inmates, administrators, and prison health-care staff tended to perceive these behaviors in terms of affect regulation or self-punishment. In other words, it may be that self-harming behaviors are a means for female inmates to engage in self-protectionism and coping, albeit unhealthy versions of these behaviors. Overall, this revelation suggests that treatment can be supported by simply altering training protocols and support for line correctional officers to better understand these behaviors and the overall importance of needing to address them in a manner consistent with models of holistic care.

Luckily, some researchers are beginning to look at unique and alternative approaches to both assess needs and explore options for mental health treatment for incarcerated women. Again, in the UK, the use of comedy has been explored when discussing mental illness within a prison of women (Wright, Twardzicki, Gomez, & Henderson, 2014). A comedy performance discussing both mental illness and race equality with the target purpose of reducing stigma was evaluated in a women's prison in England. Prior to the performance, the comedian conducted focus groups in different prisons to ensure the content would be relevant to the population. The evaluation was conducted in only one female prison using some questions from the Mental Health Knowledge Schedule (MAKS) in the form of a questionnaire before and after the individuals attended the comedy performance. Most of the findings from the comparison showed an increase in knowledge and overall positivity. One of the topics that showed some of the most improvement was the statement "Psychotherapy (e.g., talking treatment or counselling) can be an effective treatment for people with mental health problems." This appears to be an encouraging idea that those who viewed the comedy performance were able to better understand the positive role that psychotherapy can play in helping those with mental illness. While this study size was small and focused in one area, it is a positive step in showing that some alternative options may work to increase overall health for women in prison.

6.3.2   Experiences in New Zealand

The way in which the evaluation of individual needs occurs, and the subsequent execution of an individualized case planning, will vary by country, state, and even at the local level—parish/county or city. Many factors play into the level of evaluation including: funding, access to experts, education, and simply knowledge to know to look for change. Oftentimes, either an area is unwilling to change or unaware that a need for change exists (as documented by the experiences in the UK above). This is why it is pertinent to continue to evaluate the needs of women in prison, the staff working with said women, and the nature of the community in which the crimes are being committed which leads to prison stays.

One positive example of an evaluation of this sort of effort that led to a positive outcome took place in New Zealand in 2011 (McKenna et al., 2015; Pillai et al., 2016). Prior to 2011, New Zealand's prisons operated with a wide variety of outcomes and efforts in reference to incarcerated individuals with mental health needs. After evaluating the current operations at the time, officials discovered that consistency with care and resources varied depending on a litany of controllable factors. It became evident that a framework or model for care was needed to ensure consistency among facilities throughout the country.

As a result, a new prison model of care (PMOC) was created and rolled out across the two islands that comprise New Zealand in order to streamline the process of helping those with mental illness. Critically, the PMOC *did not include any new resources*, but rather provided guidelines to use the existing resources strategically and robustly throughout the country. This PMOC was implemented as a pilot study in four facilities, including one female prison.

For example, one change was to include specific pre-release planning which was not a strictly enforced element before the PMOC. In this process, incarcerated individuals were involved in case management to plan for their release within 3 months of their release date. Conversely, data was also collected on post-release, specifically in reference to engagement with mental health services. Thus, the system was better set up as a continuum of care by simply better managing individuals at critical time points as they moved/were processed by the justice system.

The results in some areas indicated statistically significant improvements—specifically for women—after the implementation of the PMOC. For example, the contact with probation revealed "significantly more engagement with residential and probation services occurred at the women's prison (residential: pre-PMOC: 5/36, 14%; post-PMOC: 12/32, 38%, $Z = 2.244$, $p = 0.03$; probation: pre-PMOC: 2/36, 6%; post-PMOC: 7/32, 22%, $Z = 1.982$, $p = 0.05$)." Additionally, for the entirety of the group in the study, "there was a significant improvement in the rate of released prisoners taking up at least one face-to-face contact with community mental health services (pre-PMOC: 43/101, 43% (7 missing cases); post-PMOC: 88/152, 58% (18 missing cases); $Z = 2.388$, $p = 0.02$)." Further, "Pre-release face-to-face contact with community agencies also improved for the women prisoners specifically, although still a minority were in contact after the PMOC implementation." Overall, it would appear that creating, and subsequently implementing, a planning guideline for individuals set to be released from prison would be beneficial for their overall success. Further, this would lend to lessen recidivism as well as increase the health of the individual. As is the case for programming throughout this book, efforts need to be managed in a way that is gender-responsive. It is clear that the efforts to remake New Zealand's continuum of care more streamlined have been executed in a way that allows women to improve in a way that works for them instead of being placed in a "once-size-fits-all" approach that has been the way of the past.

6.3.3 The American Experience

The lack of access to treatment in both the physical and monetary sense is also obviously a major obstacle for women who are incarcerated and returning home post-incarceration. Johnson et al. (2015) discuss how this is even more of an obstacle to overcome for those incarcerated women with both a mental health diagnosis and substance use disorder, i.e. co-occurring disorder (COD).

This research group conducted a survey of those working within a prison, especially with women with COD. In all, they were able to interview 14 individuals to gain insight on the struggles of women and working with them under the circumstances of incarceration and COD. These interviewees were of varying educational backgrounds (bachelor's to doctorate's) as well as levels within the hierarchy of the employment structure. The authors did well to shed light on the struggles as well as needs of the incarcerated women through the eyes of those working with them daily. The survey uncovered reoccurring themes that many individuals battle with when returning home after incarceration, but these also seemed to be amplified. The personnel of this prison remarked on the lack of support many women are facing after release. As mentioned in many chapters and topics, there is often a history of trauma and violence which limits access to housing. For example, in this prison, women are released with 2 weeks worth of medication to return home. Additionally, they are provided with a follow-up appointment. However, many were not attending those appointments upon release and therefore did not continue medication management for their needs.

Further, within the prison, many interviewed employees discussed the true lack of resources available for those in need.

6.4 Incarcerated Girls' and Women's Experiences with Pregnancy and Motherhood

Recall that the vast majority of incarcerated girls and women are of childbearing age. For American girls and women, the USA contains about 4% of the world's population of females yet has about one-third of the world's incarcerated female population. Despite the rise in the rate the USA incarcerates its girls and women, there is a void of research on the topic of pregnancy, and slightly less so, on motherhood for justice-involved females. Little is known on maternal health in this context. Yet, the vast majority of girl and women inmates are sexually active within the last 3 months (with men) before they were incarcerated for the most recent time

(Sufrin et al., 2019), thus ignoring the sexual activity of other individuals on the gender spectrum. Research also reveals that only a small proportion of incarcerated girls and women previously used a reliable form of contraception before their latest episode of incarceration, at rate between 21 and 28%. There is little doubt that girls and women will continue to be incarcerated while pregnant; yet, as of 2019, Sufrin and her colleagues reveal that there have been absolutely no systemic reviews or study of pregnancy of American inmates.

Having no systematic reports of pregnancy outcomes in US prisons presents a large gap in information in many ways. Data is crucial to impact change; therefore, the lack of data will not be effective for making adjustments to improvement of resources, programming, and services. Justice practitioners across the USA have reported an increase in maternal deaths in recent years, particularly for women outside of the prison system (e.g., jail and community corrections). With this in mind, the health and pregnancy of justice-involved girls and women is important to document for their own health outcomes let alone to their children outcomes and future generations. Racial and ethnic disparities certainly play a part in health both inside and out of prisons. As such, Sufrin and her colleagues remark that "Black women are imprisoned at twice the rate of White women, a manifestation of the racism embedded in the US criminal legal system. In addition, the pre-incarceration lives of a significant proportion of women in prison are characterized by poverty, substance use disorders, histories of trauma and abuse, and limited access to health care."

In the first study of its kind in the USA, Sufrin and her colleagues examine a year's worth of pregnancy statistics (in 2016–2017) compiled from a geographically diverse sample of 22 state prison systems and the Federal prison system in the USA (note: importantly, this lacks any coverage of American jails; yet, this research is a critical first step in filling the paucity of research in the USA). This research yielded a population of 1396 pregnant women passing through these prisons who experienced pregnancy (obviously), births, miscarriages, abortions, among other outcomes. This population represented 3.8% of all newly admitted women during 12 months in 2016–2017. These women had 753 live births, which represented 92% of all outcomes studied. Other outcomes included 46 miscarriages, or 6%, 11 abortions, or 1%, 4 stillbirths, 3 newborn deaths, and no maternal deaths (note: recall that maternal deaths are rare *in prison*, but have been becoming anecdotally more common in jails and in the community among at-risk pregnant girls and women). Of the successful live births, 6% were premature/pre-term and almost one-third were Cesarean deliveries. To date, this appears to be the first time any research has been done to systematically assess abortions, stillbirths, miscarriage, ectopic pregnancy, and neonatal/maternal death in American prisons—in 2017.

In the literature, smaller-scale studies provide a bit more context to the issue of pregnancy and the experience of justice-involved girls and women with pregnancy. For example, researchers in Indiana published a study in 2016 that addressed the experiences of women in prison nurseries in the midwestern state. In their review of the literature, Fritz and Whiteacre (2016) cited alarming trends that seem to be under-addressed in the literature; In particular:

The number of parents incarcerated in state and federal prisons increased by 79% between 1991 and mid-year 2007....In 2004, approximately 71% of mothers in prison were the sole primary caregivers for their minor children, compared to 26% of incarcerated fathers..... Between 1991 and 2007, the number of children with a mother in prison also increased 131% (Glaze & Maruschak, 2008; as cited by Fritz & Whiteacre, 2016, pp. 1–2).

These trends are significant to take note of—they reveal major changes that have occurred within the criminal justice system in the USA over the last few decades. Considering the data supporting the increased risk of incarceration for children of incarcerated parents, the number of incarcerated mothers who are primary caregivers could shed light on what could be a large proportion of the next generation of justice-involved boys, girls, men, women—and anyone regardless of how they identify.

Prison nurseries within the USA typically allow women to spend time with their children inside the prison for anywhere from the first one to 2 years of the child's life. Fritz and Whiteacre cite the Women's Prison Association (2009) to note that, at the time of their writing, about 10 state prison nursery programs existed across the USA: one at Bedford Hills Correctional Facility (first established 1901 and is the oldest program of this type), one at Riker's Island in New York City, five embedded throughout the Federal Bureau of Prisons system, collectively called Mother and Child Nurturing Together (MINT) residential parenting sites. Therefore, only a minority of jurisdictions offer this option for incarcerated women who are pregnant. Throughout their research, Fritz and Whiteacre discuss the limited literature on prison nurseries and their benefits (aside from the obvious positive mother/child relationship impact). Importantly, they cite evidence to suggest that this sort of programming is linked to reductions in recidivation upon reentry back into the communities from which the mothers came. Unfortunately, like many topics discussed related to women and prison, there is little research done on other topics surrounding incarcerated mothers.

With the help of the Indiana Department of Corrections, Fritz and Whiteacre studied women who had been enrolled in WON (Wee Ones Nursery) at Indiana Women's Prison, as well as incarcerated women who were pregnant and have given birth before the program had been created. The findings from the study showed similar experiences for both the women who had been through the program and those who had not while giving birth, specifically in the experience of pregnancy, labor, and reentry experience of women in both groups. Much of the difference between the groups were shown to be significant for the *postpartum experience* in prison, most significantly with separation between the mother and child. The more negative impact was shown with the group who were not part of WON, thus did not receive the same options for support, care, and programming to prepare for the separation. Another noted negative impact mothers both in and out of WON experienced and discussed was the use of restraints while giving birth. Women were transported to a hospital in order to give birth and restraints were used with the exception of the time during active labor. The women described the experience in terms like "inhumane" and "worthless." Many women noted the guards involved in their experience either positively or negatively impacted their experience depending upon their level of empathy.

Within the WON program, women described a much more positive experience with the staff. The staff was described as being more caring and interested in truly offering support and care. Overall, women in WON appeared to have a better experience with the process of being a mother while incarcerated. Unfortunately, like many related studies of women in prison, the sample size here was smaller which did not allow for a comprehensive study.

In 2015, public health researchers published information regarding the needs of incarcerated women in relation to pregnancy. Interestingly, they noted "because the majority of correctional policies were created when female incarceration was rare, such policies commonly fail to address incarcerated women's unique needs, especially regarding reproductive health." In other words, much of policy is not updated both in time and in the needs of women and their specific concerns. For example, these researchers also discussed the negative impact of restraints during the birth process, which was also noted by the American College of Obstetrics and Gynecology. Subsequently, laws banning or preventing the use of restraints during the birthing process have been passed in 21 states. Conversely, laws and/or policies regarding prenatal care, health, and nutrition do not exist with most states.

Increasingly, prisons are adding programming to allow for more support, care, and education for pregnant women who are incarcerated and mothers. One example is Motherhood Beyond Bars in Georgia which is a collaboration between the Department of Corrections and Emory University. In this program, faculty and students at the university work alongside other professionals and organizations to provide different types of health education to pregnant women in prison.

Despite the positive options of programs, problems are still endemic throughout many state criminal justice systems. The authors discuss, "in an analysis of state policies regarding restraints, prenatal care and alternative programs, the Rebecca Project for Human Rights and the National Women's Law Center gave 38 states failing grades." This is in reference to the lack of care offered and the lack of policy to require said care.

In a literature review search in the beginning of 2020, it appears that research on pregnant women in prison has been published more frequently (and high level of robustness) from researchers in the UK. For example, researchers there have been exploring different aspects of a woman's experience within the prison system. In the UK, a pregnant woman within the prison system can apply to be housed on a "mother and baby unit" within a facility. One study was published in 2006 discussing the mental health of women on four different "mother and baby units" in England. The study included "60 participants and an estimated prevalence of mental disorder of 50%, the true prevalence could be estimated with 95% confidence to within +13%." The study included interviews of all participants as well as a review of the prison medical records for those that could be obtained. The authors noted some interesting results:

> Women in prison mother and baby units have particular characteristics that distinguish them from the rest of the female prison population and other mothers in prison. They appear to have more stable backgrounds than their imprisoned counterparts in terms of factors such as their relationship status, employment, and accommodation. In our study a greater proportion were serving sentences for drug offences, many of whom were from ethnic minorities.

The authors went on to discuss that the process of applying to a mother and baby unit also resulted in exclusion of women with mental illness aside from depression. The hypothesis there was that women with more severe mental illness would be less likely to apply to begin with for fear of rejection or those women had longer sentences which would result in immediate disqualification for a place on the unit. The major concern with the lack of inclusion for these mothers would obviously be their lack of access to all the resources provided within the mother and baby unit. Specifically, the further access for her child or children both while in the unit and long term. The positive outcome of this study could be to explore further what obstacles exist that result in the exclusion of some mothers with mental illness. Eliminating those obstacles would result in the better care of incarcerated mothers with mental illness and their children. Further, investigating the lives of the mothers and children post-incarceration can aid in gathering insight on better options for treatment and resources while still inside the prison. Additionally, the options to offer transitional resources for women reintegrating back to their lives outside of prison would be extremely beneficial.

6.5   Innovation and Looking to the Future

In 2009, The World Health Organization (WHO) of Europe along with the United Nations Office on Drugs and Crime (UNODC) released a bold declaration titled *Women's Health in Prison: Correcting gender inequity in prison health* (WHO, 2009). This declaration came after a comprehensive review of both the needs of women in prison and the gaps in services being offered to said women—the most comprehensive global review performed to date as of this writing. The WHO released this document to discuss changes that should be made to correct inequity along with supporting evidence to defend why those corrections should be made. The WHO document states:

> Women's rights while in prison are the same as men's rights, but women seldom have equal access to these rights. As prison systems have been primarily designed for men, who comprise more than 95% of the prison population in most countries, prison policies and procedures often do not address women's health needs. Data on the health of women in prison and the health care provided for them are rare, because most prison data are not gender specific.

The declaration also discusses the human rights that should be afforded to women while in prison, yet are often compromised to some degree in systems throughout the world. While this document focused on Europe, it certainly can be basis for all countries across the world:

To offer a standard of practice and efforts to implement better options, the WHO states:

> In deciding what can, should and must be done, several important principles should be emphasized and followed.

- First, imprisonment of women should be considered only as a last resort when all other alternatives are unavailable or are unsuitable. This applies even more so to pregnant women and to women with children. Women need to be considered holistically in the context of their offending and their social situation.
- Second, health service provision and programming should specifically address mental illness, especially substance use disorders and post-traumatic stress disorder, as being essential to any prison health care system.
- Third, if children are involved, the best interest of the children must be the main and determining factor. The greater social costs to the community and the potential for long term damage must be understood and accepted. Decisions on the best interests of a child should be based on appropriate advice from a recognized source independent of the courts and prison services.
- Fourth, needs vary significantly among different groups of women; factors such as pregnancy, having responsibility for children, young or old age, dependence problems, histories of violence and/or abuse and others must be important considerations in health plans for these women.
- Fifth, the impact of separation from family and community as well as the inevitable legal and security processes involved can severely harm a woman's mental health, emotional well-being, self-esteem and social and life skills and abilities to varying extents. This is true for everyone compulsorily deprived of liberty but especially for women. Any individual health plan must include careful, comprehensive and detailed screening, including socio-economic and educational background, health and trauma histories, current health status and an assessment of skills held or required so that the individual needs are determined and can be suitably addressed.
- Sixth, although rigid policies should be avoided, given the variation in individual needs in a changing world, the underlying importance of human rights should pervade all thinking and all policy development for everyone in compulsory detention.

One major reoccurring theme when discussing women in prison, especially with relation to mental illness, is the unsuccessful use of programming geared toward men. Data shows there are far more men incarcerated across the world, especially the USA than women. It would make sense that many programs have been created for those men to aid in things like mental health, substance use, employment training, etc. These programs may serve to benefit those men both which they are incarcerated and post-release. As mentioned in previous chapters, women face struggles with trauma, domestic violence, sexual assault, and other situations that categorized them as not only a perpetrator, but also a victim. Conversely, the programs created for men often do not meet the needs of women in similar situations as it relates to the criminal justice system.

In 2009, researchers working in conjunction with the World Health Organization discussed some evidence-based practices to benefit women who are incarcerated. In response to the needs of incarcerated women, many countries have worked to establish new programming with the hopes of better outcomes.

> Punitive penal systems based on male norms routinely uphold institutionalized values of containment and subordination. The restorative and rehabilitative function is noticeably absent from such systems which, in turn, fail to attend to the trauma and mental health needs of incarcerated women. However, frameworks exist which facilitate enhanced mental well-being by utilizing evidence-based models of best practice.

To conclude, it should be helpful to review some of the changes that have occurred since this bold call to action was published. Canada, Australia, the UK, and New Zealand all made substantial changes to include programming for incarcerated women to specifically address their needs. In Canada, for example, the government established evidence-based programming for survivors of abuse and trauma to be delivered to female inmates in *all* federal instructions—meaning, all women in the system's care who need this sort of programming are eligible to receive it. This major shift was in response to the Creating Choices report published by the Task Force on Federally Sentenced Women. Further, additionally evidence-based culturally responsive programming was developed for indigenous women.

In Western Australia, a concerted effort to address characteristic issues among Australian female inmates—the intersectionality of trauma, mental illness, and substance use disorder—has been recently launched (Sodhi-Berry, Preen, Alan, Knuiman, & Morgan, 2014). These efforts have been concentrated in the Boronia Pre-Release Centre for Women and include programming for pregnant women and mothers (Botello, 2017).

In the UK, the Home Office recently funded a lofty female-specific program named Together Women Programme (TWP). In this case, officials are targeting both females at risk of offending and female offenders to disrupt offending and reoffending by targeting criminogenic needs in a gender-responsive manner (just like the method featured in New Zealand as mentioned before). By coordinating efforts across the system of care, and concentrating much of the programing at one one-stop facility, the Together Women Programme provides a comprehensive continuum of care that features psychosocial interventions and the multi-agency provision of services to build connectivity to much-needed community resources (Hedderman, Palmer, & Hollin, 2008; Jolliffe, Hedderman, Palmer, & Hollin, 2011).

Last, beyond the strategic shifts in the continuum of care in New Zealand mentioned previously, other organic efforts are blossoming that hold promise of shifting national policies. For example, in Christchurch, an interesting study explored the connection of a mother–daughter type of relationship between older and younger women while incarcerated (Goldingay, 2007). The researchers wanted to examine if this type "fictive kin" relationship was beneficial to both the older and younger women through the open embrace of a supportive, familial type of role. Again, like many efforts discussed, all previously used assessments and programming were created for men. The researchers sought to innovate. They used interviews in addition to direct observations of these budding relationships to provide some context to their findings.

In speaking with the younger incarcerated women in New Zealand, these respondents spoke about their "jail mum"—a term used to describe their paired, older incarcerated women—glowingly. Mums tended to offer "support through demonstrating understanding and empathy, derived from their own experience of being imprisoned." Interestingly, one participant in the study described having a negative relationship with her real mother but was able to have a positive one with her "jail mum." Additionally, younger women described their "jail mums" as also offering discipline much like a traditional parenting role. Further, one other interesting aspect was the idea of modeling behavior or role models. Having an older incarcerated woman for the younger women to model behavior after was seen to be beneficial and an overall success. Again, not unlike a traditional parenting role outside of prison. This sort of programming directly taps into the relational theory mentioned in previous sections.

Despite this study having a low number of participants, like many others mentioned in this chapter, it sheds like on some interesting topics for future research exploration. The article touches on the topic which is a tiny aspect of a larger conversation regarding the relationships women have and face while inside of a prison.

Expect much more of these efforts to emerge in the next decade. What is evidence from a comprehensive review of existing research is that the new millennia has seen increasing research activity, with ever increasing robustness, in the area of girl- and woman-specific criminal and victimization pathways. Collectively, we are entering a phase of exploring comprehensive ways to disrupt these maladies that can have far reaching collateral damages for generations to come. It is an exciting time to innovate given the existing knowledge that exists on the topic; yet, so much is left to explore and address.

References

Andersen, T. S. (2018). Social support and one-year outcomes for women participating in prison-based substance abuse treatment programming. *Criminal Justice Studies, 31*(1), 80–94.

Begun, A. L., Rose, S. J., Lebel, T. P., & Teske-Young, B. A. (2009). Implementing substance abuse screening and brief motivational intervention with women in jail. *Journal of Social Work Practice in the Addictions, 9*, 113–131.

Botello, C. M. (2017). *Women's imprisonment and recidivism: An illustrative analysis of Boronia Women's Pre-Release Centre (Western Australia) and progressive/open prison systems in Norway and Sweden.* Retrieved February 26, 2020, from https://researchonline.nd.edu.au/cgi/viewcontent.cgi?article=1178&context=theses

Bowles, M. A., DeHart, D., & Webb, J. R. (2012). Family influences on female offenders' substance use: The role of adverse childhood events among incarcerated women. *Journal of Family Violence, 27*, 681–686.

Bronson, J., & Berzofsky, M. (2017). *Indicators of mental health problems reported by prisoners and jail inmates, 2011–12.* Bureau of Justice Statistics. Retrieved February 24, 2020, from https://www.bjs.gov/content/pub/pdf/imhprpji1112.pdf

Drug Policy Alliance. (2018). *Women, prison, and the drug war.* Retrieved February 26, 2020, from http://www.drugpolicy.org/sites/default/files/women-and-the-drug-war_0.pdf

Federal Bureau of Prisons. (2020). *Substance abuse treatment.* Retrieved February 26, 2020, from https://www.bop.gov/inmates/custody_and_care/substance_abuse_treatment.jsp

Fritz, S., & Whiteacre, K. (2016). Prison nurseries: Experiences of incarcerated women during pregnancy. *Journal of Offender Rehabilitation, 55*(1), 1–20.

Garcia, M., & Ritter, N. (2012). Improving access to services for female offenders returning to the community. *NIJ Journal, 269*, 18–23. Retrieved February 25, 2020, from https://www.ncjrs.gov/pdffiles1/nij/237725.pdf

Glaze, L. E., & Maruschak, L. M. (2008). *Parents in prison and their minor children* (US Department of Justice. Bureau of Justice Statistics, Special Report. NCJ, 222984).

Goldingay, S. (2007). Jail mums: The status of adult female prisoners amongst young female prisoners in Christchurch women's prison. *Social Policy Journal of New Zealand: Te Puna Whakaaro, 31*, 56–73.

Hales, H., Somers, N., Reeves, C., & Bartlett, A. (2016). Characteristics of women in a prison mental health assessment unit in England and Wales (2008–2010). *Criminal Behaviour and Mental Health, 26*(2), 136–152.

Hedderman, C., Palmer, E., & Hollin, C. (2008). *Implementing services for women offenders and those 'at risk' of offending: Action research with Together Women*. London: Ministry of Justice Research Series, 12/08.

Johnson, J. E., Schonbrun, Y. C., Peabody, M. E., Shefner, R. T., Fernandes, K. M., Rosen, R. K., et al. (2015). Provider experiences with prison care and aftercare for women with co-occurring mental health and substance use disorders: Treatment, resource, and systems integration challenges. *The Journal of Behavioral Health Services & Research, 42*(4), 417–436.

Jolliffe, D., Hedderman, C., Palmer, E., & Hollin, C. (2011). *Re-offending analysis of women offenders referred to Together Women (TW) and the scope to divert from custody*. London: Ministry of Justice Research Series 11/11.

Kenning, C., Cooper, J., Short, V., Shaw, J., Abel, K., & Chew-Graham, C. (2010). Prison staff and women prisoner's views on self-harm; their implications for service delivery and development: A qualitative study. *Criminal Behaviour and Mental Health, 20*(4), 274–284.

Lucente, S. W., Fals-Stewart, W., Richards, H. J., & Goscha, J. (2001). Factor structure and reliability of the revised conflict tactics scales for incarcerated female substance abusers. *Journal of Family Violence, 16*(4), 437–450.

McKenna, B., Skipworth, J., Tapsell, R., Madell, D., Pillai, K., Simpson, A., et al. (2015). A prison mental health in-reach model informed by assertive community treatment principles: Evaluation of its impact on planning during the pre-release period, community mental health service engagement and reoffending. *Criminal Behaviour and Mental Health, 25*(5), 429–439.

National Alliance on Mental Illness. (2020). *Mental health by the numbers*. Retrieved February 24, 2020, from https://nami.org/mhstats

National Health Service Centre for Reviews and Dissemination. (1998). Deliberate self-harm. *Effective Health Care Bulletin, 4*, 1–12.

National Institute on Drug Abuse. (2014). *Principles of drug abuse treatment for criminal justice populations - A research-based guide*. Retrieved December 16, 2019, from https://www.drugabuse.gov/publications/principles-drug-abuse-treatment-criminal-justice-populations-research-based-guide

Pillai, K., Rouse, P., McKenna, B., Skipworth, J., Cavney, J., Tapsell, R., et al. (2016). From positive screen to engagement in treatment: A preliminary study of the impact of a new model of care for prisoners with serious mental illness. *BMC Psychiatry, 16*(1), 9.

Rose, S. J., Lebel, T. P., Begun, A. L., & Fuhrmann, D. (2014). Looking out from the inside: Incarcerated women's perceived barriers to treatment of substance use. *Journal of Offender Rehabilitation, 53*, 300–316.

Salisbury, E. J., Boppre, B., & Kelly, B. (2016). Gender-responsive risk and need assessment. In F. Taxman (Ed.), *Handbook on risk and need assessment: Theory and practice*. London: Routledge.

Salisbury, E. J., & Van Voorhis, P. (2009). Gendered pathways: A quantitative investigation of women probationers' paths to incarceration. *Criminal Justice and Behavior, 36*, 541–566.

Sawyer, W. (2019). Who's helping the 1.9 million women released from prisons and jails each year? *Prison Policy Initiative*. Retrieved February 24, 2020, from https://www.prisonpolicy.org/blog/2019/07/19/reentry/

Sodhi-Berry, N., Preen, D. B., Alan, J., Knuiman, M., & Morgan, V. A. (2014). Pre-sentence mental health service use by adult offenders in Western Australia: Baseline results from a longitudinal whole-population cohort study. *Criminal Behaviour and Mental Health, 24*(3), 204–221.

Substance Abuse and Mental Health Services Administration. (2018). *Mental health annual report 2016*. Retrieved February 24, 2020, from https://www.samhsa.gov/data/sites/default/files/2016_Mental_Health_Annual_Report_Revised.pdf

Sufrin, C., Beal, L., Clarke, J., Jones, R., & Mosher, W. D. (2019). Pregnancy outcomes in US prisons, 2016–2017. *American Journal of Public Health, 109*(5), 799–805.

Taxman, F. S. (2016). *Handbook on risk and need assessment: Theory and practice*. London: Routledge.

Women's Prison Association. (2009). *Mothers, infants and imprisonment: A national look at prison nurseries and community-based alternatives*. Retrieved February 26, 2020, from http://www.wpaonline.org

World Health Organization (WHO). (2009). *Women's health in prison: Correcting gender inequity in prison health*. Copenhagen: World Health Organization.

Wright, S., Twardzicki, M., Gomez, F., & Henderson, C. (2014). Evaluation of a comedy intervention to improve coping and help-seeking for mental health problems in a women's prison. *International Review of Psychiatry, 26*(4), 423–429.

Zeng, Z. (2019). *Jail inmates in 2017*. Bureau of Justice Statistics. Retrieved February 26, 2020, from https://www.bjs.gov/content/pub/pdf/ji17.pdf

Chapter 7
Sexuality and Gender: Locked in, and Out

Frances P. Abderhalden

7.1 Introduction

Sexuality in prison can be shaped by a variety of factors that are amplified, or iso-lated, by the nature of confinement. Thus, regardless of prior experiences from pre-incarceration, the experience of incarceration can lead to new sexual and gender identities. The importation and deprivation theoretical model provides some under-standing for sexuality and gender identities, from influences of the importation of prior experiences brought into the facility, as well as new sexual and gender experi-ences and identities developed through deprivations caused by the prison environ-ment and exposure to confinement (Irwin & Cressey, 1962). Furthermore, establishing just how sexual behaviors and sexual identifies that are formed while incarcerated influences future behaviors (e.g., once an inmate returns to a free soci-ety) continues to elude researchers. Practices, identities, and behaviors while incar-cerated may not translate back into the free world, but similarly, behaviors that pre-date incarceration may not translate to the confinement experience. The explo-ration of sexuality and gender in prison has largely been ignored, under-investigated, and wrongly portrayed (Tewksbury & West, 2000). Therefore, the literature on sexuality and gender for incarcerated populations is limited, in particular for incar-cerated females.

Sexual orientation is defined as the emotional and sexual attraction to a sex (male or female). Sexual orientation has a broad spectrum of categories, but there are four commonly denoted classifications for sexual orientation: heterosexual, homosexual, bisexual, and asexual. Heterosexuality is the attraction to the opposite sex from the birth sex of an individual. Homosexuality is the attraction to one's own birth sex. Bisexuality is attraction to both biological sexes. And asexuality is having no sexual attraction to either biological sex. The USA is traditionally known to be a

F. P. Abderhalden (✉)
California State University, Los Angeles, Los Angeles, CA, USA

© Springer Nature Switzerland AG 2020
J. Hector (ed.), *Women and Prison*,
https://doi.org/10.1007/978-3-030-46172-0_7

heteronormative society, meaning that heterosexual orientation is the accepted norm and most common sexual orientation identity (Ryle, 2011). Yet, sexuality in prison is somewhat distinct from general society; incarceration limits heterosexual activities by segregating prison populations by sex, confining men and women separately for a variety of stated purposes. This deprivation of heterosexual activities (Sykes, 1958) may lead to individuals seeking alternative means of sexual gratification than how they would identify outside of confinement. This can include masturbation, consensual same-sex activities, and coerced same-sex activities (Hensley, 2002).

Gender identity is how one classifies themselves as being masculine or feminine (Diamond, 2002). Gender refers to the social and cultural characteristics associated with being male or female, and sex refers to the physical, biological reproductive system that one is born with. Therefore, sex and gender are not interchangeable terms, as an individual who was born with male genitalia may identify as a female and thus their gender may be female while biologically, they are male. Similarly to sexuality, gender also occurs on a spectrum and there are multiple classification for gender identity, including (but not limited to): bigender, cisgender, gender fluid, transgender, and queer.

Bigender refers to an individual who fluctuates between social and cultural characteristics of traditional female and male behavior and identifies with both genders (Human Rights Campaign (HRC), 2019). Cisgender is a gender description for individuals who identify with the gender they were assigned at birth based on biological sex (HRC, 2019). Individuals who identify with being gender fluid are best characterized by being a mix of male and female, with variation dependent on the individual day to day (HRC, 2019). Transgender gender identity is when a person identifies with being the opposite gender from what their biological sex assignment is at birth (Stryker, 2008). Finally, queer identification can fit with either sexuality or gender identify and is an umbrella term used to classify individuals who fall somewhere within the LGBTQ+ spectrum (HRC, 2019). Furthermore, queer is often used interchangeably with LGBTQ+.

It is clear that there is a range of identities for sexual orientation and gender; however, the classification of queer females within the criminal justice system is often discussed in relation to sexual exploitation and victimization of females incarcerated in prison. However, there are a host of behaviors and attitudes that reflect across the queer incarcerated population that are not limited to exploitation and victimization, but include systemic oppression, policy exclusivity, and poor treatment. A common thread running through this chapter is the lack of information presented from an empirical standpoint on how sexuality and gender play roles in the incarceration experience of females in prison. In the following sections, we introduce sexuality and incarceration, and gender and incarceration by giving a brief overview of the existing literature. We conclude with a presentation of the challenges that sexuality and gender identity play with the female incarcerated population and what future research should further explore and expand on.

7.2 How Does Sexuality Come Into Play? Does It?

Non-heterosexual identifying individuals are marginalized in the general population, with only around 2.3–6.8% of the general population identifying as being a sexual minority (Gates, 2011). However, in prison, in particular in female prisons alone (thus not including the male population), closer to 3–4% of the population identify as a sexual minority (Gates, 2011). Furthermore, Beck and Johnson (2012) suggest that closer to 8% of the jail[1] population (which includes men and women) identify as something other than heterosexual. Some other numbers place this estimate at closer to 30% of the prison population as identifying as gay or bisexual, with female prisons having a higher proportion of sexual minorities than male institutions (Gibson & Hensley, 2013). The spread in the estimates is, in part due, to the lack of knowledge surrounding sexuality and incarceration, but also because sexuality and gender questions are often not included in correctional literature and research. It is widely suggested that the LGBTQ+ is overrepresented in prisons, because of the criminalization of LGBTQ+ individuals. In addition to the suggestion that LGBTQ+ people being criminalized is the compounding factors that LGBTQ+ identifying individuals are more likely to be actively involved in other criminal behaviors, like drug and alcohol abuse, due to comorbidity issues and lack of coping mechanisms (National Center for Transgender Equality, 2019).

In this volume, however, we are demonstrating the broad perspective of women incarcerated and for this chapter how sexuality and gender identity come into play. Sexuality in prison for females has been discussed in terms of coping mechanisms that women use to handle the stress of their incarceration. Families-like units are often formed among females who are incarcerated together, which may have an underlying sexual connotation to them (Van Wormer, 1981). These families are typically made up of traditional family roles, grandmothers, father, mother, children, and babies. The women incarcerated take on a role from the family unit and work together functioning as a family to provide support, conduct tasks and chores, and can even be sexual in nature (Van Wormer, 1981). However, while these families are often cited in literature for female coping in prison and for sexual deviance while incarcerated, a discussion of imported sexuality is often overlooked by literature, with much of the existing literature focusing on sexual behavior as a result of the environment.

The prison environment can lead to adapted sexual behavior. Sexual behaviors can be consequential of incarceration, referred to as situational homosexuality (Pardue, Arrigo, & Murphy, 2011). There is a range of sexual behavior studies for incarcerated females that examine sexual consequences from a viewpoint of prison

---

[1] It is important to note that jail and prison are not synonymous terms. Jails are shorter term, house pre-conviction and post-conviction individuals and are typically more chaotic facilities. Jails also often have high turnover rates of both incarcerated individuals and correctional staff. Prisons are more stable environments, with post-conviction individuals with longer term sentences (typically over 14 months). The focus for this chapter is on prison, but the information also applies and is significant for individuals in jail.

safety (Tewksbury & West, 2000), but an exploration of the imported sexual identities and situation-based sexuality are narrower in scope. Females who are incarcerated may adapt to a sexual minority identity in order to cope and adapt to the removal of heterosexual behaviors. The media likes to sexualize prison, through unrealistic narratives, to distract from the stark and harsh nature of the correctional system in the USA. For example, in the television show, Orange is the New Black, sexual minorities are shown to be the majority population. Women are consistently engaging in sexual and romantic relationships with other women, displaying a sense that all women incarcerated have fluid sexual identities while incarcerated. However, this is grossly overestimating the actual behaviors of women incarcerated. Furthermore, most sexual relationships while incarcerated are not displayed as publicly as they are portrayed on shows, like Orange is the New Black, for fear of retaliation from other incarcerated individuals, correctional staff, and administration. Finally, while it should be applauded that this show did have a transgender woman in a female prison, this is even less accurate, given that most transgender individuals are housed with their biological sex, not with their identity.[2] Even with data reporting that up to 30% of people incarcerated fall somewhere on the queer spectrum, the harsh reality is that in prison, sexual minorities are still sexual minorities and the treatment can be driven by the stigma of having a sexual minority identity.

Sexuality comes into play in other ways within the confines of the institution. In female prisons, heterosexual behavior has just as strong a relationship with the history of prison, as homosexual behaviors. Concerns about sexual relationships between incarcerated females and those controlling them have been a factor since the birth of female only institutions (Kahn, 2006; Kunzel, 2008). However, research on homosexual behaviors did not appear to be a concern for incarcerated females until the early 1970s, and often is deemed harmless, compared to homosexual behaviors in male only facilities (Kunzel, 2008). In part this is due to the nature of sexual behaviors for females, which is considered "noninvasive" compared to male homosexuality in prison. It is critical to note that the method of sexual behavior does not determine the harm that may occur.

Furthermore, homosexuality identity is often different than situational sexual behaviors, as someone can behave with homosexual behaviors while incarcerated but still identify as heterosexual, while an individual who identifies as homosexual, or as a sexual minority, is more likely to identify that way regardless of incarceration (Reiter, 1989). Situational homosexuality is often used as a trade tool for incarcerated females to gain economic exchanges (Kahn, 2006; Owen, 1999), whereas true homosexuality is not commonly used for economic gain. Furthermore, the research on female sexuality in prison focuses heavily on masturbation, mutual masturbation, homosexual relationships, and custodial sexual abuse, with little examination into the importation of sexual minorities and the impact of incarceration on individuals with preexisting sexual identities. Finally, it is critically

---

[2] See chapter two for a greater discussion of media and female incarceration.

important to note that the majority of the literature on female sexuality in prison has been conducted by predominately male identifying researchers.[3]

7.3   How Does a Woman's Sexual Identity Impact Life Within Prison?

Anecdotally, while the author of this chapter was collecting data in a Texas jail in the spring of 2019, Susan[4], a woman identifying as homosexual approached her and told her story of being out, while in jail. Susan is a middle-aged female who was in jail on a drug-related parole violation. At the time, she had been sitting in jail for about 2 months awaiting revocation. Susan spoke of the hatred she felt from the staff and other females she was incarcerated with due in part to her sexuality. Susan said she is a gay, masculine feeling, female. She reported being called a host of derogatory names, include "dyke," "butch," and "faggot," from other females incarcerated and also from the correctional staff. When asked about how this impacted her incarceration experiences, as well as her future upon release, she noted that she felt like she had little self-worth and felt like she did not matter, and no one would care what happened to her.

Susan's experience is not an outlier, and not unfamiliar. Sexual minorities in prison are at an increased risk for violence and discrimination. Prison staff, administration, and other people incarcerated often overlook the needs of sexual minorities, and even further, there is a routine of overlooking the protection policies and rules that are instated directly to protect sexual and gender minorities among people incarcerated. In female prisons, women identifying on the sexual spectrum that do not identify as heterosexual are more at risk for physical, emotional, and sexual abuse, sexually related violence, and violence (McNamara, 2014; Otis, Oser, & Staton-Tindall, 2016).

LGBTQ+ individuals may be disproportionately subjected to suffering compared to the heterosexual identifying population due a variety of penalties that apply directly to the LGBTQ+ community. For example, access to family visitations may be limited if someone is in a partnership and not a legally recognized marriage. In more recent years, the discussion surrounding incarceration and sexuality has been centralized under the binary definitions of male and female, assuming all individuals fall into the binary. Furthermore, there is an overwhelming assumption that male offenders are all at men's prisons and all female offenders are at women's prisons, which is simply untrue. Due to the spectrum of gender identity, there are not only two gender identities. Thus, the correctional system only having classification based

---

[3] For reference, 10 of the 35 citations from this chapter are written by a female identifying first author. The remaining 25 are written by a male identifying first author (at the time of publication).

[4] Name changed for anonymity.

on the binary means that individuals are housed in male or female facilities, that do not correspond to their actual gender identity. There are fully transitioned males, for example, that are housed in female facilities (Vitulli, 2013). The focus of the field has largely neglected the oppression of the LGBTQ+ community through the classification of individuals and the penalties from a systematic approach, through beginning with sentencing individuals on the sexual and gender spectrum to their sex assigned at birth facilities (Vitulli, 2013). As the scholarship moves forward in sexuality and non-gender normative research, looking at the system that corrections have been built on in the USA is a start to see how the housing of individuals is deeply ingrained with racial oppression and heteropatriarchy.

7.4   The Full Spectrum: Woman Identities and the Impact on Prison Experiences

The gender spectrum provides even more complexities for facilities to address. Females who identify on the gender spectrum are often misgendered, or forced to conform to the feminine/masculine experience based on birth sex assignment (Pardue et al., 2011; White Hughto et al., 2018). In some narrative reports, gender fluid and transgender women report being forced into conversion therapy by facilities, told they are not allowed to be called their preferred pronouns, and forced to be gender binary (White Hughto et al., 2018). In the work by White Hughto et al., (2018), a theme among all the narratives presented includes the negative impact on the overall mental health of the non-gender binary participants.[5]

The inadequate understanding of the gender spectrum often leads facilities to poorly identify and report on individuals on the gender spectrum, leading to misclassifications, trauma through asking invasive questions, and lack of appropriate medical treatment. Furthermore, the risk that individuals on the gender spectrum have for violence from other people incarcerated is increased over gender conforming individuals. While prisoners who identify on the gender spectrum overwhelmingly say that their gender is not affirmed how they would identify, there are some that note being on the gender spectrum is easier than being transgender. Susan, the women from the Texas jail, noted that while she struggled with mental health as a result of her gender fluidity and sexual identity, she was "lucky compared to some of the trans girls who are stuck with the men."

---

[5] Please see chapter six for a greater discussion of mental health and female incarceration.

7.5   What About Those That Identify as Queer?

In recent years, queer identities have become more of a conversation for females incarcerated. Prisons are the perfect breeding ground for being a queer space because queer individuals are criminalized and disproportionately incarcerated compared to the heteronormative population (Kunzel, 2008). However, there is a lack of empirical research being done on queer identities in prison only pushes the disparities to be ingrained in correctional scholarship. There has been a progression of research which began with asking binary questions of sexuality and gender, only asking about heteronormative relationships and male and female gender status. With the introduction of Sykes (1958), some researchers began to dive into the homosexuality that emerged in prison, primarily with male only samples. Following some de-stigmatization in the general public, prison research began to look at sexual deviance and situational homosexuality within incarceration more consistently in the late 1970s and early 1980s. However, more currently, the terminology, expansion of LGBTQ+ identity definitions, and acceptance in the general public have not progressed research proportionally. It is recognized that asking personal sexuality and gender questions to individuals currently confined is difficult and personal, being able to understand and build knowledge on the spectrum of queer identities within prisons and jails will help push policies forward to protect the queer community and ask the appropriate questions.

There is an overall lack of queer literature with the female prison population. While queer criminology is an emerging subcategory of research, the focus on the female incarceration population has yet to be deeply examined. The prison system in the USA needs to be examined with a critical lens to look at the treatment of queer identifying individuals, both male and female, to look at the impact that confinement is having on the queer population and community. Kunzel (2008) argues that supporting queer prisoners can help the entire queer community by addressing the oppression that exists resulting in an overrepresentation of queer individuals being incarcerated to begin with.

7.6   Transgender and Prison

The past decade has seen high-profile news stories regarding the appropriate treatment of transgender individuals in society, from bathroom use to competition in athletics. However, in the realm of corrections, the dilemma of transgender persons has individual and institutional safety repercussions. The classification of transgender individuals is often cited as a difficulty for the correctional system, partially due to the spectrum of transitioning. Transgender women, or women who were biologically male at birth but now identify as female for the gender expression, experience extreme stigma within the correctional system. There is no clear policy to address the sentencing and handling of transgender women (or men) within the United

States Correctional System. This poses many restrictions based purely on birth sex, which can be dangerous, physically, mentally, sexually, and emotionally for transgender women who are confined to male facilities simply due to their sex organs from birth.

Many transgender individuals are on a spectrum of transition, from dressing and tailoring their mannerisms towards that of the other sex, to hormone therapy, and gender reassignment surgery. While this is a medically recognized process, it still poses a challenge to corrections institutions. Lydon, Carrington, Low, Miller, and Yazdy (2015) cite numerous examples of individuals who began hormone therapy on the outside but could not sustain it while confined, either due to an inability to access medical records, having performed self-administered hormone care, etc. The repercussions of ceasing this treatment so abruptly are compounding, physically and mentally (devalued as the person you identify with) (rapid hormonal changes/withdraw) which can be challenging at best with the worst cases result in serious self-harm or suicide (Brown, 2010; Huft, 2008; Spicer, 2010; Summers & Onate, 2014). Coupled with the hostile environment that individuals on the gender identity spectrum experiences, like Susan mentioned, the compounding nature of prison and transgender can be extremely dangerous. Thus the restrictive hormone policies that are widespread throughout United States prisons should be examined and more supportive policies should be put in place.

Transgender women are at particular risk because they are overrepresented in criminal behaviors, due in part to stigma and access concerns in the general population. Transgender women may rely on street economies for survival, turning to sex work, substance use to handle the emotional and physical toll, and other activities that place this community at a heightened risk for arrest, and finally, incarceration (Grant et al., 2011; Nemoto, Bödeker, & Iwamoto, 2011). Estimates suggest that transgender women have a lifetime incarceration rate at between 19–65%, which is astronomically higher than the 3% that is estimated for the general population (Grant et al., 2011; Glaze & Kaeble, 2013; respectively).

Furthermore, transgender women often need routine healthcare to meet the needs of the physical transition, mental stability, and other health needs. In 2010, Italy proposed a specialty prison to house and treat only transgender persons, the concept was applauded and supported widely according to the BBC (2010). However, this facility has yet to be built as of 2019. Italy does have progressive means of offering care to individuals who are transgender, housing them in a protective area with other transgender identifying individuals, allowing them to wear clothing that aligns with their gender identity, and offering continued hormonal treatments (Hochdorn, Faleiros, Valerio, & Vitelli, 2018). Healthcare in prison is notoriously poor, and access to transition needs like estrogen and other hormones is often either lacking, or nonexistent. In addition, the mental health care of transgender women should be conducted by trained professionals who can handle the unique concerns and needs of the transcommunity, which most institutional clinicians and practitioners are not equipped to handle. There is a history of restrictive policies and procedure for transgender individuals while they are incarcerated. However, according to The Standards of Care report that transgender individuals should be provided an option for the following treatment(s) while incarcerated: "(1) changes in gender expression and role; (2) hormone therapy; (3) surgery; and (4) psychotherapy" (as referenced in *Keohane v. Jones, 2017*, p.4). Even with legislation to support ongoing medical concerns of the transgender community, Lydon et al. (2015) report that transgender women were mistreated by correctional providers and face biased interactions that limited their voice and autonomy about their gender identity. Many of the women from the study report being misgendered, belittled, and demeaned (Lydon et al., 2015).

Beyond the interpersonal mistreatment and stigma, transgender women are also restricted, or placed on long delays, to gain access to the proper transition-related care and hormone therapy that they require (Emmer, Lowe, & Marshall, 2011). Facilities' policies often claim that hormone therapy is not medically necessary, especially compared to the other diseases that plague the incarcerated population like mental health medications, HIV medications, regulatory medications, but the prioritization of hormones for a transgender individual is medically necessary according to the Human Rights Campaign (HRC, 2019). According to HRC (2019) transgender individuals who are not receiving the proper access to hormones can have a host of negative health and mental health outcomes. Therefore, it is crucial to provide access and treatment to medically necessary hormones for transgender prisoners. While politically correct labels continue to evolve, the fact that there is a portion of individuals incarcerated who are transgender means that research and policy cannot stop at a prison's door. The discussion must continue.

7.7 Challenges of Sexual and Gender Identity

The challenges that queer women in prison face are extensive. Factors that restrict access for medically necessary care to systemic phobia against transgender and non-conforming females limit access to the appropriate channels for treatment. Furthermore, beyond the structural access challenges, many sexual minorities face a host of interpersonal challenges, based on lack of policies in place to remove the social stigma from staff and the protection policies from other people incarcerated. In turn, queer women in prison are forced to adapt, to change who they are in order to fit the system, and become resilient enough to survive.

Another challenge for individuals who identify as part of the LGBTQ+ community are at an increased risk for suicide (WHO, 2014). The general population has approximately 3.5% that identify as LGBTQ+ but in jail almost 8% identify as LGBTQ+, meaning that this population is already at a higher risk for suicidality and then are also exposed to the carceral environment which may lead to an even greater suicidality risk (Beck, Berzofsky, Caspar, & Krebs, 2013). LGBTQ+ persons are at an elevated risk for suicidality compared with heterosexual identifying persons also incarcerated (Silenzio, Pena, Duberstein, Cerel, & Knox, 2007). Given the larger proportion of incarcerated individuals who identify as LGBTQ+, risk factors that may be exclusive to sexual orientation are a necessity to identify in order to address the underlying gap.

When discussing what options there are to improve the challenges faced by transgender women, there is a strong need for health care reform within prisons, as well as education and training. Educational efforts are suggested to help increase understanding of the barriers faced by sexual and gender identity minorities, as well as to destigmatize within the confines of corrections. Healthcare providers, prison administration, and correctional staff can be more aware and understand how to help transgender individuals when they are aware and informed on the barriers that transgender people face in the correctional system (Hanssmann, Morrison, & Russian, 2008). These techniques could serve to better inform corrections officers, but the administration of this training to a correctional population would prove challenging. Perhaps most important is establishing policy baselines so that an individual is not seen as simply male or female, straight or queer; there is a spectrum in between that must be recognized in order to begin to solve the problem. From education, to housing options or medical treatment, nothing can begin, and a right answer cannot be found until the first action of institutional recognition is taken.

The blurring lines of sexuality and gender make the identification of proper policies and access to treatment difficult. The experiences of women incarcerated that fall on the sexuality and gender spectrum are harsh, dangerous, and leave long-term negative impacts. The concerns for women of all communities need to be further explored. As Susan stated, it is unnecessarily hard to be out, in prison.

References

Beck, A. J., Berzofsky, M., Caspar, R., & Krebs, C. (2013). *Sexual victimization in prisons and jails reported by inmates, 2011–12*. Washington, DC: US Bureau of Justice Statistics.

Beck, A. J., & Johnson, C. (2012). *Sexual victimization reported by former state prisoners, 2008*. Washington, DC: U.S. Department of Justice, Office of Justice Programs, Bureau of Justice Statistics.

Brown, G. R. (2010). Autocastration and autopenectomy as surgical self-treatment in incarcerated persons with gender identity disorder. *International Journal of Transgenderism, 12*, 31–39.

Diamond, M. (2002). Sex and gender are different: Sexual identity and gender identity are different. *Clinical Child Psychology and Psychiatry, 7*(3), 320–334.

Emmer, P., Lowe, A., & Marshall, R. B. (2011). *This is a prison, glitter is not allowed: Experiences of trans and gender variant people in Pennsylvania's prison systems* (Hearts on a Wire Collective). Philadelphia, PA.

Gates, G. J. (2011). *How many people are lesbian, gay, bisexual, and transgender?* Los Angeles: The Williams Institute.

Gibson, L. E., & Hensley, C. (2013). The social construction of sexuality in prison. *The Prison Journal, 93*(3), 355–370.

Glaze L, & Kaeble D. (2013). *Bureau of justice statistics* (US Department of Justice; 2014. Correctional Populations in the United States). Washington, DC.

Grant, J. M., Mottet, L., Tanis, J. E., Harrison, J., Herman, J., & Keisling, M. (2011). *Injustice at every turn: A report of the national transgender discrimination survey*. Washington, DC: National Center for Transgender Equality.

Hanssmann, C., Morrison, D., & Russian, E. (2008). Talking, gawking, or getting it done: Provider trainings to increase cultural and clinical competence for transgender and gender-nonconforming patients and clients. *Sexuality Research & Social Policy, 5*(1), 5.

Hensley, C. (Ed.). (2002). *Prison sex: Practice and policy*. Boulder, CO: Lynne Rienner.

Hochdorn, A., Faleiros, V. P., Valerio, P., & Vitelli, R. (2018). Narratives of transgender people detained in prison: The role played by the utterances "not" (as a feeling of hetero- and auto-rejection) and "exist" (as a feeling of hetero- and auto-acceptance) for the construction of a discursive self. A suggestion of goals and strategies for psychological counseling. *Frontiers in Psychology, 8*, 2367. https://doi.org/10.3389/fpsyg.2017.02367

Huft, M. (2008). Statistically speaking: The high rate of suicidality among transgender youth and access barriers to medical treatment in a society of gender dichotomy. *Children's Legal Rights Journal, 28*, 53.

Human Rights Campaign. (2019). *Sexual orientation and gender identity definitions*. Retrieved October 14, 2019, from https://www.hrc.org/resources/sexual-orientation-and-gender-identity-terminology-and-definitions

Irwin, J., & Cressey, D. R. (1962). Thieves, convicts, and the inmate culture. *Social Problems, 10*, 142–155.

Kahn, M. (2006). *Punishment, prisons, and patriarchy: Liberty and power in the early Republic*. New York: New York University Press.

Kunzel, R. (2008). *Criminal intimacy: Prison and the uneven history of modern American society*. Chicago: University of Chicago Press.

Lydon, J., Carrington, K., Low, H., Miller, R., & Yazdy, M. (2015). *Coming out of concrete closets: A report on Black and Pink's LGBTQ prisoner' survey*. Boston: Black and Pink.

McNamara, M. (2014). Better to be out in prison than out in public: LGBTQ prisoners receive more constitutional protection if they are open about their sexuality while in prison. *Tulane Journal of Law and Sexuality, 23*, 135.

National Center for Transgender Equality. (2019). *LGBTQ people behind bars*. Retrieved 2020, from https://transequality.org/sites/default/files/docs/resources/TransgenderPeopleBehindBars.pdf

Nemoto, T., Bödeker, B., & Iwamoto, M. (2011). Social support, exposure to violence and transphobia, and correlates of depression among male-to-female transgender women with a history of sex work. *American Journal of Public Health, 101*(10), 1980–1988.

Otis, M. D., Oser, C. B., & Staton-Tindall, M. (2016). Violent victimization and substance dependency: Comparing rural incarcerated heterosexual and sexual minority women. *Journal of Social Work Practice in the Addictions, 16*(1-2), 176–201.

Owen, B. A. (1999). *In the mix: Struggle and survival in a women's prison*. Albany: SUNY Press.

Pardue, A., Arrigo, B. A., & Murphy, D. S. (2011). Sex and sexuality in women's prisons: A preliminary typological investigation. *The Prison Journal, 91*(3), 279–304.

Reiter, L. (1989). Sexual orientation, sexual identity, and the question of choice. *Clinical Social Work Journal, 17*(2), 138–150.

Ryle, R. (2011). *Questioning gender: A sociological exploration*. Thousand oaks, CA: Sage Publications.

Silenzio, V. M., Pena, J. B., Duberstein, P. R., Cerel, J., & Knox, K. L. (2007). Sexual orientation and risk factors for suicidal ideation and suicide attempts among adolescents and young adults. *American Journal of Public Health, 97*(11), 2017–2019.

Spicer, S. S. (2010). Healthcare needs of the transgender homeless population. *Journal of Gay & Lesbian Mental Health, 14*(4), 320–339.

Stryker, S. (2008). *Transgender history*. Seal Press.

Summers, S. M., & Onate, J. (2014). New onset psychosis following abrupt discontinuation of hormone replacement therapy in a trans woman. *Journal of Gay & Lesbian Mental Health, 18*(3), 312–319.

Sykes, G. (1958). *The society of captives: A study of a maximum security prison*. Princeton, NJ: Princeton University Press.

Tewksbury, R., & West, A. (2000). Research on sex in prison during the late 1980s and early 1990s. *The Prison Journal, 80*, 368–378.

Van Wormer, K. S. (1981). Social functions of prison families: The female solution. *The Journal of Psychiatry & Law, 9*(2), 181–191.

Vitulli, E. W. (2013). Queering the carceral: Intersecting queer/trans studies and critical prison studies. *GLQ: A Journal of Lesbian and Gay Studies, 19*(1), 111–123.

White Hughto, J. M., Clark, K. A., Altice, F. L., Reisner, S. L., Kershaw, T. S., & Pachankis, J. E. (2018). Creating, reinforcing, and resisting the gender binary: a qualitative study of transgender women's healthcare experiences in sex-segregated jails and prisons. *International Journal of Prisoner Health, 14*(2), 69–88. https://doi.org/10.1108/IJPH-02-2017-0011

World Health Organization. (2014). *Preventing suicide: a global imperative*. Geneva: World Health Organization, Department of Mental Health and Substance Abuse.

Chapter 8
Intersectional Pathways: The Role Victimization Plays in Women's Offending and in Prisons

Katherine Lorenz and Rebecca M. Hayes

8.1 Introduction

In 2017, women comprised 7% of the US prison population, totaling approximately 111,360 women (Bronson & Carson, 2019), a figure that has drastically increased in the past three decades (The Sentencing Project, 2019). In the USA, women of color (WOC) are incarcerated at disproportionate rates. For example, in 2017, Black women were incarcerated at twice the rate of White women, and Hispanic women at 1.3 times the rate of White women (The Sentencing Project, 2019). Transgender women are also disproportionately incarcerated, though there is a lack of research examining the incarceration of these individuals (Reisner, Bailey, & Sevelius, 2014). Historically, most discussions of women who are incarcerated have focused on women as a homogenous group, failing to explore differences in race, ethnicity, gender identification, sexuality, disability status, and class, and have largely neglected the intersections of marginalized social identities.

Given the incarceration rate of women, particularly WOC, it is important to consider the role of victimization in women's offending. Most women who are incarcerated have experienced some form of sexual or physical victimization as a child, an adult, or both, prior to their incarceration (Courtney & Maschi, 2013; Bradley & Davino, 2002; Raj et al., 2008; Walsh et al., 2012) and have physical and mental health issues as a result of these experiences (Aday, Huey Dye, & Kaiser, 2014; Green et al., 2016; Lynch, Fritch, & Heath, 2012; Sheridan & Nash, 2007). There is a clear connection between victimization and offending, and this chapter will

K. Lorenz (✉)
California State University Northridge, Northridge, CA, USA
e-mail: katherine.lorenz@csun.edu

R. M. Hayes
Central Michigan University, Mt Pleasant, MI, USA

© Springer Nature Switzerland AG 2020   97
J. Hector (ed.), *Women and Prison*,
https://doi.org/10.1007/978-3-030-46172-0_8

explore the theoretical and empirical support for the victim-to-offender pathway. It is necessary to consider the victimization experiences of women in the context of their offending, but we also must consider the differences in victimization and pathways to offending for WOC and transgender women, and the intersections of these social identities.

Although victimization prior to incarceration is common for women, the issues stemming from these experiences often go unaddressed while incarcerated. Indeed, many women's mental and physical health issues can be exacerbated while incarcerated due to revictimization by correctional officers or re-traumatization triggered by prison conditions (Aday et al., 2014; Covington, 2008; Maeve, 2000; Struckman-Johnson & Struckman-Johnson, 2002). Because the US correctional system disproportionately houses women of marginalized social identities, it is important to consider how this system perpetuates disadvantage through lack of support and resources to women who are incarcerated. The vast majority of women who are incarcerated will return to society and without addressing these issues during incarceration, they will likely reenter the community in a worsened state of mental and physical health, at an increased risk for recidivism (Messina & Grella, 2006). Therefore, we must explore physical and mental health consequences of victimization among women who are incarcerated and the availability for treatment in correctional facilities to address these issues.

In this chapter, we critically review the theoretical and empirical research on the role of victimization in women's offending and incarceration. Victimization, offending, and incarceration experiences differ based on social identity, and we explore these topics through an intersectional lens. First, we present the theoretical research on women's pathways to offending. Second, we discuss victimization experienced by women prior to incarceration and the related physical and mental health outcomes. Third, we review the (lack of) treatment provided to women in addressing these physical and mental health issues in the correctional facility. Finally, we discuss the perpetuation of violence in correctional facilities via victimization perpetrated by correctional officers.

8.1.1   The Dual Role of Being an Offender and Victim

Most people in American prisons are men, but the incarceration rate for women rose 700% from 1980 to 2017 (The Sentencing Project, 2019), mainly due to harsher policies that especially targeted men of color and also WOC. In order to understand the victimization of women in prison, we need to discuss the victimization of women outside of prison and the role that it plays in their offending. This is explained in research literature as the "dual role of being an offender and a victim" (von Hentig, 1948) or the victim/offender overlap (DeLong & Reichert, 2019; Jennings, Piquero, & Reingle, 2012; see Fig. 8.1). This is especially true for girls/women, as

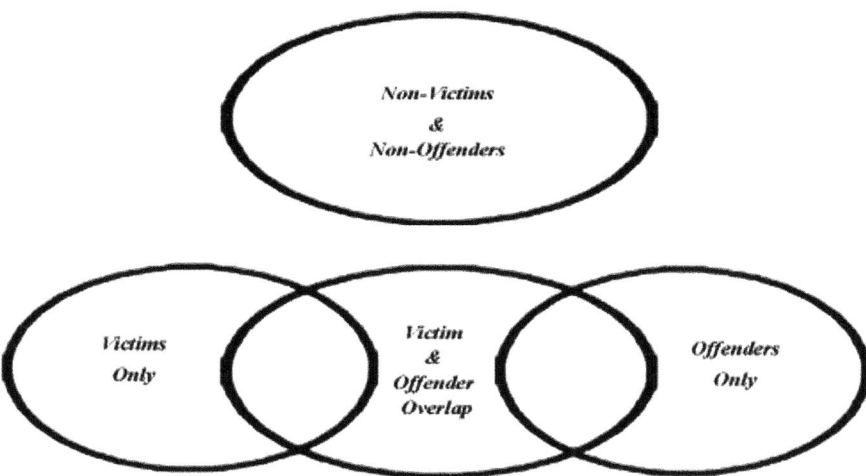

Fig. 8.1 Overlap of victimization and offending (Jennings et al., 2012)

research continues to establish how often they become a victim[1] first and an offender later (Widom, 1995, 2000; Verrecchia, 2009). We are not insinuating that all victims become offenders, just like not all victims become substance abusers; but there is a clear correlation.

Over half of women who are incarcerated have a sexual or physical victimization prior to their incarceration (Bradley & Davino, 2002; Green, Miranda, Daroowalla, & Siddique, 2005; Walsh, DiLillo, & Scalora, 2011), and once incarcerated the victimization is not being treated (Lynch et al., 2017; Wolff et al., 2011). If the victimization played a role into why a girl or woman began offending, then not treating the effects of victimization further perpetuates recidivism (Messina & Grella, 2006). In society, there is a stigma around being an offender, but there is also a stigma in being a victim. Women who are incarcerated and also survivors of sexual or domestic victimization face multiple societal stigmas. These identities are concealable, but if revealed could be stigmatizing (termed *concealable stigma*; other examples: LGB membership, HIV status; Goffman, 1963). Both victim and offender stigmas are further complicated depending on mental health or substance use issues which are related to both victimization and offending. Theoretical propositions attempt to explain and untangle these complicated trajectories.

Historically, criticisms of mainstream criminological theory have been about how they tend to be written by, for, and about boys/men (Belknap, 2015; Chesney-Lind & Pasko, 2013; Daly & Chesney-Lind, 1988). When women and girls were

---

[1] Throughout this chapter, we use the terms "victim" and "survivor" deliberately and not interchangeably. When we use the term victim, we are referring to the victim label and associated stigma. Survivor, the more commonly used term in advocacy, is used to represent those who have been victimized and the journey in working to address the short and long-term effects of victimization.

included in research it was largely through the "add women and stir approach" (Covington & Bloom, 2003; Feminist Criminology, 2019), which causes the "generalizability problem" (Daly & Chesney-Lind, 1988). The generalizability problem is questioning whether theories that are made for boys and men actually can apply to women and girls. The generalizability problem is different than the gender-ratio problem, which asserts that women and girls commit less crime than boys and men (Daly & Chesney-Lind, 1988). Yet, there is an increase in girls' and women's crimes, but little research and theory examining women and girls' offending. The myth regarding the increase in girls' and women's incarceration was initially lauded as a side effect of girls'/women's empowerment (Chesney-Lind, 1986).

Mainstream theoretical approaches to understanding why and how women commit crimes does not consider women/girls and their gendered experiences and socialization. Even further, many mainstream theories do not disaggregate experiences for Black, Hispanic, or Native American women/girls either and the intersections of race/ethnicity with gender. While the "adding women and stirring approach" is unacceptable, so is the "adding race/ethnicity and stirring approach" (Simpson, 1989). Intersectional theory (explained below) (Crenshaw, 1991) purports the importance of understanding the nuances of how race as a social construct (among other social locations) intersects with gender and impacts crime and victimization. After research had identified the frequency of victimization that many women and girls had experienced and its correlation to substance abuse/drug addiction and other deviant or criminal activities (Browne, Miller, & Maguin, 1999; Wood, Foy, Goguen, Pynoos, & James, 2002; Wood, Foy, Layne, Pynoos, & Boyd, 2002; Widom, 1995, 2000), theorists then paid attention to the "pathway" that women and girls take to crime (Belknap, 2015; Belknap & Holsinger, 1998; Owen & Bloom, 2000).

8.1.2   Feminist Pathways

Arguably a theoretical approach (Holtfreter & Wattanaporn, 2014), "*feminist pathways research* attempts to gain data that are quasi-longitudinal by asking girls and women to discuss their lives and attempt to sequence major events (e.g., abuse by parents, school experiences, delinquent and criminal behavior, and so on)" (Belknap, 2015, p. 71). Since the 1970s, research has collected girls' and women's voices to assess what life events indicate risk of criminal offending. However, Belknap (2015, p. 71) lists research studies in her section on feminist pathways, but calls this list "a bit tenuous" because many studies may not necessarily be labeled feminist pathways or even feminist. The point, however, is to group together studies that center girls' and women's lived experiences as "pathways" into deviant and criminal behavior.

Research is not arguing that there are not similarities between boys and girls, or men and women when it comes to some identifying risk factors (such as lower SES, family disruption, etc.) but that we need to pay attention to the different crimes that boys and girls or men and women commit, and how gendered experiences are associated with these crimes (Belknap, 2015; Chesney-Lind & Pasko, 2013; Owen & Bloom, 2000). A girl's pathway into crime can often begin after she runs away from home to avoid abuse (Chesney-Lind & Shelden, 1992; Chesney-Lind & Pasko, 2013). Research continues to indicate the role abuse plays into future criminal activity (Chesney-Lind & Pasko, 2013; Gilfus, 1992; Gehring, 2018; Widom, 2000), in fact the abuse itself could be the forcing of the girl into criminal activity (DeHart, 2008).

Early research examined data collected from sex workers (aka prostitutes[2]) and attempted to compare whether early childhood sexual experiences among them differed from the general population (Belknap, 2015). The research by James and Meyerding (1977) did find that rates of troubling sexual experiences for sex workers differed from the "normal" population. Gilfus (1992) interviewed 20 women who were incarcerated and found that their survival techniques were often criminal, and their victimization (such as child abuse) did lead them to offend, and the offending led them into more victimization. This theme is echoed in DeHart's (2008) qualitative research with women who are incarcerated, some of the women's victimization related directly to their involvement in criminal activities. For example, many of the illegal activities the women committed could be described as defensive or retaliatory to the direct physical victimization they had received. We must also consider the indirect effect of victimization onto criminal activities via mental and physical health impacts. When a person is victimized, they may turn to drugs or alcohol to self-medicate especially in circumstances where other resources are unavailable to them, which in lower socio-economic environments this tends to be the case. There are also pathways from crime to victimization, such as in the case where a woman is a sex worker and then gets victimized by one of her clients (DeHart, 2008).

While a lot of pathways research is qualitative, which is in line with feminist methodologies, there are some studies who examine pathways quantitatively (Gehring, 2018: Jones, Brown, Wanamaker, & Greiner, 2014; Salisbury & Van Voorhis, 2009; Van Voorhis, Wright, Salisbury, & Bauman, 2010). These quantitative studies further corroborate the qualitative research that suggests girls and women have a different pathway to crime and deviance than do boys and men. Gehring (2018) compared male and female pretrial defendants and found that for the females child abuse, mental illness, and substance abuse were all indicators for pretrial failure. Likewise, Jones et al. (2014) examined pathways among male and female juveniles and confirmed the unique gendered pathway (e.g., abuse) for female juveniles. While the research highlights the differing role that gender plays into offending pathways, we need to take it even further and pay attention to the intersecting role that race/ethnicity, sexuality, etc. also play into victimization and offending for women.

---

[2] Even though the research cited here uses the word prostitute it is not the preferred academic or societal term. Sex worker is more appropriate.

8.1.3   Intersectionality

Related to feminist pathways, intersectionality is distinct in assisting to understand how women from multiple social identities experience incarceration and victimization within prisons. Social identities can include but are not limited to race, ethnicity, color, gender identification, gender expression, neurodiversity, and sexuality; all can impact how one is treated by institutions and individuals in our society. Intersectionality, a term attributed to Kimberlé Crenshaw in the 1980s, "was initially presented to recognize the legal dilemmas faced by Black women being recognized as facing employment-related discrimination different than that faced by Black men and by White women" (Potter, 2013, p. 305). Intersectionality is also applicable to criminology, and the tenets of this theory are argued to have been in place long before Crenshaw brought them all together (Potter, 2013). We are purporting this as a theory even though it has also been lauded as a method or a concept (Davis, 2008; Potter, 2013; Tomlinson, 2013). As theories/concepts/methods tend to be complicated and definitionally disputed, we use Hill Collins and Bilges's explanation from their book, *Intersectionality* (2016, p. 2):

> Intersectionality is a way of understanding and analyzing the complexity in the world, in people, and in human experiences. The events and conditions of social and political life and the self can seldom be understood as shaped by one factor. They are generally shaped by many factors in diverse and mutually influencing ways. When it comes to social inequality, people's lives and the organization of power in a given society are better understood as being shaped not by a single axis of social division, be it race or gender or class, but by many axes that work together and influence each other. Intersectionality as an analytic tool gives people better access to the complexity of the world and themselves (Hill Collins & Bilge, 2016, p. 2).

A more succinct definition, and applicable to criminological inquiry where we focus on explanations of crime and victimization, is from Hattery and Smith (2019, p. 8), where they argue that intersectionality focuses on the "multiple systems of oppression that independently and collaboratively create complex systems of stratification that produce interlocking systems of inequality." Hopefully not disputed is that intersectional theory derived from Black Feminist thought, and therefore much of the discussion surrounds the oppression of Black women even though the applicability reaches beyond those intersectional identities (Hill Collins & Bilge, 2016; Potter, 2013). To explain it in applicable terms, while Black men suffer from racism they still benefit from male privilege, whereas Black women suffer from racism and sexism which intersect to create oppressive experiences that differ from those of Black men. Potter (2015) also highlights the importance of examining colorism (the shade of one's skin) when interrogating the role that racism plays in oppression. Due to White supremacist ideology, colorism intersects with racism and is where skin color matters beyond simply Black and White, the shade of a person's skin can impact the treatment they receive in society, such as in the criminal justice system. The darker a person's skin the more harshly they are treated by individuals and institutions. For example, Slaughter-Acey (2019) found in their preliminary findings of predictors of preterm birth among women that their skin tone mattered.

While public health research is investigating colorism and it is still in its infancy (Slaughter-Acey, 2019), criminological research also needs to examine the impacting intersections of race and color on criminal justice outcomes, such as victimization outside and within prisons.

Intersectional theoretical analysis has been occurring for the past two decades and occurs within criminology, with earlier works not necessarily identifying it as intersectional analysis (much like pathways research) (Potter, 2013, 2015). While Potter (2013) highlights some very important intersectional research (that will be discussed in detail below), Richie (1996) has conducted some of the most important pathways research (Belknap, 2015) that is also intersectional. Richie (1996) examined the differences between Black and White women who were in abusive relationships and found while there are similarities, the differences are very impactful. The context of the differences is directly related to race and the role that institutional racism plays into the daily lives of men and WOC. She developed her theory of *Gender Entrapment* which draws connections among violence against the women in her study, the construction of their gender identity (and that is related to race), and how these contribute to their criminal activity. Similarly, Potter (2008) conducted research that centered the experiences of 40 African American women and their experiences with intimate partner abuse. The women often experienced child abuse and multiple relationships that involved abuse by an intimate partner. The socioeconomic status of the women ranged from low-income, working-class to middle-class backgrounds. Her sample also ranged in level of education with most having at least some college. The importance of examining the intersection of race and class in Potter's (2008) work is highlighted by the number of abusive relationships. Women who were raised middle-class had 1.8 abusive relationships, and women who indicated they were middle-class at the time of the interview averaged 1.7. Whereas, women who grew up working-class averaged 2.7 abusive relationships and those in lower-class homes averaged 2.3 abusive relationships. Regarding race, Potter (2008) highlights how the women who participated often fought back and escaped these relationships. She argues that,

> Because Black women are raised in the United States with the stereotype of being strong, angry, and more masculine than White women, I maintain that many battered Black women can express angry feelings and communicate their anger in a physically resistant manner with less difficulty than other women, (Potter, 2008, p. 136).

Of course, then, it is important to examine this notion in regards to incarceration of Black women, if Black women are more likely to fight back than other women this could be related to the over-incarceration of Black girls and women. With the expectations of White gender roles being that of passive, the fighting back that may very well save Black girls and women's lives also may lead to a lowered likelihood of being viewed as a survivor.

Black women subjected to racialized stereotypes, dating back to slavery Black Codes, and Jim Crow, are oversexualized and stereotyped as promiscuous (i.e., "jezebel") and subsequently deemed "unrapeable" arguably meaning that it is impossible to rape them because they are inherently sexual objects (see Broussard,

2013 for review). This fits into Smith's (2015, p. 3) analysis of the sexual violence American Indian[3] women where she states that, "sexual violence is a tool by which certain peoples become marked as inherently "rapeable"". While she is discussing how "sexual violence is used as tool of patriarchy and colonialism" to destroy Native communities (Smith, 2015, p. 2), the intersections of oppression of race/ethnicity and gender in each of these communities demonstrate how WOC are not deemed "true" victims. With gendered expectations being tied to White patriarchal values, WOC who act beyond the scope of emphasized femininity find themselves on the receiving end of racist policies and practices. Further, these expectations and stereotypes serve to silence Black women (and other WOC) from seeking services needed to address physical and mental health issues that occur as a result of victimization (Tillman, Bryant-Davis, Smith, & Marks, 2010).

While Potter's (2013) article is to encourage criminologists to use intersectional analysis, the positivistic focus of much criminological research uses sociodemographic variables as fixed categories where certain identities and their intersections are excluded. Even when there is mediation and moderation, research social factors such as colorism, ethnicity, and race become confounded. This results in a general lack of research on the experiences of women who are of differing race/ethnicities outside of the Black/White dyad and the experiences of non-gender-binary identifying individuals. Mainstream criminological analysis often excludes intersectional analysis or avoids terming it that while studying social identities in research. Intersectional theory is not only important for examining understanding crime and victimization, but is paramount to understanding the impacts of both on different communities. The reasons we chose both feminist pathways and intersectional theory is the overlap they have with each other, and the focus on victimization that impacts women and girls' crime commission. They place a spotlight on the role that victimization plays into offending through individual victimization (feminist pathway) or institutional (intersectional). Without considering the overlap of these two, we argue that we cannot effectively develop crime prevention or rehabilitation programming and policies.

8.2   Victimization Experiences and Related Outcomes Among Women Who Are Incarcerated

For many women who are incarcerated, the correctional facility is a safer environment than being in the community, due to the volume and severity of abuse experienced prior to incarceration (Bradley & Davino, 2002). Women who are incarcerated have elevated levels of interpersonal violence and other traumatic experiences than non-incarcerated women, particularly domestic abuse and sexual assault. Women

---

[3]American Indian is the term used in the research. First Nations people is a more appropriate term, and where applicable is what we use when discussing this ethnicity.

who are incarcerated commonly experience repeated sexual and/or physical victimization prior to incarceration (Aday & Huey Dye, 2019; Aday et al., 2014; Bradley & Davino, 2002; Courtney & Maschi, 2013; Green et al., 2005; Tripodi & Pettus-Davis, 2013; Walsh et al., 2011). Like we mentioned above regarding intersectionality, victimization experiences are commonly compounded by intersecting disadvantaged social locations that puts one at a greater risk for being revictimized (e.g., being homeless and sexually abused and a WOC; Cook, Smith, Poister Tusher, & Raiford, 2005) and multiple trauma experiences (Courtney & Maschi, 2013). Experiences of multiple occurrences and forms of victimization is termed poly-victimization, whereas one episode of victimization is termed simple victimization (Finkelhor et al., 2007). It is important to note that those who are sexually or physically abused as children are the most likely to become poly-victims, as is the case for many women who are incarcerated (Aday et al., 2014; Courtney & Maschi, 2013; Raj et al., 2008). For many women who are incarcerated, sexual and physical abuse is a lifetime experience, beginning in childhood and continuing through adulthood.

Women who are incarcerated have higher childhood experiences of physical and/or sexual abuse than women who are not incarcerated. About half of women who are incarcerated who have victimization experiences report that the abuse began in childhood or adolescence, with events including (but not limited to): witnessing family violence, physical abuse, sexual touching, sexual assault, and neglect (Aday & Huey Dye, 2019; Cook et al., 2005; Courtney & Maschi, 2013; Hartsfield, Sharp, & Conner, 2017; Lynch et al., 2012; Tripodi & Pettus-Davis, 2013; Walsh et al., 2011). The abusive experiences, on average, begin at around 9 or 10 years of age (Courtney & Maschi, 2013) and are often perpetrated by family or friends (Raj et al., 2008). Raj et al. (2008) report that there is a decline in sexual assault in adolescence among women who are incarcerated, with the highest rates of assault occurring in childhood and adulthood, in contradiction to sexual assault rates in the general population. They speculate that this decline could be due to abused children leaving home in adolescence, subsequently being separated from the abuser, yet facing other stressors and traumas associated with homelessness or foster care, creating a pathway for future crime perpetration in response to trauma (see feminist pathways discussion above; Chesney-Lind & Shelden, 1992; Chesney-Lind & Pasko, 2013). Again, we must recognize that childhood abuse often takes place as or leads to poly-victimization. Poly-victimization can impact brain development, leading to more thrill-seeking and instant gratification, potentially criminally offending behaviors. As such, experiencing child sexual abuse (CSA) can not only create a pathway to offending, but also places women at increased risk for victimization as an adult (de Lint & Marmo, 2018).

Many survivors of childhood abuse report revictimization as an adult (Aday et al., 2014; Courtney & Maschi, 2013; Raj et al., 2008), suggesting that sexual assault across the lifespan is common among women who are incarcerated (aka poly-victimization). Indeed, CSA is predictive of adult sexual victimization among women who are incarcerated more so than women outside of correctional facilities (Raj et al., 2008). Most research to date examines this connection while controlling for racial/ethnic variation, or comparing experiences to those of White women, rather than specifically examining the experiences for WOC (aka the "add race/ethnicity and stir approach" we discussed above). As such, the child/adult revictimization experiences of individuals with intersecting marginalized identities are somewhat unknown. Jones, Worthen, Sharp, and McLeod (2018) established a connection between childhood Adverse Childhood Experiences (ACEs) and intimate partner violence (IPV) victimization as an adult among women who are incarcerated, with consideration of racial/ethnic differences. Several individual ACEs such as sexual abuse, physical and emotional neglect, and emotional abuse, and an accumulation of ACEs (five or more) all increased the likelihood of experiencing sexual, physical, and psychological IPV as an adult, more so for White women than Native American, African American, and Hispanic women (Jones et al., 2018). Abuse suffered as a child often continues into adulthood, but may even occur during incarceration, as women may be blamed or emotionally abused by family members while serving time (Maeve, 2000), which demonstrates that domestic abuse can continue into adulthood.

Intimate partner violence is a common form of victimization among women who are incarcerated. In a study examining trauma exposure using a primarily African American[4] woman sample (82%), violence perpetrated by an intimate partner was the most common form of trauma experienced (71%; Green et al., 2005). Transgender women who are incarcerated report high rates of IPV as well. Experiences of IPV victimization are diverse, including behaviors not limited to stalking, manipulation, emotional abuse, threats to kill, sexual violence, and/or physical violence (e.g., shoving, grabbing, punching, choking, etc.) that occurs on an ongoing basis and often causes women to fear for their life (Cook et al., 2005; Lynch et al., 2012; O'Keefe, 1997). In a study of 102 women serving time, 90% reported physical and sexual violence perpetrated by an intimate partner within the year prior to incarceration. When asked about lifetime experiences of IPV, 79% described at least one experience of physical violence without a weapon, 70% indicated forced sexual intercourse, 55% experienced forced sexual contact, and 43% had been attacked with a weapon, with 23% experiencing all four types of violence (Lynch et al., 2012). Experiencing ongoing IPV ultimately leads many women to perpetrate violence against their partner in self-defense or feeling that they had no other options to escape the abuse (i.e., lack of social support and resources), leading to the woman's incarceration (O'Keefe, 1997). Though sexual violence is prevalent as a form of IPV, women experience sexual violence outside of the confines of IPV as well.

Sexual victimization is a common experience for women in general (Kilpatrick, Resnick, Ruggiero, Conoscenti, & McCauley, 2007), though women who are incarcerated experience sexual victimization at a higher rate than women in the community (Aday et al., 2014; Blackburn, Mullings, & Marquart, 2008). Using a nationally

---

[4] We use the racial terminology used by the researchers in their study. However, we recognize that the term Black is more appropriate, as Black insinuates more than just African American and highlights the need to assess race, ethnicity, and colorism separately.

representative sample of women who are incarcerated, Aday et al. (2014) found that 42% of women who are incarcerated reported being sexually victimized prior to incarceration. The majority of survivors in their sample (72%) had experienced abuse on more than one occasion with more than one perpetrator (38%), highlighting that sexual assault experiences often include revictimization. Rates of sexual victimization among women who are incarcerated are higher among younger, lesbian, and bisexual women (Blackburn et al., 2008). Generally, WOC face increased risk for sexual victimization compared to White women. This risk is even higher for WOC who have intersecting marginalized identities, including being low-income, HIV-positive, bisexual, and/or incarcerated (West & Johnson, 2013), illustrating the importance of considering intersectionality in assessing victimization and offending.

Overall, women who are incarcerated commonly experience abuse, often IPV, child abuse/neglect, or sexual assault, that is greater than that of the general population. Indeed, many women who are incarcerated report victimization beginning in childhood and spanning to adulthood, evidencing the prevalence of compound trauma experiences (Aday & Huey Dye, 2019; Courtney & Maschi, 2013). Domestic abuse and sexual violence can create lifelong consequences for those with such histories.

8.2.1   Victimization History and Health Outcomes

Most women who are incarcerated are poly-victims when they enter the correctional facility and have mental and physical health issues as a result of their victimization experiences. In both policy and practice, there is often a disconnect between experiences of victimization, health, and offending where the trauma histories of women are not considered in providing treatment in correctional facilities. It is important to note that the physical and mental health issues tied to victimization often go unaddressed; while incarcerated, the unique treatment needs of women based on race, ethnicity, class, and/or LGBTQIA+ identity in addition to victimization, also go unaddressed (Lynch et al., 2012; Reisner, Bailey, & Sevelius, 2014; Young & Reviere, 2001). The result is that the issues women had when they entered the correctional facility are worse when they reenter the community, leading to additional problems (Messina & Grella, 2006). The application of an intersectional approach to identifying and treating mental and physical health issues has been minimal, and subsequently the problems experienced by women when they are released may be worse for transgender women and WOC. The following section details the mental and physical health issues stemming from victimization experiences and gives an overview of the treatment provided to these issues in correctional facilities.

8.2.1.1 Mental Health

Correctional facilities are known for housing populations suffering from mental health conditions. Mental health issues do not necessarily arise once incarcerated (though incarceration can be a determining factor for mental illness), but are often tied to victimization experiences that occurred prior to incarceration (Aday et al., 2014; Green et al., 2005; Green et al., 2016; Lynch et al., 2017; Tripodi & Pettus-Davis, 2013). For instance, correctional facilities housing only women with chronic physical or psychological health issues show higher rates of childhood and adult sexual and physical abuse experiences than the general population, with only 5% of women not reporting an abusive experience (Bradley & Davino, 2002). Generally, incarcerated women who are survivors of abuse or other traumatic experiences are more likely than their non-abused counterparts to be vulnerable to mental health issues.

A substantial number of women enter correctional facilities with high rates of Post-Traumatic Stress Disorder (PTSD) and other mental health issues due to histories of victimization or other traumatic events (Aday & Huey Dye, 2019; Green et al., 2005; Green et al., 2016). Mental health issues among women who are incarcerated are linked specifically to experiences of domestic abuse or IPV (Green et al., 2005; Lynch et al., 2012) and sexual violence (Aday et al., 2014; Hartsfield et al., 2017; Green et al., 2016). Indeed, research concludes that PTSD is more prevalent among women who are incarcerated than women outside of correctional facilities, and this has been tied to experiences of IPV and/or sexual violence (Green et al., 2005; Lynch et al., 2012). Bipolar disorder has also been linked to trauma histories among women who are incarcerated, suggesting that exposure to trauma may influence the genetic manifestation of the disorder (Green et al., 2016). Women who are incarcerated who have multiple IPV experiences, recent IPV (within 12 months prior to incarceration), and long-term IPV experiences are at a greater risk of multiple negative psychological outcomes including depression and distress (Lynch et al., 2012). In general, depressive symptoms are reported more frequently by women who are incarcerated who have sexual assault histories than those without. One half of women who are incarcerated who have histories of sexual abuse have received a diagnosis associated with a depressive disorder, compared to 29% of women who had not been sexually abused (Aday et al., 2014). Adult sexual assault survivors are 153% more likely to report a mental health diagnosis prior to incarceration (Hartsfield et al., 2017). Sexual abuse is also associated with increased risk of developing schizophrenia and personality disorders (Aday et al., 2014). Mental health consequences to sexual and physical victimization also take place outside of diagnosable conditions.

Sexual assault survivors who are incarcerated also experience consequences such as changes in sleep habits, appetite, sexual interest, temper issues, and daily activity functioning more so than women who are incarcerated without sexual assault histories (Aday et al., 2014). Further, survivors who are incarcerated report frequent periods of numbness/emptiness, episodes of paranoia, anxiety, and destructive behavior (Aday et al., 2014). It is common to experience issues tolerating, expressing, and/or modulating emotions, termed "emotional dysregulation" (Covington, 2008). Women who are incarcerated who have experienced multiple sexual victimizations report greater emotion dysregulation than those who have not been victimized and those who have been victimized once (as opposed to multiple victimization experiences; Walsh et al., 2011). Issues labeling and regulating emotions can lead to frustration and other emotional issues that exacerbate negative mental health impacts, further highlighting the cumulative impact of victimization that can potentially have life-threatening consequences.

Physical and sexual victimization experiences are predictive of suicidality among women who are incarcerated (Aday et al., 2014; DeCou, Lynch, & Cole, 2017; Tripodi & Pettus-Davis, 2013) and this is related to race/ethnicity. Among women with victimization histories, one study found 25% had attempted suicide (Tripodi & Pettus-Davis, 2013). This association between physical and sexual victimization and suicidality is present for White women, but not African American and Latina women who are incarcerated, further illustrating the importance of examining racial/ethnic differences in victimization experiences and related mental health outcomes. DeCou et al. (2017) speculate that racial/ethnic differences in suicidality in trauma survivors may be due to higher levels of intra-individual variables such as shame, self-blame, or guilt. However, it is also possible that this is due to cultural differences in coping with the effects of trauma. Overall, the association between suicidality and victimization among White women who are incarcerated not only highlights the severe mental health impact of victimization within this population, but also the unique influence of sexual and physical victimization relative to other traumatic or stressful life experiences.

There may be differences in the effects of abuse on mental health for individuals who were abused as a child, as an adult, or both. Women who are incarcerated who have histories of CSA or both CSA and adult sexual assault experiences have higher levels of depression, paranoia, behavior changes, attempt or consider suicide more than women without such experiences (Aday et al., 2014). Childhood victimization is also associated with substance use issues as an adult. Women who are incarcerated and were physically or both physically and sexually abused as a child are more likely to be diagnosed with a substance use disorder (SUD) as an adult than women with no childhood victimization history or women with only CSA history (Tripodi & Pettus-Davis, 2013). This association is more pronounced for White women than WOC, where WOC are 65% less likely than White women to develop a SUD in connection with childhood abuse experiences (Tripodi & Pettus-Davis, 2013). Women with CSA or CSA and adulthood victimization experiences are more likely to be diagnosed with a greater number of mental health conditions than women without CSA histories (Aday et al., 2014; Hartsfield et al., 2017). A study of women who are incarcerated examined the likelihood of mental health diagnoses for sexual violence survivors. They found that entering prison with a mental health diagnosis is 107% more likely for CSA (but not rape) survivors; 123% more likely for women who were raped before the age of 18; and 153% more likely for women who were raped as an adult than women with no sexual abuse experiences. Though there were no differences in abuse experienced and response for White compared to Black women, the odds of receiving a mental health diagnosis was reduced by almost 50% for Black survivors (Hartsfield et al., 2017). This may be an indication of the racial disparity in mental health services, where White individuals have greater access to receiving services and diagnoses more so than Black individuals but still have the same mental health needs. Overall, CSA survivors can experience exacerbated mental health effects due to compounded trauma, and as such, treatment programs in correctional facilities should consider individual sexual violence histories in providing services.

Mental health and victimization histories of women who are incarcerated is also important to examine in light of the aging prison population, where 15% of all women who are incarcerated in the USA are over the age of 50 (Bronson & Carson, 2019) and over half have experienced physical and/or sexual victimization. Aday and Huey Dye (2019) examined risk factors for depression among women who are incarcerated ages 50–77 and found that women who are incarcerated with a history of physical or sexual abuse as a child or adult experienced depression at a higher rate than those without victimization histories. They also found that women with abuse histories were far more likely to contemplate suicide than those without. Aday and Huey Dye's (2019) sample of older women who are incarcerated revealed that White women were more likely to experience depression than WOC, which evidences the need to examine racial and ethnic differences in mental health outcomes with consideration of the intersection of other identifying characteristics such as age.

As Bloom, Owen, and Covington (2004) point out, the criminal justice system was created to deal with male offenders and therefore does not consider the aspects of the system that can retraumatize survivors who are incarcerated. Individuals with histories of abuse may be more vulnerable to the harshness of prison conditions, which may exacerbate pre-incarceration mental health conditions and potentially trigger additional anxieties or PTSD symptoms (Aday et al., 2014; Covington, 2008; Green et al., 2005; Maeve, 2000). For example, sexual assault survivors may be triggered by strip searches and adhering to male authority figures while incarcerated, or fear being sexually assaulted while incarcerated (a fear that is not unfounded), which may lead to further traumatization when facing these realities. Women with histories of childhood abuse or neglect can be triggered by being placed in solitary confinement (Maeve, 2000). It can be retraumatizing when a woman with a domestically abusive past is yelled or cursed at by a correctional officer (Covington, 2008). As Covington (2008) points out, the incarceration itself can be traumatizing, and can be especially retraumatizing for a woman with a history of victimization, but retraumatization can be compounded by institutional racial, gender, and class discrimination facing women who are incarcerated.

8.2.1.2 Physical Health

Adverse experiences, such as sexual and physical abuse, are tied to mental health issues particularly in incarcerated populations. We need to pay attention to the physical health consequences of such abuse, as well as the physical health issues that arise *from mental health issues*. We also need to examine the relationship of physical health issues to socioeconomic status. Women often have limited access to health services before and during incarceration, particularly low-income and WOC (see Eliason, Taylor, & Williams, 2004 for review), exacerbating both mental and physical health issues.

Victimization can create both immediate and long-term physical health consequences. Shortly following abuse, women may experience broken bones, bruising, chipped teeth, among other injuries (see Sheridan & Nash, 2007 for review). However, physical or sexual victimization can also translate to long-term health issues. The original ACEs study examined a myriad of conditions, discovering a striking connection between ACEs and physical health issues in adulthood (Felitti et al., 1998), illustrating the connection of childhood abuse to long-term physical health consequences. In a national study of women who are incarcerated, Aday et al. (2014) discovered that women with sexual abuse histories are significantly more likely to experience chronic illnesses including cancer, paralysis, stroke/brain injury, diabetes, heart problems, kidney problems, arthritis, cirrhosis, hepatitis, and sexually transmitted infections (STIs). Although physical health conditions reported in their study were not highly pervasive (<32% of abused women), their findings nonetheless demonstrate increased health conditions for sexual assault survivors who are incarcerated. Physical health consequences among victimization survivors can also vary based on racial/ethnic factors. Black women experience high levels of genital injuries, STIs, bruises, and reproductive issues due to sexual assault (West & Johnson, 2013; Basile et al., 2016) but also face greater risk than White women for conditions such as heart disease, stroke, breast and cervical cancer, premature delivery, and STIs (DHHS Office of Minority Health, in Barnes, 2017) that may be linked to trauma experiences. Though the association between victimization and long-term health consequences may not be totally clear, health conditions can occur as a cumulative result of repeated injury (e.g., brain injury occurring from repeated physical abuse) or arise from long-term stress responses endured by the body during and following abuse. For example, IPV victimization typically occurs on an ongoing basis, forcing a physiological fight/flight/freeze response in the body, something that is stressful on the body. This stress response occurring on a repeated basis, potentially over a long period of time, can contribute to physical health conditions (Felitti et al., 1998), especially if left untreated which is often the case for women of low socioeconomic status (Enders, Paterniti, & Meyers, 2005; Young & Reviere, 2001; West & Johnson, 2013). Physical health issues may also stem from the mental health issues experienced by survivors.

Women who have experienced physical and/or sexual victimization may suffer mental health issues that lead to physically damaging (maladaptive) coping mechanisms. Research documents an association between past trauma and self-injury (e.g., cutting, head banging, and burning) among women who are incarcerated (Borrill et al., 2003), as well as substance abuse and addiction (Borrill et al., 2003; Covington, 2008; Langan & Pelissier, 2001; Tripodi & Pettus-Davis, 2013). Women with traumatic victimization histories may use substances to self-medicate and numb distressing feelings associated with the experience (Langan & Pelissier, 2001). Indeed, women often enter correctional institutions with substance abuse issues or histories (Enders et al., 2005) and this is often due to previous victimization. Borrill et al. (2003) discovered that although substance use is less common among African American female inmates, women in this population who are drug dependent have the highest rates of self-harm of any other racial/ethnic group. Substance use and self-harm can be coping mechanisms used simultaneously, but these findings also illustrate the vulnerability of self-harm among Black women with victimization histories. Unfortunately, maladaptive coping mechanisms such as self-harm and substance use can further mental health issues while creating physical health consequences. If untreated, both physical and mental health conditions can potentially be exacerbated and continue throughout time served and after release from correctional institutions.

Most women who are incarcerated have experienced years of poverty, racism, substance abuse, and physical, sexual, and/or emotional abuse. The physical health consequences that arise from such abuse and disadvantaged social conditions can be compounded by lack of access to healthcare. Women who are incarcerated often lack access to health care prior to imprisonment (Aday & Krabill, 2011). For example, low-income women may lack access to reproductive and physical health services and enter prison with sexually transmitted infections, substance abuse issues, and histories of poor nutrition (Enders et al., 2005). Women may not receive treatment to address these issues while incarcerated.

8.3 Treating Victimization with Mental and Physical Health Services in Prison Facilities

Women who are incarcerated often enter the correctional system needing treatment. Frequently, women who are incarcerated have limited personal coping skills, lack informal social support, and had difficulty accessing health care prior to incarceration for various reasons (e.g., lack of health insurance, abusive partners preventing use of health care services, low-income status) (Blitz, Wolff, & Paap, 2006). This lack of access to resources can lead to self-medication through drugs or alcohol which survivors argue can be very helpful to them (de Lint & Marmo, 2018). Survivors of sexual or domestic abuse are likely to have mental health issues that may be compounded by other treatment needs, such as a co-occurring substance use disorder or physical health problems tied to the abuse experienced (Courtney & Maschi, 2013; Lynch et al., 2012). Indeed, about half of women who are incarcerated report treatment needs specific to their experiences of domestic violence and childhood abuse (Lynch et al., 2012) and are more likely to utilize services while incarcerated than women without abuse histories (Aday et al., 2014). Women who are incarcerated who have experienced victimization have unique and complex treatment needs and recognize their need for treatment to overcome these experiences. Yet, the screening and treatment of prior victimization experiences are lacking in women's correctional facilities despite the overwhelming evidence of the negative impacts of trauma.

Most women who are incarcerated have greater access to healthcare in the correctional facility than they did in the community (Blitz et al., 2006), but there are barriers to receiving such services. Correctional facilities often fail to identify offenders with mental illness upon entry into the system or may make a misdiagnosis, and therefore women may not even have the opportunity to receive services (Lynch et al., 2017; Young & Reviere, 2001). Women may not be able to receive the healthcare they need due to inability to articulate their healthcare needs and physical health issues to healthcare providers (Enders et al., 2005). Women who are incarcerated tend to lack autonomy in their healthcare, limiting the services they can receive to address their physical health issues. When receiving treatment, women report that physicians tend to "tell" them rather than "ask" about their symptoms, something that not only limits autonomy but can also contribute to trust issues (Enders et al., 2005). Developing trust can be a barrier to receiving healthcare for women who are incarcerated, often due to issues of consistency and availability of physicians (Enders et al., 2005), particularly among women needing healthcare arising from sexual victimization. It is common for women who are incarcerated to report feeling unable to advocate for their own healthcare and feeling that their physician would not advocate for them either. Literacy issues and a lack of knowledge about healthcare treatment limit autonomy, the ability to self-advocate and make health-related decisions, subsequently limiting access to treatment for physical and mental health issues arising from victimization (Enders et al., 2005). As such, provision of information would be helpful in enhancing patient–physician communication and treatment. While these barriers can be the reality of any woman who is incarcerated, there are additional barriers in seeking health services experienced by WOC and transgender women.

Women of color face additional barriers to receiving mental and physical health services than White women. White women are twice as likely as WOC to seek mental health treatment (Kirkner, Relyea, & Ullman, 2018), including rape crisis centers and sexual assault hotlines offered in the community (Weist et al., 2014). Indeed, Black women have more trauma experiences than other racial/ethnic groups, but are the least likely to receive mental health services (Alvidrez, Shumway, Morazes, & Boccellari, 2011). This is likely, in part, due to the stereotypes and gendered expectations, such as those discussed above relative to Black women, but also practice-based barriers such as trust, intimidation, and concern of stigmatization. In the course of seeking healthcare, women report experiences of helplessness, guilt, shame, confusion, intimidation, and embarrassment (Enders et al., 2005), which may be more present in low-income women who have less experience "talking out" their problems or WOC who are concerned about the added cultural stigma of needing mental health care on top of the stigma of being a victim and being incarcerated. WOC also may be intimidated by the wide status difference between themselves and the therapist (Young & Reviere, 2001), which is particularly pronounced in correctional facilities, especially in White-dominated professions like mental health and medical care. Interestingly, women ethnically matched with their clinician are more likely to engage in mental health treatment (Alvidrez et al., 2011), illustrating the importance of representation in medical care settings. Little to no research exists that examines the barriers to receiving healthcare for women who are incarcerated, specifically WOC and intersecting marginalized identities such as women who identify as LGBTQIA+ and women with cognitive or physical disabilities. As explored by Torres, Mata-Greve, Bird, and Herrera Hernandez (2018) intersectional research and clinical practice in addressing mental health issues, particularly within Latinx, is lacking. However, examining these barriers facing women of different identities or intersecting identities is the first step in overcoming them to provide the necessary treatment. Even identifying these barriers and increasing the accessibility of services for marginalized women does not ensure that they will receive the treatment they need.

Though women who are incarcerated may have greater access to physical and mental health care while serving time than they did in the community (despite barriers to receiving correctional facility care), the quality of care is often lacking (see Mignon, 2016 for review) and many women's needs go unmet (Wolff et al., 2011). Young and Reviere (2001) explored the available services in 65 correctional facilities to determine if the healthcare services meet the unique needs of women paying attention to intersectionality, including older women, WOC, and women with substance use issues. They found that most facilities offered basic services but were unprepared to address the needs of certain populations including individuals with disabilities and HIV-positive patients. They concluded that one out of three staff failed to screen for physical and sexual abuse, sickle cell anemia, or breast cancer, as well as other medical conditions that are all common in Black women (Young & Reviere, 2001). Transgender women are often denied healthcare while incarcerated. For example, Asian/Pacific Islander transgender women are often denied hormones required for gender affirmation while incarcerated, and this leads to coping via substance use (Reisner et al., 2014). These findings suggest that facilities are ill-equipped to address the physical health issues stemming from victimization experiences, including the specialized needs of those with marginalized identities that call for additional screening and knowledge of risk factors. Indeed, medical professionals should routinely screen for sexual and physical victimization, especially when examining WOC who have higher risk than White women for victimization and certain physical health consequences. West and Johnson (2013) recommend that medical professionals explain invasive procedures and ask permission before touching patients to avoid retraumatizing survivors and increase their sense of safety and trust. Regarding mental health, most facilities are staffed with mental health professionals and there are available services (Young & Reviere, 2001), though facilities may only offer services to women who will most likely re-enter society (Maeve, 2000). Generally, however, research is limited in terms of the quality of these services specifically in addressing victimization histories. For example, to our knowledge, the neurological treatment that could address issues stemming from poly-victimization is not offered in correctional facilities, despite the volume of women who may benefit from it. Thus, while services may be more accessible than they were in the community, the services are likely lacking, particularly for the vast majority of women who are incarcerated with physical and mental health needs stemming from victimization.

As women who are incarcerated have a high frequency of sexual and physical abuse histories that translate to mental and physical health consequences, this means that they have subsequently unique and potentially complex treatment needs. Researchers and clinicians have begun to explore variations in treatment that can address the needs of women who are incarcerated with abuse histories. For example, treatment programs that incorporate social interaction (e.g., group sharing/group therapy) and creative processing of trauma (e.g., writing) have been proven effective at reducing mental health issues such as depression (Bradley & Follingstad, 2003). Similarly, Karlsson, Bridges, Bell, and Petretic (2014) piloted an 8-session weekly therapy group among 33 women who are incarcerated with histories of sexual trauma, where women shared their sexual abuse memories one at a time with group leaders helping to process their experiences. The researchers found significant decreases in depression and general anxiety disorder from pre- to post-treatment and the majority of participants were no longer above the clinical cutoff for PTSD, depression, and general anxiety disorder (Karlsson et al., 2014). These findings collectively illustrate that women who are incarcerated may benefit from treatment programs specifically designed to address domestic and sexual abuse histories.

Physical and mental health services in women's correctional facilities often fail to consider the intersection of social location, trauma, and mental and physical illness. Subsequently, mental health issues and associated physical health issues often go unaddressed. Without appropriate identification or care, pre-incarceration physical and mental health issues (such as those stemming from sexual and/or physical victimization histories) can be exacerbated while incarcerated. Researchers propose that clinicians and others working in the correctional setting adopt a trauma-informed system of care (Harner & Burgess, 2011; Lynch et al., 2017). Originally set forth by Harris and Fallot (2001), being "trauma informed" means having knowledge of the role that victimization has played in one's life and using this knowledge to provide services that accommodate the vulnerabilities associated with such victimization. The guiding principles of trauma-informed care include: (1) understanding trauma; (2) understanding the survivor; (3) understanding available services; and (4) understanding the service relationship (Harris & Fallot, 2001). Rather than only treating the symptoms that arise from trauma, trauma-informed care works to create a safe and sustainable system of care that considers victimization experiences, as well as how victimization can contribute to a person's interactions, behaviors, health, and choices, and treats the survivor as an active participant in treatment. Harner and Burgess (2011) suggest that a trauma-informed approach in correctional facilities may reduce the need for services over time and increase the chance that women may leave the correctional facility in better physical and mental health than when they arrived.

Women who have histories of multiple sexual or domestic violence victimizations are more likely to have lifelong mental health issues than those with one victimization, and those without any victimization experience (Aday et al., 2014). Women who are incarcerated with abuse histories are also likely to experience comorbid mental health and substance abuse issues (Courtney & Maschi, 2013; Lynch et al., 2012). Research indicates that substance abuse is often fueled by underlying trauma, providing further support for trauma-informed programming that considers victimization histories in addressing substance use and mental health issues (Harner & Burgess, 2011; Langan & Pelissier, 2001). Langan and Pelissier (2001) argue that substance abuse treatment programs may be inappropriate for the treatment of women who are incarcerated because programs have generally been designed to treat men, and therefore do not consider that women differ in frequency and type of substance abuse and the underlying reasons for substance abuse. As such, correctional facility treatment programs should consider the compound effects of trauma and co-occurring disorders when treating women who are incarcerated. Yet, many correctional facilities are not equipped to treat substance abuse issues in general. Although facilities may list substance abuse treatment programs, many do not have readily available professional help, and even fewer have counselors specializing in substance abuse (Young & Reviere, 2001). Therefore, abstinence from drugs and alcohol may occur while incarcerated but the women are not equipped with the tools to sustain that abstinence upon leaving the system.

Correctional facilities may be the last and perhaps only opportunity for survivors to receive medical and mental health care to address the issues stemming from their victimization. Failure to address mental health, substance use, and physical health issues among victimized women who are incarcerated can exacerbate these issues, increasing the likelihood that these problems will continue after release. Reentry to the community without addressing the physical and mental health issues that women entered the system with can lead to additional issues such as joblessness, homelessness, child custody issues, and recidivism (Messina & Grella, 2006). Young and Reviere (2001) suggest that addressing factors that contribute to worsened health conditions such as diet, inability to avoid stress, and failure to take medications may be an important aspect of care. As such, health education, including self-care strategies, may benefit women who are incarcerated by equipping them with the tools they need to manage their health and stress during and after incarceration. However, for many women, victimization continues through incarceration.

8.4   Sexual Assault/Sexual Harassment and Correctional Officers

It is clear from our review that women frequently enter correctional facilities with previous experiences of victimization. However, little attention is given to the victimization that occurs *after* women enter these facilities. Once incarcerated, women, particularly WOC and trans women, are at risk for being sexually assaulted or harassed by correctional officers (COs). This is because women who are incarcerated are at a further disadvantage that makes them vulnerable to assault and harassment by correctional officers that occurs on an ongoing basis, as women who are incarcerated face many barriers to reporting despite legislation geared toward prevention of violence in correctional facilities (Reisner et al., 2014; Hearn & Parkin, 2001; Hattery & Smith, 2019; Beck, Rantala, & Rexroat, 2014; Calhoun & Coleman, 2002; Pimlott Kubiak, Brenner, Bybee, Campbell, & Fedock, 2017; Rantala, 2018). Violence in correctional facilities extends beyond those incarcerated to the COs, who face harassment and assault by fellow COs, or experience violence perpetrated by incarcerated persons that is enabled by fellow COs ("Correctional Officers at High Risk", 2018; Dickerson, 2018), suggesting that correctional facilities are not safe for those who reside there nor those employed to protect them. The research presented in this section evidences the notion that violence is perpetuated in correctional facilities.

8.4.1 Sexual Assault and Harassment by Correctional Officers

Correctional facilities are total institutions (e.g., confined organization with rules, norms, and regulations separate from larger society), and therefore are at elevated risk for violence and misuse of power by those in positions of authority (Goffman, 1961; Hearn & Parkin, 2001; Hattery & Smith, 2019). Simply being incarcerated, women are in a position that makes them vulnerable to exploitation and misuse of power by correctional staff. According to the Bureau of Justice Statistics (BJS) staff-on-inmate sexual misconduct includes "sexual misconduct or harassment perpetrated on an inmate by a facility employee, volunteer, contractor, official visitor, or other agency representative" (Rantala, 2018, p. 2). However, most attention is paid to the misconduct perpetrated by COs, who tend to have most access to inmates where harassment and assault could occur. These acts include:

> Any consensual or nonconsensual behavior or act of sexual directed toward an inmate by staff including romantic relationships...touching directly or through clothing...completed, attempted, threatened, or requested sexual acts, occurrences of indecent exposure, invasion of privacy...repeated verbal comments or gestures of sexual nature (Rantala 2018, p. 2).

Based on this definition, sexual assault and harassment can take many forms. Inappropriate touching and groping in the context of pat and strip searches is the most common form of sexual assault experienced by women who are incarcerated, though attempted and completed rape is also common. In exploring sexual abuse among women incarcerated in Hawaii, Calhoun and Coleman (2002) discovered that sexual abuse takes place in three contexts: (1) "trading" (i.e., coercion) refers to performing sexual act in exchange for items or privileges such as telephone calls, goods not provided in the facility (e.g., perfume, drugs, etc.), or preferential treatment; (2) "love" or lust that leads to "consensual" sexual contact; and (3) sexual contact "in the line of duty" which occurs during frequent, routine, pat and strip searches and even "sexually motivated" searches. However, sexual victimization occurs outside of these contexts as well, including through blackmail, bribe, and physical force (Blackburn et al., 2008; Struckman-Johnson & Struckman-Johnson, 2002).

Most of the focus on sexual assault in correctional facilities focuses on inmate-on-inmate sexual violence, primarily among men. Even so, sexual victimization while incarcerated is often dismissed as an inevitable aspect of punishment where victims are blamed for being an offender, and as such victimization while incarcerated is not given due attention. Women comprise only 7% of the inmate population, but 33% of victims of staff-perpetrated sexual victimization in prisons are women (Beck et al., 2014) and have experiences of victimization perpetrated by both male and female staff (Struckman-Johnson & Struckman-Johnson, 2002). Black and White women who are incarcerated experience victimization by staff at similar rates, though research has largely neglected to explore the victimization experiences of WOC and transgender[5] women. Transgender women are at a heightened vulnerability to be assaulted by COs, as they are often assigned to facilities based on genitalia (i.e., transgender women in male facilities; Tarzwell, 2006), and then put in segregation (Jenness, 2009). Indeed, research shows that almost half of transgender women in correctional facilities report being harassed, physically assaulted, or sexually assaulted by COs (Reisner et al., 2014). Black, Latina/Hispanic, and mixed-race/ethnicity transgender women disproportionately report violence while incarcerated (Reisner et al., 2014), extending the characterization of being "over-policed and under-protected" from the community to correctional facilities and from WOC to transgender WOC (Crenshaw, 2012, p. 1419). Researchers caution that the frequency of sexual victimization in correctional facilities may vary depending on the characteristics of the facility, the composition of the inmates and staff, security, and facility culture (Struckman-Johnson & Struckman-Johnson, 2002). Despite variation in prevalence, it is clear that for many women, correctional facilities are a place of continued victimization.

Despite the prevalence of sexual assault and harassment perpetrated by correctional officers against women who are incarcerated, these events are unlikely to be reported (approximately 8%; Calhoun & Coleman, 2002; Pimlott Kubiak et al., 2017). This is not surprising, as sexual assault among women outside of correctional facilities has a low reporting rate (Kilpatrick et al., 2007) and women who are incarcerated face additional barriers to reporting, particularly if the perpetrator is a CO. Women who are incarcerated may not interpret the incident as sexual assault, particularly if the act occurs in the context of a "trade" or if they consider the violation simply a part of prison life (Calhoun & Coleman, 2002). Women may also feel that no one would believe them, especially if they perceive they have no credibility as an incarcerated person, termed "bad girl syndrome" (Struckman-Johnson &

---

[5] Like other terms used in this chapter, we want to explain that we use the terms that are presented in the research for accuracy. Gender identification, presentation and orientation and therefore one's personal identifying label is complicated. Read Lenning (2009) for an introduction to this topic.

Struckman-Johnson, 2002; Baro, 1997). Women who rely on the perpetrator for some type of good or resource are less likely to report (Pimlott Kubiak et al., 2017), highlighting the power dynamics present in staff-on-inmate assaults. Power dynamics that serve as a barrier to reporting may be more pronounced for low-income, WOC who may have low institutional trust. This low trust is because of the history of institutional racism and classism in the USA, and subsequently the women may think there will be no benefit to reporting. Reluctance to report may also stem from threats of retaliation from perpetrators, particularly among women who have longer sentences to serve (and potentially longer to face retaliation) (Calhoun & Coleman, 2002; Fedock et al., 2019; Pimlott Kubiak et al., 2017; Struckman-Johnson & Struckman-Johnson, 2002). One study examined barriers to reporting for Black women and found that retaliation is not only a common reason for not reporting, but is well-grounded, as Black women who did report frequently experienced some form of retaliation (Fedock et al., 2019). Assaults perpetrated by staff against multiple victims (i.e., "serial offenders") are unlikely to be reported as well, as women who are aware of ongoing abuse may perceive reporting as futile (Pimlott Kubiak et al., 2017). Assaults that result in physical injury and occur on multiple occasions are more likely to be reported (Pimlott Kubiak et al., 2017), perhaps because women feel that there is more evidence to substantiate their report. Barriers to reporting such as these limit opportunities for legal justice for all women who are incarcerated who experience sexual assault or harassment by COs. These barriers are more pronounced for WOC and transgender women who are subject to larger power dynamics and institutional bias, further limiting their opportunity for justice. Unfortunately, the reality is that making a formal report is the only way to prevent abuse from reoccurring, which continues the cycle of abuse for women who are incarcerated. This is an issue that until recently was not taken very seriously.

To address the issues surrounding sexual assault and harassment of incarcerated persons by staff and correctional officers, the Prison Rape Elimination Act (PREA) was enacted in 2003 and the National Standards to Prevent, Detect, and Respond to Prison Rape were issued in 2012 (Rantala, 2018). The PREA aims to improve prevention and detection of prison sexual assault. The standards require correctional facilities to educate staff and inmates on sexual victimization, refer all allegations to investigation, track information collected, and provide the information on request. Following the enactment of the national standards, reports of sexual assault and harassment rose drastically, particularly for victimizations that were perpetrated by staff. Yet, the actual abuse perpetrated likely did not rise, but incarcerated persons had greater access to reporting. However, only 8% of all 24,661 allegations across US correctional facilities in 2015 were found to be substantiated (Rantala, 2018). While this may suggest that there is a high rate of false reports being made, this is more likely an indication of investigation and attrition issues where incidents that did occur are not being treated as such. The PREA mandates that every allegation of abuse be investigated, but states are not mandated to follow these standards, leaving little accountability for correctional decision making in determining investigation outcomes. As such, correctional facility investigations are subject to bias in decision making rooted in misconceptions about rape, rape reporting, and rape victims (i.e., rape myths) that lead to a high attrition rate, just as with sexual assault that occurs outside correctional facilities (Spohn, White, & Tellis, 2014; Venema, Lorenz, & Sweda, 2019). Racial bias is present in the administration of justice for women who are incarcerated as well, with Black women having fewer reported cases investigated and fewer cases determined as substantiated than White women (Fedock et al., 2019). While the PREA and the national standards are steps in the right direction toward acknowledging and preventing sexual misconduct in correctional facilities, they provide these protections unequally and largely ignore the mental and physical health consequences of sexual victimization.

Experiencing sexual assault and/or harassment by a CO can result in mental and physical health consequences like that of any sexual assault. These effects can be exacerbated as women who are incarcerated have to continue to see their perpetrator on a day-to-day basis with the possibility of being assaulted or harassed on multiple occasions, contributing to the cumulative effects of trauma. Women may also experience added frustration of having to interact with their perpetrator knowing that they may be unable to report and therefore unable to stop the abuse from reoccurring or from happening to another individual, which can create additional feelings of powerlessness (Calhoun & Coleman, 2002). There may be newly developed physical health consequences from assault that occurs in facilities including physical injury, STIs, and pregnancy (Struckman-Johnson & Struckman-Johnson, 2002; Smith, 2003), as well as HIV-seropositivity and poorer general health conditions among transgender women (Reisner et al., 2014). Experiencing abuse while incarcerated may retraumatize women and trigger maladaptive coping mechanisms such as self-injury, suicide attempts, and/or aggression (Dirks, 2004). Transgender women in particular report more daily cigarette smoking, self-medication, and suicide attempts than transgender women who had not been victimized while incarcerated (Reisner et al., 2014). Given the barriers to reporting CO abuse, women may also be reluctant to seek help from the correctional health services or may face retaliation for doing so. Further, correctional facilities are often not equipped to provide services to women in crisis immediately or shortly following assault (VanNatta, 2001).

8.4.2   Sexual Assault/Harassment of Correctional Officers

Work as a correctional officer can be a high-stress occupation. Johnson and colleagues (2005) classify antecedents of occupational stress into eight broad categories: (1) work relationships; (2) the job itself; (3) overload; (4) control; (5) job security; (6) resources and communication; (7) work-life balance; and (8) pay and benefits. All of these can apply to prison work and, as such, COs are trained to anticipate and manage these "operational stressors" and the subsequent strain caused by these stressors (Brough & Biggs, 2010). With violence against women, particularly sexual harassment and assault being a common occurrence in society, it would be expected in an institution that is male dominated (the leaders are mostly male) that this problem exists here as well. Yet, little attention is paid to sexual harassment and assault of correctional officers, termed occupational trauma. Most attention in practice and research focuses on violence perpetrated by COs on incarcerated persons (though this research is limited as well), rather than the violence experienced by COs perpetrated by fellow officers and individuals who are incarcerated. This is a notable issue, as COs are being harassed and assaulted by those they are employed to protect and police, and this behavior is similarly perpetrated or enabled by those they work alongside.

To our knowledge, harassment and assault experienced by COs is a largely neglected research area. Most knowledge on the topic is presented through news media outlets, typically stories on "isolated" incidents of abuse in correctional facilities (e.g., Russel, 2019; Carter, 2018; Edwards, Joyner, & Peebles, 2018). Most coverage focuses on the victimization experienced by women COs in male correctional facilities (including both the perpetration by male inmates and the enabling of this behavior by male COs) and the measures women COs often take to feel safe at work (e.g., Carter, 2018; Dickerson, 2018), but not the harassment directly experienced by fellow COs. For example, Edwards et al. (2018) examined harassment and assault experienced among female COs in Atlanta, perpetrated by male co-workers, and Dickerson (2018) discussed the measures female officers take to protect themselves against abuse on-the-job perpetrated by males who are incarcerated. However, even in the era of the #MeToo movement, women's stories of assault and harassment while working as a CO do not receive the necessary attention in both research and society.

We argue that CO sexual assault and harassment goes undetected for a number of reasons. First, researchers may have difficulty accessing correctional facilities to gather data. Correctional facilities may be difficult for researchers to access for security reasons or researchers may simply be denied entry. Second, it was only recently that the USA started to pay attention to sexual assault within prisons in research, news media, and policy. Even with this recent attention, there is an arguable lack of grants geared toward funding such research. Third, COs may be reluctant to disclose abuse for a multitude of reasons. COs may fear the stigma of being a victim, and therefore be unwilling to disclose or participate in research. COs being abused by co-workers may fear retaliation from the perpetrator or from supervisors, similar to survivors of workplace harassment or assault outside of correctional facilities (Lorenz & O'Callaghan, under review). Correctional officers often work in isolated rural areas and therefore, if retaliated against, have few alternative job options (Edwards et al., 2018). In a dangerous environment like correctional facilities, COs are expected to provide back-up and support to one another to stay safe and maintain order. However, COs experiencing harassment by co-workers or harassment/abuse enabled by co-workers may feel betrayed, isolated, and/or fear retaliation that could further compromise their safety on the job (e.g., intentionally slow back-up to violent incidents). With the lack of research and societal attention on the victimization experiences of COs, we must acknowledge the intersection of marginalized identities in CO work, where COs are commonly working class, women, and African American than other criminal justice professions, with White men in leadership positions. The stratification of correctional work only serves to silence and create barriers to support for COs who are victimized on the job. However, this area is certainly worthy of research and attention, as occupational trauma such as this can result in a myriad of consequences for those affected ("Correctional Officers at High Risk", 2018; Brough & Biggs, 2010; Denhof & Spinaris, 2013).

The stressors associated with working as a CO can have mental/physical health and other job-related consequences with sexual harassment and assault exacerbating the negative impacts. However, most work examining the outcomes of these stressors looks at prison work or occupational trauma in general, rather than consequences specific to sexual assault or harassment. Correctional officers who experienced occupational trauma may feel unsafe coming to work and may be less satisfied with their job ("Correctional Officers at High Risk", 2018; Brough & Biggs, 2010). Similarly, COs who have negative perceptions of incarcerated persons, perhaps due to fear of being assaulted or experiences of being assaulted, are shown to have higher levels of job stress (Misis et al., 2013). Correctional officers experience significantly higher rates of PTSD and depression, or comorbid PTSD/depression than that of the general population (Denhof & Spinaris, 2013), and report anxiety and nightmares ("Correctional Officers at High Risk", 2018). The negative outcomes associated with occupational stressors can be further exacerbated when the victimized CO is not met with support from his/her/their colleagues and/or supervisors (see Brough & Biggs, 2010 for review). These consequences not only affect the individual, but can also extend to the families, colleagues, and the organization itself which creates a toxic environment.

Correctional facilities often provide support to officers who experience occupational trauma (e.g., debriefing and employee assistance programs), but less support is provided to staff who experience these stressors as a routine part of their job, such as if the sexual harassment or assault is occurring on a regular basis (Brough & Biggs, 2010). Even if support services are offered, officers may be reluctant to seek help out of fear of repercussion for having mental health issues ("Correctional Officers at High Risk", 2018). Having to disclose mental health issues to their supervisor may lead to forced time off, change in duties, or differential treatment. Officers may fear being perceived as "weak" for having mental health issues or being labeled a victim. When correctional facilities do not offer adequate support to COs who are victimized, this can not only exacerbate issues by the CO, but contribute to an environment conducive to violence among both officers and those incarcerated.

8.5   Conclusion

Researchers argue that prisons perpetuate gender-based violence (Hattery & Smith, 2019). As a total institution rape can be used to maintain or assert power. Rape in prisons is often joked about in the media and society, and this form of trivialization is considered part of the larger rape culture. Rape culture "is when within a particular culture or subculture rape is normalized, excused, and/or trivialized through the means of institutions which objectify people (usually women/girls) and blame victim's behavior while often sympathizing with the offender" (Hayes & Luther, 2018, p. 109). As rape culture is gendered, and with the media tending to focus on male rape ignoring other types, those who are experiencing this type of assault while incarcerated are likely silenced. Women/girls tend to come in with previous victimizations, and arguably within a total institution poly-victimization is more likely because of the type of control that is wielded.

Examining the role of violence in the histories of women who are incarcerated may shed light on how to best rehabilitate these individuals. What is clear to us from our review of the research is that in order to move forward, research needs to be more inclusive of the intersections of all the social identities of women. Within both feminist pathways and intersections is room to pay attention to the pathway of transgender women and Black transgender women, which includes rejection from family and high rates of homelessness leading to victimization and survival offending. In the USA, there has been some media attention of the seemingly high rate of violence against Black transgender women specifically (Human Rights Campaign, 2019). Research highlights the amount of incarceration that trans women and men incur that is disproportionately high compared to their representation in the general population (Buist & Lenning, 2015). Then transgender women also experience a higher amount of victimization once incarcerated. We urge researchers to undergo this necessary research in order to create programs and policies that protect this marginalized population of individuals. It is not enough to simply recognize the inequalities faced by marginalized individuals, but researchers and policymakers must acknowledge the differences in power between social groups and the systems of inequality that perpetuate disadvantage.

Race/ethnicity often becomes convoluted and colorism is an aspect of racism that needs further examination. In the USA and other parts of the world, Islamophobia appears to be on the rise. Rising Islamophobia impacts how Arab American Women or other WOC are marginalized based on the shade of their skin and/or what they are wearing. Where Islamophobia is rooted in religious prejudice, it frequently has xenophobia outcomes where individuals are afraid of Arab American individuals based on their color, their name, their dress, and/or their ethnicity. This can occur based on the perception of their social identity, regardless of whether they actually practice the Islamic faith. As such, colorism can influence racism and xenophobia, where WOC can face multiple forms of prejudice and discrimination. Yet, colorism is rarely considered in the context of addressing systemic racism in our corrections system. Research can examine the impact of racialized and xenophobic victimization on an individual's experience in the US corrections system.

As discussed in this chapter, women enter in prisons with not only victimization histories but the mental and physical health issues that result from those victimizations (Aday et al., 2014; Green et al., 2016; Lynch et al., 2012; Sheridan & Nash, 2007). Victimizations can lead to offending which can lead to incarceration which can lead to further victimizations. Treatment for the victimizations, or at the very least lessening the likelihood of poly-victimization while incarcerated, could lower the likelihood of future offending. Reducing recidivism is arguably a goal of correction, and we have known since the 1970s that rehabilitation does work if programs are carefully constructed and properly executed (Martinson, 1974). Correctional institutions that include proper programming for women's victimization will likely impact recidivism, or at the very least help women to heal.

References

Aday, R. H., & Huey Dye, M. (2019). Examining predictors of depression among older women who are incarcerated. *Women & Criminal Justice, 29*(1), 32–51.

Aday, R.H., & Krabill, J.J. (2011). Women aging in prison: A neglected population in the correctional system. Boulder, CO: Lynne Reinner.

Aday, R. H., Huey Dye, M., & Kaiser, A. K. (2014). Examining the traumatic effects of sexual victimization on the health of women who are incarcerated. *Women & Criminal Justice, 24*, 341–361.

Alvidrez, J., Shumway, M., Morazes, J., & Boccellari, A. (2011). Ethnic disparities in mental health treatment engagement among female sexual assault victims. *Journal of Aggression, Maltreatment, and Trauma, 20*, 415–425.

Baro, A. L. (1997). Spheres of consent: An analysis of the sexual abuse and sexual exploitation of women incarcerated in the state of Hawaii. *Women & Criminal Justice, 8*, 61–84.

Basile, K.C., Smith, S.G., Fowler, D.N., Walters, M.L., & Hamburger, M.E. (2016). Sexual violence victimization and associations with health in a community sample of African American women. Journal of Aggression, *Maltreatment, & Trauma, 25*(3), 231–253.

Beck, A. J., Rantala, R. R., & Rexroat, J. (2014). *Sexual victimization reported by correctional authorities, 2009-2011*. Washington DC: Bureau of Justice Statistics, U.S. Department of Justice.

Belknap, J. (2015). *The invisible woman: Gender, crime, and justice* (4th ed.). Stamford, CT: Cengage Learning.

Belknap, J., & Holsinger, K. (1998). An overview of delinquent girls. In R. T. Zaplin (Ed.), *Female offenders: Critical perspectives and effective interventions* (pp. 31–64). Gaithersburg, MD: Aspen.

Blackburn, A. G., Mullings, J. L., & Marquart, J. W. (2008). Sexual assault and prison and beyond: Toward an understanding of lifetime sexual assault among women who are incarcerated. *The Prison Journal, 88*(3), 351–377.

Blitz, C. L., Wolff, N., & Paap, K. (2006). Availability of behavioral health treatment for women in prison. *Psychiatric Services, 57*(3), 356–360.

Bloom, B. E., Owen, B., & Covington, S. (2004). Women offenders and the gendered effects of public policy. *Review of Policy Research, 21*, 31–48.

Borrill, J., Burnett, R., Atkins, R., Miller, S., Briggs, D., Weaver, T., et al. (2003). Patterns of self-harm and attempted suicide among white and black/mixed race female prisoners. *Criminal Behavior and Mental Health, 13*, 229–240.

Bradley, R. G., & Davino, K. M. (2002). Women's perceptions of prison environment: When prison is "the safest place I've ever been". *Psychology of Women Quarterly, 26*, 351–359.

Bradley, R. G., & Follingstad, D. R. (2003). Group therapy for women who are incarcerated who experienced interpersonal violence: A pilot study. *Journal of Traumatic Stress, 16*(4), 337–340.

Bronson, J., & Carson, A. (2019). *Prisoners in 2017*. Washington, DC: Bureau of Justice Statistics.

Brough, P., & Biggs, A. (2010). Occupational stress in police and prison staff. In *Cambridge handbook of forensic psychology*. Cambridge: Cambridge University Press.

Broussard, P. A. (2013). Black women's post-slavery silence syndrome: A twenty-first century remnant of slavery, Jim Crow, and systemic racism - who will tell her stories? *Journal of Gender, Race, and Justice, 16*(2), 373–421.

Browne, A., Miller, B., & Maguin, E. (1999). Prevalence and severity of lifetime physical and sexual victimization among women who are incarcerated. *International Journal of Law and Psychiatry, 22*, 301–322.

Buist, C.L. & Lenning, E. (2015). Queer Criminology. Routledge.

Calhoun, A. J., & Coleman, H. D. (2002). Female inmates' perspectives on sexual abuse by correctional personnel. *Women & Criminal Justice, 13*(2–3), 101–124.

Carter, T. J. (2018, February 8). My sexual harassers were behind bars. I was their guard. *The Marshall Project.* Retrieved from https://www.themarshallproject.org/2018/02/08/my-sexual-harassers-were-behind-bars-i-was-their-guard

Chesney-Lind, M. (1986). Women and crime: The female offender. *Signs, 12*(1), 78–96.

Chesney-Lind, M., & Pasko, L. (2013). *The female offender: Girls, women, and crime* (3nd ed.). Thousand Oaks, CA: Sage Publications.

Chesney-Lind, M., & Shelden, R. (1992). *Girls, delinquency, and juvenile justice.* Pacific Grove, CA: Brooks/Cole.

Cook, S. L., Smith, S. G., Poister Tusher, C., & Raiford, J. (2005). Self reports of traumatic events in a random sample of women who are incarcerated. *Women & Criminal Justice, 16*(1–2), 107–126.

"Correctional officers at high risk for depression, PTSD, suicide, survey finds." (2018, August 23). *Public Affairs,* UC Berkeley. Retrieved from https://news.berkeley.edu/2018/08/23/california-correctional-officers-at-high-risk-for-depression-ptsd-and-suicide-new-survey-finds/

Courtney, D., & Maschi, T. (2013). Trauma and stress among older adults in prison: Breaking the cycle of silence. *Traumatology, 19*(1), 73–81.

Covington, S. S. (2008). Women and addiction: A trauma-informed approach. *Journal of Psychoactive Drugs, 5*, 377–385.

Covington, S. S., & Bloom, B. E. (2003). https://www.stephaniecovington.com/assets/files/4.pdf

Crenshaw, K.W. (1991). Mapping the margins: Intersectionality, identity, politics and violence against women of color. *Stanford Law Review, 43*(6), 1241–1299.

Crenshaw, K.W. (2012). From private violence to mass incarceration: Thinking intersectionally about women, race, and social control. UCLA Law Review 1418. Retrieved from: https://www.uclalawreview.org/pdf/59-6-1.pdf

Daly, K., & Chesney-Lind, M. (1988). Feminism and criminology. *Justice Quarterly, 5*(4), 497–538.

Davis, K. (2008). Intersectionality as buzzword: A sociology of science perspective on what makes a feminist theory successful. *Feminist Theory, 9*(1), 67–85.

DeHart, D. D. (2008) Pathways to Prison. *Violence Against Women, 14*(12):1362–1381

de Lint, W., & Marmo, M. (2018). *Narrating injustice survival: Self-medication by victims of crime.* London: Palgrave Macmillan.

DeCou, C. R., Lynch, S. M., & Cole, T. T. (2017). Physical and sexual victimization predicts suicidality among women in prison: Understanding ethnic and trauma-specific domains of risk. *Current Psychology, 36*, 774–780.

DeLong, C., & Reichert, J. (2019). *The victim-offender overlap: Examining the relationship between victimization and offending.* Chicago, IL: Illinois Criminal Justice Information Authority. Retrieved from http://www.icjia.state.il.us/articles/the-victim-offender-overlap-examining-the-relationship-between-victimization-and-offending

Denhof, M.D. & Spinaris, C.G. (2013). Depression, PTSD, and comorbidity in United States corrections professionals: Prevalence and impact on health and functioning. Retrieved from: http://desertwaters.com/wp-content/uploads/2013/09/Comorbidity_Study_09-03-131.pdf

Dickerson, C. (2018, November 17). Hazing, humiliation, terror: Working while female in federal prisons. *The New York Times.* Retrieved from: https://www.nytimes.com/2018/11/17/us/prison-sexual-harassment-women.html

Dirks, D. (2004). Sexual revictimization and retraumatization of women in prison. *Women's Studies Quarterly, 32*(3/4), 102–115.

Edwards, J., Joyner, C., & Peebles, J. (2018, October 26). AJC exclusive: Women working in GA prisons endure harassment, groping - by male guards. *AJC*. Retrieved from: https://www.ajc.com/news/state%2D%2Dregional/women-working-prisons-endure-harassment-groping-male-guards/Gi5sTquFkOYcaxdO6Pw2GO/

Eliason, M.J., Taylor, J.Y., & Williams, R. (2004). Physical health of women in prison: Relationship to oppression. *Journal of Correctional Healthcare, 10*(2), 175–203.

Enders, S. R., Paterniti, D. A., & Meyers, F. J. (2005). An approach to develop effective health care decision making for women in prison. *Journal of Palliative Medicine, 8*(2), 432–439.

Fedock, G., Cummings, C., Kubiak, C., Bybee, D., Campbell, R., & Darcy, K. (2019). Incarcerated women's experiences of staff-perpetrated rape: Racial disparities and justice gaps in institutional responses. *Journal of Interpersonal Violence*. https://doi.org/10.1177/0886260519850531

Felitti, V. J., Anda, R. F., Nordenberg, D., Williamson, D. F., Spitz, A. M., Edwards, V., et al. (1998). Relationship of childhood abuse and household dysfunction to many of the leading causes of death in adults: The adverse childhood experiences (ACE) study. *American Journal of Preventive Medicine, 14*, 245–258.

Feminist Criminology. (2019). Retrieved from: https://criminal-justice.iresearchnet.com/criminology/feminist-criminology/3/

Finkelhor, D., Ormrod, R.K., & Turner, H.A. (2007). Polyvictimization and trauma in a national longitudinal cohort. *Development and Psychopathology, 19*(1), 149–166.

Gehring, K. S. (2018). A direct test of pathways theory. *Feminist Criminology, 13*(2), 115–137.

Gilfus, M. E. (1992). From victims to survivors to offenders: Women's routes of entry and immersion into street crime. *Women & Criminal Justice, 4*, 63–90.

Goffman, E. (1961). *Asylums: Essays on the social situation of mental patients and other inmates.* Oxford: Penguin.

Goffman, E. (1963). *Stigma: Notes on the management of spoiled identity.* New York: Simon & Schuster.

Green, B. L., Dass-Brailsford, P. D., Hurtado de Mendoza, A., Mete, M., Lynch, S. M., DeHart, D. D., et al. (2016). Trauma experiences and mental health among women who are incarcerated. *Psychological Trauma: Theory, Research, Practice, and Policy, 8*(4), 455–463.

Green, B. L., Miranda, J., Daroowalla, A., & Siddique, J. (2005). Trauma exposure, mental health functioning, and program needs of women in jail. *Crime & Delinquency, 51*(1), 133–151.

Harner, H., & Burgess, A. W. (2011). Using a trauma-informed framework to care for women who are incarcerated. *JOGNN, 40*, 469–476.

Harris, M., & Fallot, R. D. (2001). Envisioning a trauma-informed service system: A vital paradigm shift. *New Directions for Mental Health Services, 89*, 3–22.

Hartsfield, J., Sharp, S. F., & Conner, S. (2017). Cumulative sexual victimization and mental health outcomes among women who are incarcerated. *Dignity: A Journal on Sexual Exploitation and Violence, 2*(1), 1–18.

Hattery, A. & Smith, E. (2019). Gender, Power, and Violence: Responding to Sexual and Intimate Partner Violence in Society Today. Rowman & Littlefield.

Hayes, R. M., & Luther, K. (2018). *#Crime: Social media, crime and the criminal legal system.* Cham: Palgrave Macmillan.

Hearn, J. & Parkin, W. (2001). Gender, sexuality, and violence in organizations: The unspoken faces of organization violations. Sage.

Hill Collins, P., & Bilge, S. (2016). *Intersectionality.* Malden: Polity Press.

Holtfreter, K., & Wattanaporn, K.A. (2014). The transition from prison to community initiative: An examination of gender responsiveness for female offender reentry. *Criminal Justice and Behavior, 41*(1), 41–57.

Human Rights Campaign. (2019). *Violence against the transgender community in 2019.* Retrieved from: https://www.hrc.org/resources/violence-against-the-transgender-community-in-2019

James, J. & Meyerding, J. (1977). Early sexual experience and prostitution. *American Journal of Psychiatry, 134*(12), 1381–1384.

Jenness, V. (2009). Transgender inmates in California's prisons: An empirical study of a vulnerable population. In *The California department of corrections and rehabilitation wardens' meeting*. Irvine, CA: University of California, Irvine, Center for Evidence-Based Corrections, Department of Criminology, Law, and Society.

Jennings, W. G., Piquero, A. R., & Reingle, J. M. (2012). On the overlap between victimization and offending: A review of the literature. *Aggression and Violent Behavior, 17*, 16–26.

Johnson, S., Cooper, C., Cartwright, S., Donald, I., Taylor, P., & Millet, C. (2005). The experience of work-related stress across occupations. *Journal of Managerial Psychology, 20*(2), 178–187.

Jones, M. S., Worthen, M. G. F., Sharp, S. F., & McLeod, D. A. (2018). Life as she knows it: The effects of adverse childhood experiences on intimate partner violence among women prisoners. *Child Abuse & Neglect, 85*, 68–79.

Jones, N. J., Brown, S. L., Wanamaker, K. A., & Greiner, L. E. (2014). A quantitative exploration of gendered pathways to crime in a sample of male and female juvenile offenders. *Feminist Criminology, 9*, 113–136.

Karlsson, M. E., Bridges, A. J., Bell, J., & Petretic, P. (2014). Sexual violence therapy group in a women's correctional facility: A preliminary evaluation. *Journal of Traumatic Stress, 27*, 361–364.

Kilpatrick, D. G., Resnick, H. S., Ruggiero, K. J., Conoscenti, L. M., & McCauley, J. (2007). *Drug-facilitated, incapacitated, and forcible rape: A national study*. Charleston, SC: MUSC.

Kirkner, A., Relyea, M., & Ullman, S. E. (2018). PTSD and problem drinking in relation to seeking mental health and substance use treatment among sexual assault survivors. *Traumatology, 24*(1), 1–7.

Langan, N. P., & Pelissier, B. M. (2001). Gender differences among prisoners in drug treatment. *Journal of Substance Abuse, 13*, 291–301.

Lenning, E. (2009). Moving beyond the binary: Exploring the dimensions of gender presentation and orientation. *International Journal of Social Inquiry, 2*(2), 39–54.

Lorenz, K. & O'Callaghan, E. (under review). "I realized I couldn't act normal": A qualitative study of sexual assault survivors' experiences with workplace disclosure.

Lynch, S. M., Dehart, D. D., Belknap, J., Green, B. L., Dass-Brailsford, P., Johnson, K. M., et al. (2017). An examination of the associations among victimization, mental health, and offending in women. *Criminal Justice and Behavior, 44*(6), 796–814.

Lynch, S. M., Fritch, A., & Heath, N. M. (2012). Looking beneath the surface: The nature of women who are incarcerated's experiences of interpersonal violence, treatment needs, and mental health. *Feminist Criminology, 7*(4), 381–400.

Maeve, M. K. (2000). Speaking unavoidable truths: Understanding early childhood sexual and physical violence among women in prison. *Issues in Mental Health Nursing, 21*, 473–498.

Marcos Misis, Bitna Kim, Kelly Cheeseman, Nancy L. Hogan, Eric G. Lambert, (2013) The Impact of Correctional Officer Perceptions of Inmates on Job Stress. SAGE Open 3 (2):215824401348969

Martinson, R. (1974). What works? Questions and answers about prison reform. *The Public Interest, 35*, 22–54.

Messina, N. & Grella, C. (2006). Childhood trauma and women's health outcomes in a California prison population. *American Journal of Public Health, 96*, 1842–1848.

Mignon, S. (2016). Health issues of women who are incarcerated in the United States. *Ciencia & Saude Coletiva, 21*(7), 2051–2059.

O'Keefe, M. (1997). Incarcerated battered women: A comparison of battered women who kill their abusers and those incarcerated for other offenses. *Journal of Family Violence, 12*(1), 1–19.

Owen, B., & Bloom, B. (2000). *Profiling the needs of young female offenders: Instrument development and pilot study—Final report*. Washington, DC: U.S. Department of Justice.

Pimlott Kubiak, S., Brenner, H. J., Bybee, D., Campbell, R., & Cummings, C.E., Darcy, K.M., Fedock, G., & Goodman-Williams, R. (2017). Sexual misconduct in prison: What factors affect whether women who are incarcerated will report abuses committed by prison staff? *Law and Human Behavior, 41*(4), 361–374.

Potter, H. (2008). Battle cries: Black women and intimate partner abuse. NYU Press.

Potter, H. (2013). Intersectional criminology: Interrogating identity and power in criminological research and theory. *Critical Criminology, 21*(3), 305–318.

Potter, H. (2015). *Intersectionality and criminology: Disrupting and revolutionizing studies of crime.* New York and London: Routledge.

Raj, A., Rose, J., Decker, M. R., Rosengard, C., Hebert, M. R., Stein, M., et al. (2008). Prevalence and patterns of sexual assault across the life span among women who are incarcerated. *Violence Against Women, 14*(5), 528–541.

Rantala, R. R. (2018). *Sexual victimization reported by adult correctional authorities, 2012-15.* Washington, DC: Bureau of Justice Statistics.

Reisner, S. L., Bailey, Z., & Sevelius, J. (2014). Racial/ethnic disparities in history of incarceration, experiences of victimization, and associated health indicators among transgender women in the U.S. *Women & Health, 54*(8), 750–767.

Richie, B. E. (1996). *Compelled to crime: The gender entrapment of battered black women.* New York: Routledge.

Russel, J. (2019, March 16). 'I am a shell of who I used to be.' A female prison guard's tale of torment. *The Boston Globe.* Retrieved from https://www.bostonglobe.com/metro/2019/03/16/sentenced-years-gratuitous-cruelty-and-yet-she-persevered/sswaNzfz1lqniMfOYwDkxM/story.html

Salisbury, E. J., & Van Voorhis, P. (2009). Gendered pathways: A quantitative investigation of women probationers' paths to incarceration. *Criminal Justice and Behaviour, 36,* 541–566.

Sentencing Project (2019, June 6). *Incarcerated women and girls.* Retrieved from: https://www.sentencingproject.org/publications/incarcerated-women-and-girls/

Sheridan, D. J., & Nash, K. R. (2007). Acute injury patterns of intimate partner violence victims. *Trauma, Violence, & Abuse, 8*(3), 281–289.

Simpson, S. S. (1989). Feminist theory, crime, and justice. *Criminology, 27*(4), 605–631.

Slaughter-Acey, J. (2019, April 17). *Maternal and infant health at the crossroads of racism and colorism.* Retrieved from https://www.racialhealthequity.org/blog/2019/4/16/maternal-and-infant-health-at-the-cross-roads-of-racism-and-colorism

Smith, A. (2015). *Conquest: Sexual violence and American Indian genocide.* Durham: Duke Univ. Press.

Smith, B. V. (2003). Watching you, watching me. *Yale Journal of Law and Feminism, 15*(2), 225–288.

Spohn, C.C., White, C., & Tellis, K. (2014). Unfounding sexual assault: Examining the decision to unfound and identifying false reports. *Law and Society Review, 48,* 161–192.

Struckman-Johnson, C., & Struckman-Johnson, D. (2002). Sexual coercion reported by women in three midwestern prisons. *Journal of Sex Research, 39*(3), 217–227.

Tarzwell, S. (2006). The gender lines are marked with razor wire: Addressing state prison policies for the management of transgender prisoners. *Columbia Human Rights Law Review, 38*(167), 70.

Tillman, S. Bryant-Davis, T. Smith, K., & Marks, A. (2010). Shattering silence: Exploring barriers to disclosure for African American sexual assault survivors. *Trauma, Violence, & Abuse, 11*(2), 59–70.

Tomlinson, B. (2013). To tell the truth and not get trapped: Desire, distance, and intersectionality at the scene of argument. *Signs, 38*(4), 993–1017.

Torres, L., Mata-Greve, F., Bird, C., & Herrera Hernandez, E. (2018). Intersectionality research within Latinx mental health: Conceptual and methodological considerations. *Journal of Latina/o Psychology, 6*(4), 304–317.

Tripodi, S. J., & Pettus-Davis, C. (2013). Histories of childhood victimization and subsequent mental health problems, substance use, and sexual victimization for a sample of women who are incarcerated in the U.S. *International Journal of Law and Psychiatry, 36,* 30–40.

Van Voorhis, P., Wright, E. M., Salisbury, E., & Bauman, A. (2010). Women's risk factors and their contributions to existing risk/needs assessment. *Criminal Justice and Behavior, 37,* 261–288.

VanNatta, M. (2001). Conceptualizing and stopping state sexual violence against incarcerated women. *Social Justice, 37*(1), 27–52.

Verrecchia, P. J. (2009). Female delinquents and restorative justice. *Women and Criminal Justice, 19*, 80–93.

Venema, R.M., Lorenz, K., & Sweda, N. (2019). Unfounded, cleared, or cleared by exceptional means: Sexual assault case outcomes from 1999 to 2014. Journal of Interpersonal Violence. Advance online publication.

von Hentig, H. (1948). *The criminal and his victim: Studies in the sociobiology of crime*. New York: Shocken Book.

Walsh, K., DiLillo, D., & Scalora, M. J. (2011). The cumulative impact of sexual revictimization on emotion regulation difficulties: An examination of female inmates. *Violence Against Women, 17*(8), 1103–1118.

Walsh, K., Gonsalves, V.M., Scalora, M.J., King, S., & Hardyman, P.L. (2012). Child maltreatment histories among female inmates reporting inmate on inmate sexual victimization in prison: The mediating role of emotion dysregulation. *Journal of Interpersonal Violence, 27*(3), 492–512.

West, C., & Johnson, K. (2013, March). *Sexual violence in the lives of African American women*. Harrisburg, PA: VAWnet, a project of the National Resource Center on Domestic Violence. Retrieved from: www.vawnet.org

Weist, M.D., Kinney, L., Taylor, L.K., Pollitt-Hill, J., Bryant, Y., Anthony, L., & Wilkerson, J. (2014). African American and White women's experience of sexual assault and services for sexual assault. *Journal of Aggression, Maltreatment, & Trauma, 23*, 901–916.

Widom, C. (1995). *Victims of childhood sexual abuse: Later criminal consequences*. Washington, DC: U.S. Department of Justice.

Widom, C. (2000). Childhood victimization and the derailment of girls and women to the criminal justice system. In J. Samuels (Ed.), *Research on women and girls in the justice system: Plenary papers of the 1999 conference on criminal justice research and evaluation—Enhancing policy and practice through research* (Vol. 3, pp. 27–36). Washington, DC: U.S. Department of Justice.

Wolff, N., Frueh, B. C., Shi, J., Gerardi, D., Fabrikant, N., & Schumann, B. E. (2011). Trauma exposure and mental health characteristics of incarcerated females self-referred to specialty PTSD treatment. *Psychiatric Services, 62*(8), 954–958.

Wood, J., Foy, D., Layne, C., Pynoos, R., & Boyd, J. (2002). An examination of the relationships between violence exposure post-traumatic stress symptomatology and delinquent activity: An "ecopathological" model of delinquent behavior among incarcerated adolescents. *Journal of Aggression, Maltreatment and Trauma, 6*, 127–147.

Wood, J., Foy, D., Goguen, C., Pynoos, R., & James, C. (2002). Violence exposure and PTSD among delinquent girls. *Journal of Aggression, Maltreatment, and Trauma, 6*, 109–126.

Young, V. D., & Reviere, R. (2001). Meeting the health care needs of the new woman inmate: A national survey or prison practices. *Journal of Offender Rehabilitation, 34*(2), 31–48.

Chapter 9
Educational and Vocational Programming in Women's Prisons: History, Gender Disparities, and Promising Progress

Rashaan A. DeShay

9.1 Introduction

Beginning in the 1970s and 1980s, the USA began to experience an increase in incarceration rates over a period of approximately three to four decades (Clear & Austin, 2009; Mauer, 2006). This prison boom which at times led to over 1.5 million men and women incarcerated in this country is often referred to as mass incarceration (Alexander, 2010; Mauer, 2006; Tonry, 2011). Even with recent declines in the total number of individuals in state and federal prisons, recent data found that there were still close to 1.5 million individuals incarcerated in prison in 2017 (Bronson & Carson, 2019). Although more men than women were incarcerated during these decades leading to mass incarceration, women have also been impacted. In 2017, there were 111,360 women incarcerated in both state and federal prisons, which accounted for approximately 7% of the U.S. prison population (Bronson & Carson, 2019). The majority of these women—close to 90%—were serving their time in state prisons (Bronson & Carson, 2019). While these numbers represent a very slight decrease from a decade earlier, in general these numbers reflect a significant increase in the number of women being incarcerated in the USA over the past three to four decades. Since the late 1970s, women's state prisons have seen an increase of approximately 830%—this increase is more than twice the pace that was seen in incarceration among men (Sawyer, 2018; The Sentencing Project, 2019). A contributing factor to these increases in female incarceration rates is drug offenses. For instance, in 2016, a higher percentage of female inmates were serving time in state prisons for drug offenses than their male counterparts (25% versus 14%, respectively) (Bronson & Carson, 2019). The percentage was even higher for federal

R. A. DeShay (✉)
The University of Texas at Arlington, Arlington, TX, USA
e-mail: rashaan.deshay@uta.edu

© Springer Nature Switzerland AG 2020   131
J. Hector (ed.), *Women and Prison*,
https://doi.org/10.1007/978-3-030-46172-0_9

inmates; more than half of women serving time in those institutions were doing so for a drug trafficking offense (Bronson & Carson, 2019). It has also been argued that state and local policies have contributed to the significant increase in incarceration rates among women (e.g., harsher sentencing laws, expanded efforts by law enforcement) (Sawyer, 2018; The Sentencing Project, 2019).

While it is true that in recent years we have seen a decline in the number of people incarcerated in the USA, the majority of that decline has been experienced by male inmates (Sawyer, 2018). This raises questions about why policymakers have been able to find success as it relates to men but have not been as successful with women. One possible explanation is that more attention has been paid to male inmates from a policymaking perspective (e.g., few programs for women, disciplinary action while incarcerated), which has contributed to the less significant decarceration (minus a few exceptions) we have seen when comparing female inmates to males (Sawyer, 2018).

There is a need to explore the needs of female inmates to ensure that they are provided with adequate and appropriate programming while incarcerated. It is not enough to assume that what has been done for men in prison over the years is sufficient to address the needs of women. For instance, females are shown to have different histories and needs than men when they enter prison. They often have significant educational, economical, and employment deficits when they begin serving their sentences (e.g., unemployed or having held minimum-wage jobs, over half having been on public assistance, approximately 20% being illiterate) (Austin & Irwin, 2001; Messina, Burdon, & Prendergast, 2001; Owen & Bloom, 1995). In addition, while estimates vary research has indicated that close to 70% of women who are incarcerated are mothers (Gabel & Johnston, 1995; Smith, 1991). This has significant implications for the inmates, as well as the children left behind on the outside and separated from their mothers (Fogel & Martin, 1992; Pollock, 2002). These women often have plans to rejoin their children once they are released, which can significantly impact the anxieties they experience while incarcerated due to concerns about whether the reconciliation will happen (Bloom & Steinhart, 1993; Greenfeld & Snell, 1999; Hairston, 1991; Pollock, 2002). Compared to men, research has shown that women are also more likely to enter prison with a history of abuse (physical and sexual), mental health issues, trauma, and different physical health needs (Bloom, Chesney-Lind, & Owen, 1994; Blume, 1990; Islam-Zwart & Vik, 2004; James & Glaze, 2006; Rose, 2004; Sawyer, 2018).

This increase in the number of women being incarcerated in the USA has led to an increased need to provide programs and resources to them while they are in prison. There is a need for scholars to pay attention to female inmates, including their experiences while incarcerated and whether prisons prepare them for release. Further, exploring the needs of female inmates is necessary because there is a possibility that the experiences and lives of female inmates are different than those of men.

9.2   Educational Programs and Gender-Based Disparities

Research has consistently found a difference in educational programming being made available to female inmates compared to their male counterparts. Scholars have argued that providing education programs in prison is important because it can have a positive impact on what happens to inmates once they are released, including reducing recidivism and increasing the likelihood that an individual will find a job (Knepper, 1990; Harer, 1995; Lahm, 2000). A study of prisons from 15 states found differences in the availability of programming between male and female inmates (Arditi, Goldberg, Hartle, & Phelps, 1973). In terms of education, they found that more educational programs were available to men (e.g., a state offering college classes in male but not female institutions). In several of the states studied, this was explained by the fact that it was believed that the women's facilities were simply too small to handle such a program. There were also fewer teachers found in the women's institutions that did have educational programs (Arditi et al., 1973). A study conducted in the 1980s exploring educational programs in 45 states found that college classes were available in close to 75% of the women's prisons, with GED and adult basic education programs being available in close to 85% of these institutions (Ryan, 1984). Research has found that although the differences were minimal, when compared to men a larger proportion of female inmates were more likely to take college and adult basic education classes (Morash, Haarr, & Rucker, 1994). This seems to demonstrate the need to ensure that these programs are available to both female and male inmates.

Decades after Arditi et al. (1973), Lahm (2000) studied men's and women's prisons in 30 different states to determine whether there was evidence of continued disparities between educational and vocational programming that prior scholars had identified. She found that almost all of the prisons, both men's and women's, did indeed offer basic educational programming for its inmates. This demonstrated a significant shift from what prior scholars had found decades earlier (see Arditi et al., 1973, for example). In terms of access to college classes, they found similar numbers again, with about half of both the female and male prisons offering such programs. She did note, however, that even though there was a lack of disparity having approximately 50% of prisons offering college programs was not ideal (Lahm, 2000). This signaled that the availability of postsecondary education in prisons may not be seen as a priority. It is possible that this lack of concern may be attributed to "tough on crime" legislation, with the Violent Crime Control and Law Enforcement Act playing a significant role (Lahm, 2000).

A more recent study exploring the availability of programs to female inmates in Texas noted that the state still has significant disparities between male and female inmates. Linder (2018) found that in terms of academic programs, women only had the option of earning an associate degree, while programs for associate, bachelor's, and master's degrees were available to men. The Texas Department of Criminal Justice (TDCJ) disputed these findings, arguing that they do indeed offer opportunities for female inmates to receive a bachelor's degree from a 4-year state university

(Greene, 2018). In addition, TDCJ says they are continuing to explore ways to provide more programming to women which will include an individual appointed to have oversight of programs for female inmates (Barajas, 2018).

Attempts have been made to identify factors that may play a role in program availability in general, but not necessarily based on gender. That being said, these reasons may also influence limited program availability to female inmates. Scholars have identified varying explanations for why these limitations exist. Several studies have found that southern institutions were less likely to have college programs than prisons categorized as non-southern (Lahm, 2000; Morash et al., 1994; Rafter, 1995). Location may also be a factor due to a significant number of prisons being built in rural areas, which may make it difficult for institutions to find qualified instructors in these isolated areas (Huling, 2002). In addition, security level has been identified as a factor that impacts program availability (Lahm 2000). Budget cuts and lack of funding are also important in explaining limited program availability, with some scholars noting reductions in program availability over time (Batchelder, O'Neill, Rodriguez, & Tibbs, 2018; Davis, Bozick, Steele, Saunders, & Miles, 2013; Hobby, Walsh, & Delaney, 2019; McCarthy, 2006; Palmer, 2012). Lastly, one study examining the use of educational programs in prison discussed that one issue impacting inmates being able to complete these programs was due to the transfer of inmates to other institutions often with very brief notice, causing them to abandon their studies before they were done. As such, it was noted that some institutions in North Carolina had decided to limit their offering of programs in that state to locations where inmates would be able to complete them, leading to a reduced number of prisons where they were available (Zoukis, 2014).

9.2.1 Why Education in Prison Matters

Because less attention has been paid to female inmates, some of the research exploring the value of providing education in prison are not gender specific. This demonstrates the need for scholars and corrections officials to explore issues specific to incarcerated women. Research, however, has found that participating in educational programs while in prison can lead to better outcomes upon release (Aos, Miller, & Drake, 2006; Davis et al., 2013; MacKenzie, 2006; Wilson, Gallagher, & Mackenzie, 2000). It has been found that when comparing them to inmates who did not, those who did participate in these programs while incarcerated were 43% less likely to recidivate (Davis et al., 2013). This includes various types of education programs, including adult basic education programs, high school/GED programs, postsecondary programs, and vocational programs. A more recent study suggests that participation in a postsecondary program in prison can reduce the likelihood of recidivating by 48% (Bozick, Steele, Davis, & Turner, 2018). Participation in education programs (including both vocational and academic) has also been found to improve one's chances of securing employment post-release (Davis et al., 2013; Wilson et al., 2000). For those that participated in academic programs, they had 8% higher odds of finding a job when compared to those who did not (Davis et al., 2013). Research also suggests that providing these programs to inmates is actually cost-effective in the long-term because it is cheaper than paying for the potential costs associated with the individual being sent back to prison (Davis et al., 2013; Oakford et al., 2019). Further information is needed regarding the specific characteristics of these programs that may make some more effective than others (Davis et al., 2013).

Participating in educational programs can improve one's job prospects (e.g., higher earnings, higher employment rates) after release (Cho & Tyler, 2010; Duwe & Clark, 2014; Oakford et al., 2019). As such, the argument has been made that reinstating Pell Grant opportunities for inmates would increase their potential regarding employment and earnings (Oakford et al., 2019). This could prove to be beneficial not only for those that are formerly incarcerated, but for their families as well. Further, as research has shown that being incarcerated tends to reduce employment opportunities as well as income earned compared to individuals who have not been in prison (see Western & Pettit, 2010), it is vital that everything possible is done to improve job prospects for formerly incarcerated people. With women having the added concern of caring for children and trying to regain custody of children upon release (Bloom & Steinhart, 1993; Greenfeld & Snell, 1999; Hairston, 1991; Pollock, 2002), ensuring they can secure employment is paramount.

As noted, lack of educational attainment can be a barrier to formerly incarcerated people in general, but research has shown this can be particularly problematic for women who have been to prison. One study found that for formerly incarcerated women, having neither a high school diploma nor GED led to unemployment rates of close to 30% for white women, just over 45% for Hispanic women, and 60% for black women (Couloute, 2018). This signifies the need to prioritize educational programs for female inmates, fund these programs, and encourage these women to participate in the programs.

9.2.2 Issues with Program Participation

Although education has been shown to have significant value, data has shown that close to 60% of incarcerated individuals do not obtain a higher level of education during the time they are in prison (National Center for Education Statistics, 2016; Oakford et al., 2019). One explanation given for this lack of participation is based on limited time available to inmates to attend classes because they may have conflicts with job assignments (Batchelder & Pippert, 2001). According to a 2014 survey of state and federal inmates (1,315 inmates—1,048 were male and 267 were female), 68% of the women surveyed completed no further education than what they had when they entered prison---12% obtained a high school diploma or GED, 9% received a certificate from college or trade school (National Center for Education Statistics, 2016). While fewer females than males were surveyed for this study, the researchers made an effort to target a nationally representative sample of inmates in the USA (National Center for Education Statistics, 2016). A survey of female inmates in Texas also found limited participation, with only 39% of them having participated in educational programs made available to them (Linder, 2018). This lack of participation, however, may have been due to inmates' feeling as though the Texas Department of Criminal Justice (TDCJ) was not doing enough for them to prepare them for release. For instance, just over 50% of the survey respondents did not believe the Texas prison system was providing them with what they needed in terms of employment training (Linder, 2018).[1] This suggests that institutions need to do a better job at not only providing programs to these women, but also in terms of communicating to them that the institution itself is invested in their future success. One way this could be done is to share success stories of formerly incarcerated women who participated in the programs while they were in prison. This may help encourage women to believe these programs are worth the effort and could be beneficial to them long-term.

Research has explored why female inmates may not participate in educational programming. Though not completely responsible for it, the elimination of Federal Pell Grants (see discussion in the next section) in the 1990s contributed to a decline in participation among female inmates in postsecondary education during that decade (Rose, 2004). The significant increase in the female inmate population in the USA has also contributed to a lack of participation among women because the increase likely put a strain on the already limited programs that were available (Rose, 2004). This is particularly troubling considering that scholars have found that female inmates are often in need of more educational programs than their male counterparts when they get to prison, making it even more important that proper resources are made available to them (Austin & Irwin, 2001). Prior research has found that when compared to men's facilities, women have fewer options and that what is available may not be as good as what is offered to men (Janusz, 1991; Ross & Fabiano, 1986). The lack of availability and quality may contribute to female inmates deciding not to participate in educational programs because they may be viewed as a waste of one's time (Rose, 2004).

The quality of education offered in an institution can impact how inmates respond to the material that is being disseminated. Formerly incarcerated women identified their opinions of the characteristics of good teachers, including: (1) those that did not merely just teach out of books, (2) those that made an effort to connect with students, (3) those that encouraged students to become aware one's self and others, and (4) teachers that allow students to have some control and demonstrate that they have the ability to be responsible for their education (Mageehon, 2006). The belief is that if these characteristics are displayed by teachers in correctional facilities, this may improve the value of the education that female inmates receive. It may also increase participation if these women are confident that the education they receive will be beneficial to them, as opposed to being a waste of their time.

Federal inmates have provided information that may help answer the question of why some inmates do not participate in programming. In terms of federal

---

[1] This could involve vocational programs in addition to education programs.

institutions, the availability of educational programs varies from institution to institution and they are often taught by other inmates calling into question the value of the education one receives. This may discourage inmates from wanting to participate. Further, federal inmates have reported that being able to earn a college degree while incarcerated is extremely difficult due to the small numbers of programs available, financial considerations, and lack of access to computers to do work for their classes (Ring & Gill, 2017). Federal inmates also suggested that there would likely be a higher level of participation in available programs if doing so provided a desirable incentive (e.g., sentence reduction) (Ring & Gill, 2017). This suggests that there may be different issues at the state and federal level, and that policymakers need to consider making education in federal prisons more accessible, improving the quality, and encouraging federal inmates to participate by communicating the long-term value of these programs. The Federal Bureau of Prisons (BOP), however, has acknowledged that male and female inmates have different needs and argue that they tailor their programs with that in mind. For instance, they work to address issues related to past trauma and abuse that women are more likely than men to have experienced prior to incarceration (Federal Bureau of Prisons n.d.).

9.2.3   Budget Cuts/Changes in Legislation and Funding Availability

A significant event related to funding for postsecondary education for inmates is based on changes to the Federal Pell Grant program in the 1990s. For decades, the program offered an opportunity for inmates to receive financial assistance to be used toward obtaining a postsecondary education (Mercer, 2004). This changed in the mid-1990s due to tough on crime policies and legislation, including the Violent Crime Control and Law Enforcement Act of 1994 (Oakford et al., 2019). The U.S. recession of 2008 was also found to have an impact on the availability of these programs due to budget cuts. While some states have since seen either increases in funding or at least no further decreases in funding, the possibility of reduced funding is something that correctional administrators should likely anticipate and plan for going forward (Davis et al., 2013).

After the Federal Pell Grant program was eliminated for inmates in the 1990s, a number of states did the same by cutting off access to state funds for inmates that could be used to pursue a college education (Hobby et al., 2019). Limited funding has complicated attempts to provide postsecondary education to inmates (Hobby et al., 2019). At times, this has left facilities relying on support from private funders or relying on inmates to pay tuition themselves, which significantly limits the number of inmates that would be able to enroll (Hobby et al., 2019). Data has also shown that despite the majority of inmates being interested in postsecondary education, a small portion of them do participate (National Center for Education Statistics, 2016). While explanations for why they do not participate even though they express a desire to do so needs to be further explored, one possible explanation is a lack of funding.

While the elimination of funding by some states and through the Federal Pell Grant program made it challenging for inmates to pursue postsecondary education, some states have made an effort to provide postsecondary education to inmates. A recent study, however, noted that more than half of states currently have laws or policies that stand in the way of inmates receiving funding to assist in pursuing postsecondary education, with only 17 states having no barriers (Hobby et al., 2019). These barriers include legislation preventing incarcerated students from being able to obtain state funds from at least one of the available programs, and those limiting state inmates from accessing federal funds. Some states have taken steps to further limit access to state funds by disqualifying inmates from receiving these funds if they do not also qualify for federal funds (Hobby et al., 2019). Some barriers may also be less straightforward while still essentially standing in the way of inmates receiving funds (e.g., requiring that funded recipients are a full-time student, taking classes at a state 4-year university or community college, having certain requirements regarding one's high school GPA). As such, it is important for states to explore multiple funding options so postsecondary education can be provided to their inmates. For instance, veterans' benefits are being used in Wisconsin, Texas, and California (Hobby et al., 2019). While this will not help all inmates, these states have also combined other sources of funding (e.g., state financial aid, federal funding from Second Chance Pell Grants, private funding) to make these opportunities available to more incarcerated individuals (Hobby et al., 2019).

9.2.4   Bright Spots: Promising Legislation and Programs

While we continue to see gender-based disparities in terms of availability and access to programming, as well as issues regarding funding of programs, there are some encouraging developments. Some states as well as the federal government have made efforts that signal a desire to assist inmates in general, and at times specifically female inmates. For instance, there is a bit of hope in terms of seeing a return of federal funding being made available to inmates to help them pursue postsecondary education. In 2015, the Obama administration announced the development of a pilot program—known as the Second Chance Pell Pilot Program—that would once again provide funding for education through Pell Grants (U.S. Department of Education, 2016). The following year, the Department of Education announced that 12,000 inmates would be participating in this program through partnerships with colleges and universities (U.S. Department of Education Press Release, 2016). While further evaluation of this program is needed (Government Accountability Office, 2019), early evidence indicates that these programs have been beneficial to individuals upon release, particularly in terms of securing employment in varying fields (Haynes, 2018). This can contribute to helping them avoid recidivating while also being able to provide for themselves and their families during the reentry process (Oakford et al., 2019). In May of 2019, the U.S. Secretary of Education Betsy DeVos announced that the pilot program was going to be expanded, which would allow more inmates to participate while also providing more data for the evaluation of the program (U.S. Department of Education Press Release, 2019a). The following month while speaking at a commencement ceremony at a prison in Oklahoma, DeVos expressed her support of making the Second Chance Pell program permanent (U.S. Department of Education Press Release, 2019b). It has been argued that permanently reinstating this program for inmates would not be unduly burdensome on the government (Oakford et al., 2019). Instead, the existing research on the value of providing education to inmates suggests that it would favor both the inmates and society as a whole to provide this opportunity (Aos et al., 2006; Davis et al., 2013; MacKenzie, 2006; Wilson et al., 2000). Estimates suggest that more than 450,000 inmates in state prisons could benefit from the Pell Grant program if it is fully reinstated, including male and female inmates (Oakford et al., 2019). There also appears to be at least some bipartisan support in Congress, and legislation has been introduced that would restore this funding past the existence of the pilot program.[2]

It may be argued that California could be viewed as a model of offering educational programming to inmates, including females, and that doing so may help confront the national problem of mass incarceration (Mukamal & Silbert, 2018). Between the years 2014 and 2017, California made moves to expand offerings to incarcerated college students. This was done to move beyond the high school and GED classes, and career technical classes that had been offered at the time (Mukamal & Silbert, 2018). In 2014, the state of California implemented a policy providing funding that would allow thousands of inmates to pursue their education at a community college while still incarcerated (Rivera, 2015). The program paired four of the state prisons with community colleges to offer classes; one of these prisons was a women's institution (Rivera, 2015). This also included providing educational opportunities to inmates upon release. As such, not only were community college classes being taught in person inside the institutions, there were also support groups and programs for formerly incarcerated individuals upon release (Mukamal & Silbert, 2018). An important aspect of these programs is that they are available in both male and female prisons. Arambula and LeBlanc (2018) conducted an evaluation of the new program in California that allowed inmates to take community college classes face-to-face. They found an increase in the number of students taking these types of classes, and an increase in the number of courses being offered to these inmates. They also found that the classes offered in prison had higher retention rates than those classes offered on the actual community college campuses; the inmates also had higher success rates for degree-eligible classes (Arambula & LeBlanc, 2018). One promising aspect of the evaluation was the finding that the rigor of the classes offered at the prisons was at the same level as that offered on the community college campuses. Further, the inmates seemed to appreciate the

---

[2] Restoring Education and Learning (REAL) Act.

challenge and worked hard to rise to meet the expectations. While the evaluation acknowledged there was room for improvement (e.g., funding, providing textbooks, making sure there was enough space available, making technology available to the incarcerated students), the overall findings were extremely optimistic about the future of the program and the potential for continued provision of these resources to inmates (Arambula & LeBlanc, 2018).

In addition, UCLA began a prison education program in 2016 which provides an opportunity for traditional UCLA students to learn from and along with inmates from several institutions, including the California Institute for Women (CIW). During the first two years of the program, 13 women from CIW participated in the program alongside 22 UCLA students and 12 inmates from juvenile hall. The students can take classes including creative writing, philosophy, and urban planning. In addition, at some point during the program six law students will be paired with 10 incarcerated students to evaluate the resources and opportunities available to inmates as they reintegrate into society. The hope is that this program will provide valuable learning opportunities for both inmates and the UCLA students (UCLA Prison Education Program, 2019).

Through the funding of various organizations, several states were given an opportunity to participate in what would be known as the Pathways from Prison to Postsecondary Education. The pilot programs in three states, including North Carolina, provided funding to be used for educational programming and reentry services for individuals who were incarcerated. This was made available to both male and female inmates (Davis & Tolbert, 2019). The one female institution involved was a minimum-security prison, and the program offered courses that could be used for these inmates to pursue an Associate degree (e.g., developmental courses, core technical courses, and general education courses) (Davis & Tolbert, 2019). One finding of this program was that both male and female inmates needed help at times during the program but were often hesitant to seek assistance. They did note, however, that females found asking for help less challenging than their male counterparts. The report made it clear that it was important for these students to have someone they trusted that they could vent to and felt comfortable talking to about issues and concerns they had regarding the material presented in class. This suggests the need to have instructors that are invested in the success and outcomes of the students (Davis & Tolbert, 2019).

As previously discussed, budgeting crises have contributed to significant cuts to program availability in prisons. For instance, back in 2012, a women's institution in Pennsylvania discontinued its GED program due to budget cuts (Zoukis, 2017). While going years without a GED program, they did implement other programs aimed at assisting these women and preparing them for release. The programs include a sexual assault education program, a program that allows inmates to take classes along with college students studying criminal justice, and a creative writing program (Zoukis, 2017). An added benefit of the creative writing program was the production of a play performed by both formerly incarcerated inmates and college students who had not been incarcerated. This play provided an opportunity to make others aware of the challenges faced by these women before and after being incarcerated (Zoukis, 2017).

These examples of recent efforts at educating incarcerated individuals are promising. They also demonstrate that through state and private funding, prisons may indeed find ways to provide these services to inmates. A crucial aspect of providing funding to inmates, however, would likely be the permanent reinstatement of Federal Pell Grants (Hobby et al., 2019).

9.2.5 Policy Recommendations: Educational Programs for Female Inmates

The history of program availability for female inmates as well as recent developments set forth several policy recommendations in the operation of these programs: (1) securing state legislation/funding to assist in running these programs, (2) ensure no barriers to admission are in place to prevent current and formerly incarcerated inmates from becoming eligible to enroll, (3) enacting legislation that makes tuition free at community colleges for low-income students, including those who are incarcerated, (4) creating an environment that is conducive to learning, involves mutual respect among students and faculty, and encourages the students to be engaged, (5) hiring the right faculty and staff, and making space available for classes to be held, (6) making an extra effort to help prepare those inmates who are not yet ready for postsecondary education (e.g., those without a high school diploma or GED, those who may need developmental classes to prepare them for college classes), (7) ensuring that any credits earned while in prison would be transferrable to a 4-year university if the student so desired, (8) being sure that any educational or vocational programming made available to students will help set them on a path to a career or academic outcome that will not be blocked by barriers created by the state that would keep them from taking advantage of what they had learned in prison, and (9) continued evaluation of these programs, especially in terms of understanding how they impact the lives of these women post-release (Dortch & James, 2019; Erzen, Gould, & Lewen, 2019; Mukamal & Silbert, 2018). These have the potential to expand postsecondary education to inmates across the county while also ensuring that these programs are effective and help inmates upon release.

While not necessarily a policy recommendation, a policy consideration is related to the Second Chance Pell pilot program. The program gives funding priority to inmates taking classes with expected release dates within the following 5 years. One of the issues that has been raised in determining whether this program should be reinstated permanently is whether it is reasonable to make this experience available to inmates who will likely never be released from prison (Dortch & James, 2019). This would impact slightly more than 6,700 female inmates in the USA, which accounts for approximately 3.5% of all USA inmates serving virtual life or life sentences (Carson & Anderson, 2016; Nellis, 2017). As such, policymakers need to determine what limitations should be in place if this program is indeed restored on a permanent basis.

9.3   Vocational Programming and Gender Disparities

Differences have also been identified between men and women's prisons in terms of the availability of vocational training programs. First, men often were given a wider variety of programs from which to choose. Second, the vocational programs offered were often aligned with gender stereotypes. This may include men being offered programs to learn how to fix cars, while women were offered programs such as cosmetology services and typing classes (Arditi et al., 1973). The programs available to male inmates were more likely to provide them with skills that would serve them upon release (i.e., likely being able to earn more upon release). In addition, Arditi et al. (1973) found that decisions related to which institution an inmate should be sent also differed by gender. This included sending men to prisons according to their rehabilitation needs, while women were not given the same option. In exploring the types of vocational programs available at the women's prison they studied, Glick and Neto (1977) also found that the programs likely to be offered were related to food service, office skills, and cosmetology. Scholars did note an increase in the availability of vocational programs for female inmates during the 1980s in comparison to prior decades (Crawford, 1988; Ryan, 1984; Weishet, 1985). Even with this increase, however, there were still disparities between the number and type of programs being offered to women (Morash et al., 1994). A limitation of programming and opportunities for rehabilitation while the women are in prison can prove to complicate matters once they are released, making reintegration more difficult than it is already likely to be (Simon, 1975; Sobel, 1982).

Decades after the Arditi et al. (1973) study, scholars still noted that formerly incarcerated women expressed complaints that the availability of vocational programs during their time in prison was limited and gendered (e.g., cosmetology and office skills) (Case & Fasenfest, 2004). In her study of vocational programming in prisons in 30 states, Lahm (2000) found continued disparities in the types of programs being offered to men and women. For instance, women were still more likely to be trained for secretarial, telemarketing, medical assistants, seamstress, and custodial jobs (Lahm, 2000). She did note, however, that there was an increase among female institutions providing inmates with opportunities to be trained in professional and managerial programs. Male prisons were more likely to offer programs such as farming, forestry, auto repair, plumbing, electrical, etc. (Lahm, 2000). Morash et al. (1994) also found that the offerings of programs were based on gender stereotypes. While Lahm (2000) found that female inmates were more likely to be offered training in technical/sales and service-oriented jobs, she also noted that these types of jobs were dominated by women employees on the outside. As such, she suggested that these institutions may be attempting to help these women find a job working in an industry predicated on gender stereotypes upon release (Lahm, 2000). Unfortunately, these tend to be jobs that do not pay well and are often unstable thereby suggesting that these women may be ill-prepared to be successful in the workforce once they reenter society. This issue may be complicated by the fact that these women may seek to regain custody of their children once they are released and will need to find a way to support them while also working to reintegrate into society (Gabel & Johnston, 1995).

It has been argued that almost two decades after Lahm's (2000) study, even with some improvements, issues still exist (Harris, 2018). Insufficient and ineffective programming in women's prisons can contribute to difficult reentry experiences, limiting one's prospects post-release (Harris, 2018). A recent study exploring the availability of academic and vocational programs to female inmates in Texas noted that the state still has significant disparities between male and female inmates. Linder (2018) found that while two vocational programs offering certificates were made available to women, 21 were available to men. Texas also provides technical education programs through what is known as the Windham School District (WSD); disparities were present there as well. While female inmates in Texas had access to 21 courses, their male counterparts were given access to 48 courses (Linder, 2018). To be fair, the technical education courses offered to women included such options as HVAC, carpentry, electrical trades, and copper network cabling, among others. That being said, there were 27 technical education courses that were not available to them, including welding, sheet metal, small engine repair, among others (Linder, 2018). A survey of 400 female inmates in Texas was conducted to ask about their participation in programs, as well as their thoughts on the quality and usefulness of these programs. Fewer than half of the respondents acknowledged that they had participated in programs that were intended to assist them with finding employment in the future—only 29% of them participated in vocational or job training programs (Linder, 2018). As previously noted, TDCJ has disputed the findings of Linder's report regarding program disparity, while also declaring their goal of making more programming available to female inmates in the state of Texas (Barajas, 2018). This is supposed to include an individual whose specific responsibility will be to oversee the programs for female inmates (Barajas, 2018). While there are improvements that need to be made—a few of the women who have been able to participate in these programs recently made available to them (e.g., HVAC, plumbing) have expressed gratitude for the opportunity and believe the training could be helpful to them upon release (Greene, 2018).

In terms of programming, it has also been suggested that apprenticeships should be offered to inmates to provide them with skills that will make them appealing in the labor market once released (Hanks, 2016). This is based on recent research acknowledging the financial benefit over the course of their careers to individuals who complete apprenticeships (Reed et al., 2012). In addition, apprenticeships have been found to be beneficial to employers while also being a sound government investment (Helper, Noonan, Nicholson, & Langdon, 2016). There is, however, a significant disparity based on gender related to these opportunities with male inmates having more access to these programs than their female counterparts. For instance, women accounted for only 2% of construction apprentices in the year 2013 which is unfortunate because those apprentices have been known to earn the highest wages. Instead, women often find themselves in apprenticeships that offer the lowest wages (Hanks, 2016). As such, opportunities should be expanded to female inmates to increase employability.

9.3.1 Why Vocational Programs in Prison are Needed

The participation in a vocational training program while in prison has been shown to reduce recidivism upon release (Lattimore, Witte, & Baker, 1990; Lawrence, Mears, Dubin, & Travis, 2002; Anderson, 1995; Steurer & Smith, 2003; Wilson et al., 2000), while others have not found this to be the case (Van Stelle, Moberg, & Welnetz, 1998). A meta-analysis exploring the impact of prison vocational programs found no significant evidence that these programs reduced recidivism, but they do seem to improve post-release employment options (Davis et al., 2013). As such, even if recidivism rates are not impacted, there may still be benefits in other areas (i.e., employment).

While some research has included both men and women in their samples, there is limited research that specifically focuses on the impact of vocational programming post-release for female inmates. Even Saylor and Gaes (1997) noted that due to the small number of women prisoners they studied, they were unable to determine whether participation in the programs did indeed play a role in recidivism rates. Even though there appears to have been an increase in these programs since early scholars began to explore the issue, too many of these programs still appeared to offer gendered training opportunities (Young & Mattucci, 2006). As such, it has been argued that prisons should be training women for professions that will provide them a chance to secure employment and a livable wage post-release (Young & Mattucci, 2006). For instance, plumbing has been identified as a vocation that may need skilled workers to fill available positions (MacGillis, 2001).

Participation in education programs (including both vocational and academic) has also been found to improve one's chances of securing employment post-release (Davis et al., 2013; Wilson et al., 2000). One study found that the prospects appear to be better for those who participate in vocational programs. Davis et al. (2013) found that when compared to those who did not, inmates who trained in vocational programs had 28% higher odds of securing employment. For those that participated in academic programs, however, they only had 8% higher odds of finding a job when compared to those who did not (Davis et al., 2013). The study suggests that there may indeed be true benefits for participating in vocational programs.

9.3.2 Participation and Access to Programs

Studying both educational and vocational programs, Rose (2004) found that at no point between the years of 1979 and 1997 did a majority of incarcerated women participate in either of these programs. Further, during the 1990s (1991–1997), Rose (2004) noted a decrease in the participation in vocational programs among women. One of the explanations for why this may have happened was due to the discontinuation of Federal Pell Grants during the 1990s because some community colleges had been providing this type of training through the grant (Lawrence et al., 2002; Rose, 2004). Further, recent survey data indicated that while vocational programs are appealing to federal inmates, access to these programs is limited and an inmate has to be close to release date in order to qualify (Ring & Gill, 2017). The Federal Bureau of Prisons, however, says that they do indeed attempt to address the vocational needs of incarcerated women because they are aware that men are more likely to have vocational skills not possessed by women (Federal Bureau of Prisons n.d.). Regardless, it appears that we need a better understanding of why there is not more participation among female inmates when it comes to these vocational programs at both the state and federal level.

In a study exploring the quality and effectiveness of vocational programs in California prisons, Tesfai (2014) acknowledged that the California Department of Corrections and Rehabilitation (CDCR) had set a goal of providing programming to its inmates that would be beneficial to them upon their release. As such, they had set a goal of offering educational programming to a significant percentage (i.e., 70%) of the inmates that qualified for such programming. Inmates are not forced into participation in these programs, and instead volunteer. However, there is not even funding to cover all the inmates who would like to participate. As such, in deciding who gets to participate, the CDCR has chosen that inmates who are nearing release should be given priority (Tesfai, 2014). Access to these programs varies by institution, with some facilities having as few as two percent of inmates with access. For female institutions in California, the range is 4–10% of the inmate's population having access to vocational programming. Of these programs in female institutions, the percent of enrollment ranges from 45 to 91%, but it is unclear as to why these differences exist especially considering they all have waitlists (Tesfai, 2014). An interesting aspect of the data was that female inmates have more access than their male counterparts (36.6% versus 6.3%, respectively). A caveat, however, is that women were not able to participate in all the programs available through the CDCR (i.e., they had access to 13 of the 16 programs). While they did have access to the majority of the programs available, the ones they were not able to participate in (i.e., small engine repair, machine shop, and sheet metal work) were the ones found to offer some of the highest pay. It is important to note, however, that CDCR did offer training to female inmates in such areas as auto mechanics, carpentry, electric work, HVAC, and plumbing, among others that are often associated with only being available to men. There were very few female institutions offering these programs, however (Tesfai, 2014). Further, the study found that the training programs made available to inmates in CDCR were those for which California had no restrictions for ex-offenders in terms of obtaining professional licenses (Tesfai, 2014). This was significant because prior research has expressed concern about training inmates for jobs they will not be able to get once released due to states' licensing requirements (Glick & Neto, 1977; Hersch & Meyers, 2019; Rodriguez & Avery, 2016).

9.3.3 What Do Vocational Programs Need?

In addition to providing job training, it has also been argued that these programs need to offer these women other skills that will serve them well as they attempt to find and keep a job post-release (e.g., being able to work with others in a team setting, pro-social norms) (Bazos & Hausman, 2004; Tonkin, Dickie, Alemagno, & Grove, 2004). Young and Mattucci (2006) explored a 16-h plumbing training program offered to female inmates in several jails in the state of New York. Their findings suggest that the women did indeed learn something from the program that could assist them once they were released from jail (e.g., fixing toilets and sinks, using plumbing tools, teamwork) (Young & Mattucci, 2006). In addition, the women who participated in this program reported enjoying the hands-on aspect of the program, expressed a desire for more time to do so, as well as noting how the program had given them feelings of hope and helped improve their self-esteem (Young & Mattucci, 2006).

Several factors have been found that could help make vocational programming more successful including: (1) sufficient buy-in from the correctional staff, (2) adequate physical space for the training, (3) learning materials that accommodate the reading levels of inmates, and (4) having fellow inmates serve as mentors (Young & Mattucci, 2006).

Hersch and Meyers (2019) argue that formerly incarcerated women may experience more of a burden than formerly incarcerated men in terms of securing a stable income due to their circumstances and experiences (e.g., increased likelihood of being a single parent, history of abuse, issues with mental health). There needs to be a significant effort made by states across the country to remove some of the obstacles that inmates face post-release, including being ineligible for occupational licenses either permanently or for a set period of time (Hersch & Meyers, 2019; Rodriguez & Avery, 2016). For instance, decades ago research discussed concerns that inmates had about whether the vocational programs provided in prisons had any value post-release. Scholars noted that at times inmates would be trained for professions that would unlikely be available to them once they were released (Glick & Neto, 1977).

An issue faced by former inmates seeking employment is that employers are often hesitant to hire them (Hersch & Meyers, 2019; Holzer, Raphael, & Stoll, 2006). This may differ based on the occupation. For instance, it has been found that the construction industry is one that is likely more willing to hire formerly incarcerated individuals (Hunt, Smart, Jonsson, & Tsang, 2018). This industry, however, often employs men as opposed to women putting formerly incarcerated women at a disadvantage. A policy that several states have employed has been to issue certificates of rehabilitation to formerly incarcerated inmates to improve their chances of securing post-release employment (Hersch & Meyers, 2019). This could be achieved by inmates participating in educational and vocational programs during their incarceration (Hersch & Meyers, 2019). It can also be valuable to listen to incarcerated women about their needs and suggestions for policies that will be helpful to them while in prison and upon release (Hersch & Meyers, 2019).

The fact that when compared to men, women make up such a small percentage of the prison population likely helps explain why fewer programs have historically been available (Harris, 2018). This, however, needs to be addressed because it has the potential to limit the prospects of female inmates post-release (Harris, 2018). Post-release outcomes are important, especially considering differences have been found between formerly incarcerated men and women. La Vigne, Brooks, and Shollenberger (2009) found that a fewer percentage of women than men were working after being released from prison. At the time of 2–4 months post-release, 36% of women versus 48% of men were working. Further, 34% of women versus 60% of men were working 8–10 months after being released from prison (La Vigne et al., 2009). There may also be gendered experiences post-release based on the type of offense. Research has found that having a drug conviction could be more harmful to women's chances of employment than to men's (Curcio & Pattavina, 2018). As such, these vocational programs for female inmates need to be sure they are not only providing them with the skills needed to make them employable, but likely also need to continue services post-release to help these women secure employment.

9.3.4 Expanding Vocation Programs for Women

Just as has been seen with educational programs in prisons, some institutions have made some efforts to expand vocational programs for incarcerated women. For instance, data from the state of Washington showed that between fiscal years 2006 and 2009, they were expanding their vocational programs in women's prisons (Paris, 2009). Further, in fiscal year 2009, these three women's institutions saw close to 100% of available hours being used in these vocational programs (Paris, 2009). As previously noted, California is now offering training to female inmates in areas such as carpentry, electric work, HVAC, and plumbing (Tesfai, 2014). Texas has also expanded its programming to female inmates. While also offering carpentry, electrical trade training, and HVAC, they still do not offer welding, sheet metal, among other programs (Linder, 2018).

A program now being made available to women that had formerly only been available to men is coding. Providing inmates knowledge about the tech industry could be an extremely valuable skill upon release. In 2014, a nonprofit in California began a prison coding program available only to men. They have since expanded this program to several women's facilities (Stone, 2018). Additional efforts are being made outside of California to offer skills training to female inmates that had previously only been offered to men. For instance, a pilot coding program at a women's prison in Delaware began in 2017 (Stone, 2018). For three years prior, this opportunity had only been open to male inmates. This hopefully signals a change and move in the right direction that will continue to see women in prison being given expanded job training opportunities to provide them with skills they would not ordinarily receive. The nonprofit offering the training to inmates in Delaware points to the importance of technology in today's society, and the value that it can have on employment prospects for formerly incarcerated individuals (Stone, 2018). As with all programming, funding is key and additional/continued funding is needed to keep these programs going, make them available to more female inmates, and to ensure that the training lasts long enough for these women to grasp the material being offered (e.g., the initial class at the Delaware facility was only 12.5 h) (Stone, 2018). While we have seen improvements and increased offerings to incarcerated women, there is still work to be done.

9.3.5 Policy Recommendations: Vocational Programs for Female Inmates

The available information regarding vocational programming in women's prisons lends to a number of policy recommendations, including: (1) removing gender disparities and expanding program availability to women, (2) providing adequate funding, (3) making sure sufficient physical space is available for training, (4) sufficient buy-in from correctional staff, (5) thinking beyond just basic job skills (e.g., teamwork), and (6) removing obstacles to licenses and/or make sure that training provided is not in a profession that an individual will be blocked from upon release (Bazos & Hausman, 2004; Hersch & Meyers, 2019; Tesfai, 2014; Tonkin et al., 2004; Young & Mattucci, 2006). The goal is to improve the quantity and quality of these programs while also increasing the likelihood that these women will be successful upon release.

References

Alexander, M. (2010). *The new Jim Crow: Mass incarceration in the age of colorblindness.* New York: The New Press.
Aos, S., Miller, M., & Drake, E. (2006). *Evidence-based adult corrections programs: What works and what does not* (Washington State Institute for Public Policy, #06-01-1201, January 2006).
Anderson, S.V. (1995). Evaluation of the impact of correctional education programs on recidivism. Columbus, OH: Ohio Department of Rehabilitation and Corrections.
Arambula, R., & LeBlanc, L. (2018). *Inmate education: Encouraging results from pilot program.* Sacramento, CA: California Community Colleges Chancellor's Office.
Arditi, R., Goldberg, F., Hartle, M., & Phelps, J. (1973). The sexual segregation of American prisons. *Yale Law Journal, 82*, 1229–1273.
Austin, J., & Irwin, J. (2001). *It's about time: America's imprisonment binge* (3rd ed.). Halifax, Nova Scotia, Canada: Wadsworth Thomson Learning.
Barajas, M. (2018, April 24). Women in Texas prisons denied same academic, job training opportunities as incarcerated men. *Texas Observer.* Retrieved September 13, 2019, from https://www.texasobserver.org/women-in-texas-prisons-denied-same-academic-job-training-opportunities-as-incarcerated-men/
Batchelder, J. S., O'Neill, A., Rodriguez, A. D., & Tibbs, R. (2018). Overcoming the barriers to successful completion of GED programs among prison and jail inmates. *International Journal of Social Science Studies, 6*, 1–6.

Batchelder, J. S., & Pippert, J. M. (2001). Hard time or idle time: Factors affecting inmate choices between participation in prison work and education programs. *Prison Journal, 82,* 269–280.

Bazos, A., & Hausman, J. (2004). *Correctional education as a crime control program* (Prepared for the United States Department of Education, Office of Correctional Education).

Bloom, B., Chesney-Lind, M., & Owen, B. (1994). *Women in California prisons: Hidden victims of the war on drugs.* San Francisco: Center on Juvenile and Criminal Justice.

Bloom, B., & Steinhart, D. (1993). Why punish the children? A reappraisal of the children of incarcerated mothers in America. San Francisco: National Council on Crime and Delinquency.

Blume, S. (1990). Alcohol and drug problems in women: Old attitudes, new knowledge. In H. B. Milkman & L. I. Sederer (Eds.), *Treatment choices for alcoholism and substance abuse.* New York: Lexington.

Bozick, R., Steele, J., Davis, L., & Turner, S. (2018). Does providing inmates with education improve postrelease outcomes? A meta-analysis of correctional education programs in the United States. *Journal of Experimental Criminology, 14,* 389–428.

Bronson, J., & Carson, E. A. (2019). *Prisoners in 2017.* Washington, DC: Bureau of Justice Statistics.

Carson, E. A., & Anderson, E. (2016). *Prisoners in 2015.* Washington, DC: Bureau of Justice Statistics.

Case, P., & Fasenfest, D. (2004). Expectations for opportunities following prison education: A discussion of race and gender. *The Journal of Correctional Education, 55,* 24–39.

Cho, R. M., & Tyler, J. H. (2010). Does prison-based adult basic education improve post-release outcomes for male prisoners in Florida? *Crime & Delinquency, 59,* 975–1005.

Clear, T. R., & Austin, J. (2009). Reducing mass incarceration: Implications of the iron law of prison populations. *Harvard Law & Policy Review, 3,* 307–324.

Couloute, L. (2018). Getting back on course: Educational exclusion and attainment among formerly incarcerated people. *Prison Policy Initiative.* Retrieved Saturday 11, 2019, from https://www.prisonpolicy.org/reports/education.html

Crawford J. (1988). *Tabulation of a Nationwide survey of state correctional facilities for adult and juvenile female offenders.* College Park, MD: American Correctional Association.

Curcio, G., & Pattavina, A. (2018). Still paying for the past: Examining gender differences in employment among individuals with a criminal record. *Women & Criminal Justice, 28,* 375–396.

Davis, L. M., Bozick, R., Steele, J. L., Saunders, J., & Miles, J. N. V. (2013). *Evaluating the effectiveness of correctional education: A meta-analysis of programs that provide education to incarcerated adults.* Santa Monica, CA: RAND Corporation.

Davis, L. M., & Tolbert, M. C. (2019). *Evaluation of North Carolina's pathways from prison to postsecondary education program.* Santa Monica, CA: RAND Corporation.

Dortch, C., & James, N. (2019). *Prisoners' eligibility for pell grants: Issues for congress* (Congressional Research Service. R45737).

Duwe, G., & Clark, V. (2014). The effect of prison-based educational programing on recidivism and employment. *Prison Journal, 94,* 454–478.

Erzen, T., Gould, M. R., & Lewen, J. (2019). *Equity and excellence in practice: A guide for higher education in prison* (Prison University Project; The Alliance for Higher Education in Prison).

Federal Bureau of Prisons. (n.d.). *Female offenders.* Retrieved September 13, 2019, from https://www.bop.gov/inmates/custody_and_care/female_offenders.jsp#female_facilities

Fogel, C., & Martin, S. (1992). The mental health of incarcerated women. *Western Journal of Nursing Research, 14,* 30–40.

Gabel, K., & Johnston, D. (1995). *Children of incarcerated parents.* New York: Lexington.

Glick, R., & Neto, V. (1977). *National Study of Women's Correctional Programs (National Institute of Law Enforcement and Criminal Justice).* Washington, DC: U.S. Government Printing Office.

Government Accountability Office. (2019, April 4). Federal student aid: Actions needed to evaluate Pell Grant pilot for incarcerated students. Retrieved September 12, 2019, from https://www.gao.gov/mobile/products/GAO-19-130?utm_campaign=usgao_email&utm_content=daybook&utm_medium=email&utm_source=govdelivery

Greenfeld, L., & Snell, T. (1999). Special Report: Women Offenders. Washington, DC: U.S. Department of Justice, Bureau of Justice Statistics. https://www.bjs.gov/content/pub/pdf/wo.pdf

Greene, S. (2018, May 21). "Women can do this": Female inmates in Texas find fulfillment in learning technical skills, but they have fewer options than men. *The Texas Tribune*. Retrieved September 11, 2019, from https://www.texastribune.org/2018/05/21/women-are-offered-variety-programming-while-prison-gender-disparities-/

Hairston, C. F. (1991). Family ties during imprisonment: Important to whom and for what? *Journal of Sociology and Welfare, 18*, 87–104.

Hanks, A. (2016, November 18). *Now is the time to invest in apprenticeships*. Retrieved September 11, 2019, from https://www.americanprogress.org/issues/economy/reports/2016/11/18/292558/now-is-the-time-to-invest-in-apprenticeships/

Harer, M. D. (1995). Recidivism among federal prisoners released in 1987. *Journal of Correctional Education, 46*, 98–128.

Harris, A. (2018, April 30). Women in prison take home economics, while men take carpentry. *The Atlantic*. Retrieved September 11, 2019, from https://www.theatlantic.com/education/archive/2018/04/the-continuing-disparity-in-womens-prison-education/559274/

Haynes, D. D. (2018, July 27). Throw the books at them: How more training for Wisconsin's prisoners could help companies. *Milwaukee Journal Sentinel*. Retrieved from https://perma.cc/MH86-MPT4

Helper, S., Noonan, R., Nicholson, J. R., & Langdon, D. (2016). *The benefits and costs of apprenticeship: A business perspective*. Case Western Reserve University. Department of Commerce. Retrieved September 11, 2019, from https://www.commerce.gov/sites/default/files/migrated/reports/the-benefits-and-costs-of-apprenticeships-a-business-perspective.pdf

Hersch, J., & Meyers, E. E. (2019). *The gendered burdens of conviction and collateral consequences on employment*. Vanderbilt University Law School, Legal Studies Research Paper Series. https://papers.ssrn.com/sol3/papers.cfm?abstract_id=3397309

Hobby, L., Walsh, B., & Delaney, R. (2019). *A piece of the puzzle: State financial aid for incarcerated students*. New York: Vera Institute of Justice.

Holzer, H. J., Raphael, S., & Stoll, M. A. (2006). Perceived criminality, criminal background checks, and the racial hiring practices of employers. *The Journal of Law and Economics, 49*, 451–480.

Huling, T. (2002). Building a prison economy in rural America. In Mauer, M. & Chesney-Lind, M. (Eds.), Invisible punishment: The collateral consequences of mass imprisonment (pp. 197–213). New York: New Press.

Hunt, P., Smart, R., Jonsson, L., & Tsang, F. (2018). *Incentivizing employers to hire ex-offenders: What policies are most effective?*. Santa Monica, CA: RAND Corporation. https://www.rand.org/pubs/research_briefs/RB10003.html

Islam-Zwart, K. A., & Vik, P. W. (2004). Female adjustment to incarceration as influenced by sexual assault history, criminal justice and behavior. *American Association for Correctional Psychology, 31*, 521–541.

James, D. J., & Glaze, L. E. (2006). *Special report: Mental health problems of prison and jail inmates*. Washington, DC: U.S. Department of Justice, Bureau of Justice Statistics. https://www.bjs.gov/content/pub/pdf/mhppji.pdf

Janusz, L. (1991). *Separate but unequal: Women behind bars in Massachusetts* (pp. 6–17). Odyssey (Fall).

Knepper, P. (1990). Selective participation, effectiveness, and prison college programs. *Offender Counseling, Services, and Rehabilitation., 14*, 109–135.

Lattimore, P. K., Witte, A. D., & Baker, J. R. (1990). Experimental assessment of the effect of vocational training on youthful property offenders. *Evaluation Review, 14*, 115–133.

La Vigne, N. G., Brooks, L. E., & Shollenberger, T. L. (2009). *Women on the outside: Understanding the experiences of female prisoners returning to Houston, Texas*. Washington, DC: Urban Institute.

Lahm, K. F. (2000). Equal or equitable: An exploration of educational and vocational program availability for male and female offenders. *Federal Probation, 64*, 39–46.

Lawrence, S., Mears, D. P., Dubin, C., & Travis, J. (2002). *The practice and promise of prison programming*. Washington, DC: Urban Institute.

Linder, L. (2018). *An unsupported population: The treatment of women in Texas' criminal justice system*. Austin, TX: Texas Criminal Justice Coalition.

MacGillis, A. (2001, September 3). *Union plumbing for new members: United Association taking novel steps to fill its ranks*. https://www.baltimoresun.com/news/bs-xpm-2001-09-03-0109030114-story.html

MacKenzie, D. (2006). *What works in corrections: Reducing the criminal activities of offenders and delinquents*. New York: Cambridge University Press.

Mageehon, A. (2006). What makes a "good" teacher "good": Women in transition from prison to community reflect. *The Journal of Correctional Education, 57*, 145–157.

Mauer, M. (2006). *Race to incarcerate*. New York: The New Press.

McCarthy, H. J. (2006). Educating felons: Reflections on higher education in prison. *Radical History Review, 96*, 87–94.

Mercer, C. (2004). *Federal Pell grants for prisoners*. Washington, DC: Congressional Research Services. https://perma.cc/6SNY-9BFP

Messina, N., Burdon, W., & Prendergast, M. (2001). *A profile of women in prison-based therapeutic communities* (Draft). Los Angeles: UCLA Integrated Substance Abuse Program, Drug Abuse Research Center.

Morash, M., Haarr, R., & Rucker, L. (1994). A comparison for women and men in U.S. prisons in the 1980s. *Crime and Delinquency, 2*, 197–221.

Mukamal, D., & Silbert, R. (2018). Don't stop now: California leads the nation in using public higher education to address mass incarceration. In *Will we continue?* Stanford: Law School, Stanford Criminal Justice Center (SCJC).

National Center for Education Statistics. (2016). *Highlights from the U.S. PIAAC survey of incarcerated adults: Their skills, work experience, education and training*. Washington, DC: U.S. Department of Education

Nellis, A. (2017). *Still life: America's increasing use of life and long-term sentences*. Washington, DC: The Sentencing Project.

Oakford, P., Brumfield, C., Goldvale, C., Tatum, L., diZerega, M., & Patrick, F. (2019). *Investing in futures: Economic and fiscal benefits of postsecondary education in prison*. Georgetown Center of Poverty and Inequality & Vera Institute of Justice.

Owen, B., & Bloom, B. (1995). *Profiling the needs of California's female prisoners: A needs assessment*. Washington, DC: National Institute of Corrections.

Palmer, S. M. (2012). Postsecondary correctional education. *Adult Learning, 23*(4), 163–169.

Paris, M. (2009). *Offender education services: Performance report fiscal year 2009*. Tumwater, WA: Washington State Department of Corrections.

Pollock, J. (2002). *Women, prison, and crime* (2nd ed.). Pacific Grove, CA: Brooks/Cole.

UCLA Prison Education Program. (2019). Retrieved September 13, 2019, from https://prisonedu-program.ucla.edu/

Rafter, N. (1995). *Partial justice: Women, prison, and social control* (2nd ed.). Boston: Northeastern University Press.

Reed, D., Liu, A. Y., Kleinman, R., Mastri, A., Reed, D., Sattar, S., et al. (2012). *An effectiveness assessment and cost-benefit analysis of registered apprenticeship in 10 states*. Oakland, CA: Mathematica Policy Research.

Ring, K. A., & Gill, M. (2017). *Using time to reduce crime: Federal prisoner survey results show ways to reduce recidivism*. Washington, DC: Families Against Mandatory Minimums.

Rivera, C. (2015, August 5). Four prisons in California to get community college programs. *Los Angeles Times*. Retrieved September 11, 2019, from https://www.latimes.com/local/education/la-me-pell-inmate-column-20150805-story.html

Rodriguez, M. N., & Avery, B. (2016). *Unlicensed & untapped: Removing barriers to state occupational licenses for people with records*. New York: National Employment Law Project.

Rose, C. (2004). Women's participation in prison education: What we know and what we don't know. *The Journal of Correctional Education, 55*, 78–100.

Ross, R., & Fabiano, E. (1986). *Female offenders: Correctional afterthoughts*. Jefferson, NC: McFarland.

Ryan, T. (1984). *Adult female offenders and institutional programs: A state of the art analysis*. Washington, DC: National Institute of Corrections.

Sawyer, W.. (2018, January 9). The gender divide: Tracking women's state prison growth. *Prison Policy Initiative*. Retrieved from https://www.prisonpolicy.org/reports/women_overtime.html.

Saylor, W. G., & Gaes, G. G. (1997). Training inmates through industrial work participation and vocational and apprenticeship instruction. *Corrections Management Quarterly, 1*, 32–43.

Simon, R. (1975). *The contemporary woman and crime*. Washington, DC: U.S. Government Printing Office.

Smith, S. (1991, March). *Women in prison* (Bureau of Justice Statistics Special Report).

Sobel, S. (1982). Difficulties experienced by women in prison. *Psychology of Women Quarterly, 82*, 107–117.

Steurer, S. J., & Smith, L. G. (2003). *Three-state recidivism study: Executive summary*. Lanham, MD: Correctional Education Association; Centerville, UT: Management & Training Corporation Institute.

Stone, Z. (2018, August 3). Women-led initiatives are closing the gender gap in prison coding programs. *Vice*. Retrieved September 13, 2019, from https://www.vice.com/en_us/article/zmkqe8/women-learning-to-code-prison-program

Tesfai, L. (2014). *California's in-prison vocational education: An analysis of program access and alignment to labor market demands*. Legislative Data Center, California Senate Office of Research. Retrieved September 13, 2019, from https://sor.senate.ca.gov/sites/sor.senate.ca.gov/files/Tesfai%20APA.pdf

The Sentencing Project. (2019). *Fact sheet: Incarcerated women and girls*. https://www.sentencingproject.org/wp-content/uploads/2016/02/Incarcerated-Women-and-Girls.pdf

Tonkin, P., Dickie, J., Alemagno, S., & Grove, W. (2004). Women in jail: "Soft skills" and barriers to employment. *Journal of Offender Rehabilitation, 38*, 51–71.

Tonry, M. (2011). *Punishing race: A continuing American dilemma*. New York: Oxford University Press.

U.S. Department of Education Press Office. (2016). *12,000 incarcerated students to enroll in postsecondary educational and training programs through department's new second chance Pell pilot program*. https://perma.cc/BU4R-UQ3D.

U.S. Department of Education Press Release. (2016, June 24). *12,000 incarcerated students to enroll in postsecondary educational and training programs through education department's new second chance Pell pilot program*. Retrieved September 12, 2019, from https://www.ed.gov/news/press-releases/12000-incarcerated-students-enroll-postsecondary-educational-and-training-programs-through-education-departments-new-second-chance-pell-pilot-program

U.S. Department of Education Press Release. (2019a, May 20). *Secretary DeVos builds on "Rethink Higher Education," agenda, expands opportunities for students through innovative experimental sites*. Retrieved September 12, 2019, from https://www.ed.gov/news/press-releases/secretary-devos-builds-rethink-higher-education-agenda-expands-opportunities-students-through-innovative-experimental-sites

U.S. Department of Education Press Release. (2019b, June 25). *Prepared remarks by Secretary Devos at Tulsa Community College's second chance commencement*. Retrieved September 12, 2019, from https://www.ed.gov/news/speeches/prepared-remarks-secretary-devos-tulsa-community-colleges-second-chance-commencement

Van Stelle, K.R., Moberg, D.P., & Welnetz, T. (1998). Specialized Training and Employment Project (STEP): Outcome evaluation report. Madison, WI: University of Wisconsin Center for Health Policy and Program Evaluation.

Weishet, R. (1985). Trends in programs for female offenders: The use of private agencies as service providers. *International Journal of Offender Therapy and Comparative Criminology, 1*, 35–42.

Western, B., & Pettit, B. (2010, September 28). *Collateral costs: Incarceration's effect on economic mobility*. Washington, DC: The Pew Charitable Trusts. https://perma.cc/N75T-XGRS.

Wilson, D. B., Gallagher, C. A., & Mackenzie, D. L. (2000). A meta-analysis of corrections-based education, vocation, and work programs for adult offenders. *Journal of Research in Crime & Delinquency, 37*, 347–368.

Young, D. S., & Mattucci, R. F. (2006). Enhancing the vocational skills of incarcerated women through a plumbing maintenance program. *The Journal of Correctional Education, 57*, 126–140.

Zoukis, C. (2014). *College for convicts: The case for higher education in American prisons*. Jefferson, NC: McFarland & Company, Inc. Publishers.

Zoukis, C. (2017, April 17). Innovative prison programs boost opportunities for female inmates. *HuffPost*. Retrieved September 12, 2019, from https://www.huffpost.com/entry/innovative-prison-programs-boost-opportunities-for_b_58f4ff4ee4b048372700da4a?guccounter=2

Chapter 10
Women Working in Male Prisons and Jails

Catherine Fontenot

10.1   An Insider's Voice

Much like the rise of the female incarcerated population, so too has the number of female professionals increased inside our jails and prisons. Careers for women in the field of corrections are limitless today. The first female warden in America, Mary Weed, like so many other women who became the first of anything, had elevated to the title because of the untimely death of her husband in 1793. It would take more than another couple dozen years for the first female correctional officer to be hired in 1822 (Winters, 2014). Our pioneer women trickled in for decades after that and most were employed solely in female institutions to "babysit" the weaker sex. As equal opportunity spread so did the chances increase for women to become incarcerated and as a consequence more matrons, as they were called, reported for duty.

However, in male facilities, female correctional officers were still a rarity 50 years ago. Then came the 1970s and major USSC decisions provided that women had the right to seek equal opportunity in employment without unfair treatment (Feder, 2015). Prior to these important promises of protection, female corrections officers (or guards as we were called once upon a time) were assigned to posts outside the secure perimeter, like towers, and if assigned inside were working inside secure, locked control centers or "cages" as they are commonly referred. Most women remained at entry-level positions until their retirements due to the few positions open to them in these male jails and prisons. For years this continued as correctional unions, mostly occupied and headed up by men clinging to the ways of the past, considered allowing women more access to jobs placing them in contact with male prisoners a threat to the security and stability of the institution.

C. Fontenot (✉)
East Baton Rouge Sheriff's Office, Baton Rouge, LA, USA

© Springer Nature Switzerland AG 2020   155
J. Hector (ed.), *Women and Prison*,
https://doi.org/10.1007/978-3-030-46172-0_10

As more and more women divorced from traditional gender roles, breaking into the work force at record numbers to support their families, entry level jobs no longer paid their bills. The creation of a union in one of the most infamous state penitentiaries in the Deep South by a courageous, newly divorced woman who wanted to apply for a supervisor position resulted in Shirley Coody becoming the first female supervisor of the Main Prison at the Louisiana State Penitentiary at Angola in the early 1980s (Turner, 2000). She, now an Assistant Warden, continues to fight for the rights of and has opened many locked gates for both female and male employees and is known and respected across the country. Following her example, once the ceiling was broken, many future stars emerged to shine light upon the old myths that women could not succeed in this male dominated world. While some men remained in the dark ages, more men (first of which were the male inmates) came to see that women, who calmed the environment and assisted in the collection of intel due to their attention to detail and their promotion of more verbal communication, could make their jobs safer. While the powers proclaimed, "nothing works," it clearly appeared that "women worked."

The following decades would see women soar to positions far higher than first line supervision. Across the USA, there were first captains, majors, colonels, assistant wardens, wardens, assistant secretaries, and secretaries of corrections. The occupation of women throughout the field did not cause the "softening" of security or safety as it had been predicted. In fact, as incarcerated male, female and juvenile populations increased both in numbers and in years to be served, having a strong female presence balanced the ability to create a more normative atmosphere where compassionate corrections could occur. It can be argued that male and juvenile minority demographic populations take instructions and orders from females better than they do those from males or those who approach with a more paternalistic style. The matriarchal style is said by many, including the FBI LEEDA, to be the more preferred method of obtaining compliance (Wane, 2019). However, the availability of both sexes and styles is optimal to the mission. With both present, the ever-changing dynamics of the many characters and behaviors present when staff and inmates come to share such secured and secluded spaces, correctional environments accomplish accountability and rehabilitation more effectively.

Most people unfamiliar with corrections seem to think that physical strength is required more than mental strength and emotional intelligence to survive and thrive in the prison or jail setting. Shockingly, it is actually the opposite. Women excel in male prisons largely because the majority of inmates are used to female authority figures. Women tend to be more patient and less threatening which can lead to greater communication, especially when de-escalating a critical situation, but the presence of women stabilizes and norms the environment, making it more like free world society, which allows space and time for inmates to practice better interpersonal skills. The presence of women also softens the way men interact with each other—many inmates throughout the years have commented that they would not want their mothers, wives, or sisters exposed to crudeness and violence and they in turn policed each other in an effort to protect female officers. The logic being that they (the prisoners) would continue to be vilified by the public if they victimized their female overseers and if they could be overseen by women then they must be worthy of a second chance to live among the law abiding.

Inmate living areas changed as a result of cross gender supervision once women began spreading in number among all ranks and posts. There were gender specific jobs established so that appropriate supervision could occur in a way that respected the privacy of male inmates when they were using bathroom facilities. Females entering male housing areas were announced so that inmates could have time to make themselves decent. While some critics believe this takes away from security, practitioners (those in the trenches) know that it contributes to reinforcing the respect men and women should have for one another.

Even male correctional staff who were hesitant about female staff seemed to grow in appreciation for the fact that inmates seemed less combative when a woman was present making for more peaceful shifts. Male and female co-workers' relationships improved as well because the proverbial white elephant was now like the bull in the china shop—out and about everywhere one turned, impossible to hide from. Realistically, at any point in the day or night, you could possibly be in the presence of someone who reminded you of your mother, wife, sister, or daughter (Lambert, Paoline, Hogan, & Baker, 2007).

Women also make intelligence gathering more successful. Men simply like to talk to women. Men love to brag to women, especially about dramatic events such as fights, escape plans, and suicide attempts. Recaptured inmates would generously and delightfully recount their escape tales—step by step—if there was a woman in their presence. Lessons learned from these interchanges result in corrective actions and policies following to repair breaches in security as well as to improve chase team protocols.

As women continue to move into the bowels of the prison—we see them in kitchens, sewing industries, administrative offices, timekeeping, control centers, armories, and transportation. Now, 225 years after Mary Weed became the first female warden in America and 196 years after the first female correctional officer was hired at Sing Sing prison we can challenge the original belief that women cannot contribute positively to corrections because of their smaller, weaker frames, and their perceived propensity to be attracted to "bad boys."

The website of the *Correctional Peace Officer's Foundation* (cpof.org) noted deaths of 27 female correctional officers/employees (nurses, clerks, and teachers included) killed by inmates indicate that most were strangled and/or stabbed. More were attacked and assaulted during escape attempts than were victims of a sexual assault. Deaths from 1977 to 2018 indicated that the deadliest assignment within a prison setting were kitchens and industry training/work areas. Two were killed in prison chapels and a warden's wife (who was also employed as a clerk) was murdered along with her husband in their home on the grounds of the prison. The number of female officers shot and killed by inmates during transports are also increasing. None of these murders occurred at a female facility.

In addition to those murdered by inmates, two women were killed by a deranged male co-worker who shot them in their employee housing area. Female correctional officers also died from disease, heart attacks, and aneurism. Others died in work related motor vehicle crashes (CPFO, 2020). Compared to their male counterparts, women are not more likely to die in the line of duty nor be taken hostage simply because they are female. The statistics also show that compared to female patrol officers, women working in prisons and or probation and parole for that matter are less likely to die in the line of duty than males.

As for falling in love, it is a fact that male officers have lost their reputations, careers, and freedom from engaging in inappropriate relationships with those under their care and custody in ever more increasing numbers since the increased use of direct supervision, community corrections, and from prolonged jail and prison stays. It is less about gender and more about length of experience and training. A role played by officers with <3 years is common denominators in most major security breaches. And in the more rare case, of a seasoned correctional staff member crossing the line, he/she has become too comfortable with a trusted inmate and sharing and revealing too much over the course of a 12 h shift causing them to become isolated from their family and friends who they struggle to see while splitting their waking, remaining hours with sleep. Free people, men and women alike, find themselves most alert in the inmate world in order to survive and ironically sleeping through their outside relationships. It is not surprising nor shocking that we become close to those we work with especially if the work is done in an intense fishbowl. Speaking of the fishbowl, all officers should be on guard for the piranha in the tank.

Of course let us not believe that there are women who have failed to live up to professional standards and due to their shortcomings and sometimes outright criminal activity, they have further supported the argument that women will fall short and cannot perform well because they simply do not belong in a male prison (Fantz, 2015). Again, these types of officers do not belong in a female prison either and have fallen in these traditionally acceptable arenas as well. Therefore, beyond gender, providing training that is constantly evolving and is fluid and flexible to work in the ever changing and always challenging penal environment is paramount. It is better to promote and support mentors of both genders who can share their experiences of what works in modern corrections, which more so now than ever is focused on providing an atmosphere conducive to peaceful, citizen oriented, successful reentry. In order to achieve this we must inspire those working in the field to record their stories so that others entering this line of work can build upon the progress they helped to create. There is no doubt that we have come a long way—not only women, but the professional correctional officer and administrator who continue to stretch the boundaries of what can be accomplished when we create a safe place where true crisis intervention of every sort imaginable can occur. One gender alone cannot achieve peace for all—just as one gender alone cannot serve to protect the other.

10.2   And Thank Goodness There Are Others

Fortunately, we have mentors; and in the below case, legends, who are easily reachable, gracious, and generous in their willingness to share their life experiences with us. Please enjoy the following interview with Corrections Consultant and former California Warden Susan E. Poole (Poole, 2019, Personal Communication).

Susan Poole, Criminal Justice Consultant: Positions and Titles Held (1972–2001)

- Teaching Assistant
- Correctional Officer
- Correctional Program Supervisor
- Correctional Sergeant
- Correctional Counselor
- Associate Personnel Analyst—Headquarters
- Staff Services Manager I (Assistant Chief of Personnel)—Headquarters
- Correctional Counselor III (Classification Staff Representative)—Headquarters
- Program Administrator/Facility Captain—Headquarters
- Assistant Transition Coordinator—Special Assignment—Headquarters
- Correctional Administrator (Chief of Institutions Services)—Headquarters
- Career Executive Assignment III (CEA III)—Assistant deputy Director, Institutions Division.
- Warden—California Institution for Women

10.2.1 Where Are Our Strengths and Where Are Our Weaknesses?

I believe that women bring an approach and style to leadership which actually helps overcome challenges that organizations routinely face. Women tend to be relationship oriented and to value relationships with others. This is often viewed as a weakness in corrections, but the ability to be inclusive and incorporate shared values into the goal setting process can result in the development of strong productive teams.

Women tend to listen more to the views of others, seek input from a variety of sources, including those who disagree with their point of view. As a result they can gain a broader perspective on issues in the decision making process. I find that women who use relationship building and listening skills to lead their teams create an environment where their staff take ownership for the results.

In corrections, information in a male dominated environment is often held close to the vest, resulting in poor communication, lost time and mismanagement of projects/resources, and even lawsuits. This is a luxury most agencies cannot afford.

Women have the ability to make everyone feel that their contributions are being valued. They value sharing information, ensuring that everyone has the information and resources they need to be successful. The leadership skills of persuasion and negotiation come quite naturally to women leaders. This partly stems from the fact that they are empathic listeners, learning about people in ways that enable them to appeal to their unique needs and sensibilities.

I am confident in my abilities and aware of my strengths and weaknesses. I have a strong work ethic and I can work both independently and as a team member depending upon the situation. I hired smart people and encouraged their participation, but it was important to give credit and recognition to subordinates who contributed to the success of a project. I enjoyed sharing my knowledge, but also learning from other members of my team.

The following are traits that women exhibit that may be construed as weaknesses.

10.2.1.1 Lack of Self-Confidence

Women sometimes fail to take on the challenges of new assignments/promotions for fear that they will not be able to compete with their male counterparts. This is a self-fulfilling prophesy that eliminates them from the process without actually knowing their real chances of achieving career success.

10.2.1.2 Vulnerability

Being vulnerable means owning up to your mistakes and admitting when you are wrong. In a power-based environment this may be perceived as weakness, but in fact, if the leader can be honest about their own mistakes and shortcomings, team members may feel more comfortable about doing the same.

10.2.1.3 Emotions

In a masculine dominated environment crying is seen as a weakness, and there is higher scrutiny of emotionality in the workplace of women in corrections. Women who want to be viewed as strong refrain from showing emotions and often avoid things that appear overly feminine. They do so at the risk of being viewed as "cold" by other women in the organization. Women who want to be viewed as strong often isolate themselves from others and fail to network or call on others for support, as they do not want to appear to be "needy." This can lead to loneliness and get in the way of true collaboration when required.

10.2.1.4 Sensitivity to Criticism

Women often overreact to feedback, taking it personally. First, it is important to consider the source, and whether or not you value their input. If so, it is worth it to consider their input objectively. Then, it is important to reevaluate the basis for your own actions. Feedback is good, and even if not accurate affords the opportunity to become aware of how you are being perceived in a given situation. Ultimately you are responsible for your decisions and actions. Evaluating feedback can help put things in perspective.

10.2.2   What Are Some of the Obstacles for Women You Have Seen Change Over the Course of Your Career?

Work flexibility is a challenge for women who are caregivers for their children. This can be true for single parent women as well as those in a married/committed relationship. These responsibilities often fall to women, thus limiting their ability to be available for some assignments. Flexible work schedules are not a hallmark of correctional work thus this limits women's ability to balance their career and personal priorities, and can contribute to absenteeism and lower productivity.

Often upward mobility and promotion require making physical moves from one part of the state or country to another. Women leaders that I spoke with tell me that they sometimes pass on these opportunities, because they fear their partners (usually male) are not willing to be uprooted to support their moves. Conversely, women have told me that their male partners often take assignments and advise them of the move, and expect their support. Women often believe that they have to make decisions between making promotions, requiring relocation versus sustaining a marriage/relationship.

An additional factor that women face is when they find themselves as the breadwinner or is in a position of higher authority than her male partner. Some men find it difficult to accept this role reversal and this may be a source of frustration for some women in their relationship. In these circumstances some may choose not to take promotions so as not to impact their relationships.

In the past, self-doubt and the belief that they have to act and behave like their male counterparts have been a deterrent for some women. In my experience, more and more women are now accepting the fact that women's ways of leading have a legitimate place in corrections and can add value.

Often, we are our worst enemies. Our self-doubt and insecurities cause women to worry that they themselves and therefore other women are not good enough. This often holds women back from applying for positions. Women should apply for and take exams that they minimally qualify for as a way to gain experience and identify where they have gaps. Following an interview, speak with the interviewer if the circumstance permits and ask in what areas there could be improvements.

In some organizations many believe that opportunities for women are limited and that one woman's success is a lost opportunity for the rest. This is a scarcity mentality and should be discouraged. Having an abundance mentality allows that when one women makes it to a position of leadership, she can pave the way for others.

Often, women in leadership positions in corrections are working in an environment where there are few female peers, and they may feel isolated and disconnected. Joining women's professional organizations and participation in single gender leadership programs such as those sponsored by the National Institute of Corrections (NIC) can provide contact with a peer groups of women leaders from other jurisdictions. These programs provide opportunities for networking and exploration of shared experiences while at the same time building leadership skills.

And just in case the reader is interested in seeing another female professional's rise up the ladder…

10.3   The Author's Career Path in Bullets

- Majored in Criminal Justice at the University of Southwestern Louisiana from 1988 to 1992.
- Started career with the Louisiana Department of Public Safety and Corrections in August 1992 at Dixon Correctional Institute.

    - Cadet, tower guard, front gate
    - Sergeant, ACA office
    - Special assignment to assist Secretary of Corrections with statewide accreditation
    - Human resource analyst
    - Classification Officer

- Transferred to Louisiana State Penitentiary in August 1995.

    - Classification officer
    - Accreditation manager
    - Public information officer
    - Executive staff officer
    - Director of classification
    - Assistant warden of treatment
    - Assistant warden of programming
    - Special assignment to director of storm recovery post Hurricanes Katrina and Rita
    - Assistant warden of Treatment Center

- Auditor with the American Correctional Association
- Certified Corrections Executive
- Earned a Master's in Criminology from Grambling State University in 2006.
- Transferred to Office of Youth Development in 2006.

    - Youth facility director, Acadiana Center for Youth project
    - Jetson Correctional Center for Youth director

- Transferred to Louisiana State Penitentiary in April 2007.

    - Assistant warden of Support Services
    - Assistant warden of Programming

- Adjunct Professor at Louisiana Technical College, Greensburg/Angola and Baton Rouge Community College
- Transferred to Department of Justice in January 2015.

- Special assistant to attorney general

- Began career in local government in March 2016 with the Lafayette Parish Sheriff's Office.

  - Warden
  - Major of corrections

- Adjunct professor at the University of Louisiana at Lafayette
- Expert witness (in jail death case in the state of Colorado)
- Transferred to East Baton Rouge Sheriff's Office in July 2018.

  - Deputy warden
  - Major of corrections

10.4 Them Too

In the wake of "Me Too," many arguments have been made for and against the facts surrounding how we protect, support, and apologize to women in hopes that victimization in the pursuit of equal opportunity and as by granted to us in the Bill of Rights is deterred. This author begs readers to consider advocating "Them Too." Those of us in corrections learned long ago that "Us vs. them" (Handel, 2013) simply does not work in the best interest of all.

Justice cannot be maintained without balance for all people no matter our individual differences. We must rethink the routes by which we advocate reform. An all-inclusive strategy, rather than picking one side over another, allows us to remain on track to obtain justice for all or community justice as opposed to criminal justice or victim justice. Precious resources will go further and accomplish more for many if applied with lasting peace rather than quick, knee-jerk appeasement in mind.

Although "it" happened to "me too," we are morally obligated to care for "them too." Fortunately not all of us will be victimized and unfortunately not all of us will be protected, we should and must still care and consider each other. Our freedom depends on it. Our lives rely on it. Equal opportunity and treatment under our laws and in our daily interactions are key to how successful we are in making corrective policies that govern and guide our actions.

Since it is women who give birth and sustain life within their bodies, it is natural for women to appreciate that overall health in total institutions are dictated by how well the keepers keep the kept. Again, not that women know it all, but women innately understand that creating an environment that enables and inspires change is within their reach and under their immediate control (most of the time). Therefore, the addition and promotion of the number of women in the field of corrections at every level, without a doubt, improve our chances to save lives both inside and outside jail and prison walls.

For this author, serving others is the ONLY reason for working in corrections. The sacrifices that come with service, although great, pale in comparison to the losses and even tragedies that would occur, if only a few of us chose to dedicate our time to do so. We are so fortunate for all those who created places for us to serve, especially in those places traditionally thought to not be places we should be or ever want to go. Jails and prisons, like the moon, needed to be explored but not only by men for all mankind. Footprints left by the women who have and continue to serve continue to lead us toward more peaceful, law abiding, healthy, and hopeful communities we long to live, grow, and love together in.

References

Correctional Peace Officers Foundation. (2020). Retrieved February 24, 2020, from http://cpof.org
Fantz, A. (2015). *Drugs, money, love and cell phones: How prison guards go bad*. Retrieved February 24, 2020, from https://www.cnn.com/2015/06/25/us/new-york-prison-break-contraband-smuggle/index.html
Feder, J. (2015). *Sex discrimination and the United States Supreme Court: Developments in the law*. Congressional Research Service. Retrieved February 24, 2020, from https://fas.org/sgp/crs/misc/RL30253.pdf
Handel, S. (2013). *The us vs. them mentality: How group thinking can irrationally divide us*. Retrieved February 24, 2020, from https://www.theemotionmachine.com/the-us-vs-them-mentality-how-group-thinking-can-irrationally-divide-us/
Lambert, E. G., Paoline, E. A., Hogan, N. L., & Baker, D. N. (2007). Gender similarities and differences in correctional staff work attitudes and perceptions of the work environment. *Western Criminology Review, 8*(1), 16–31.
Turner, J. (2000). Who's afraid of 'the walk?' *AFSEME*. Retrieved February 24, 2020, from https://www.afscme.org/news/publications/newsletters/works/novemberdecember-2000/whos-afraid-of-the-walk.
Wane, J. (2019). Mama Pam: The Auckland prison officer dishing out tough love to inmates. *Noted*. Retrieved February 24, 2020, from https://www.noted.co.nz/currently/currently-profiles/mama-pam-auckland-prison-officer-dishing-out-tough-love-to-inmates
Winters, R. (2014). *Understanding and enhancing the value of female corrections professionals*. Retrieved February 24, 2020, from http://www.corrections.com/news/article/36734-understanding-and-enhancing-the-value-of-female-corrections-professionals

Chapter 11
Concluding Remarks

Jada Hector

This work was created by both academics and practitioners coming together to discuss the needs and issues (change this word) as it relates to women and prison. Uniquely, each of the female writers featured here comes from different backgrounds and career paths to paint a unique picture of the overall state of affairs facing justice-involved girls and women across America.

One major, reoccurring, and consistent thread throughout these chapters appears to be the lack of research and information. This could stem from the lack of dialogue around the topic of justice-involved girls and women. By no means is this text a fully comprehensive work but, the goal of this text is to serve as a beginning point to spur dialogue. It should offer a beginning to conversations and sparks of insight to discover what is missing that may best serve the girls and women in jails and prisons not only in the USA, but anywhere in the world. What unique needs do females face that can be tackled in future programming? How do stakeholders come together to best serve the needs of girls and women, and subsequently, our future generations?

- *If the vast majority of incarcerated girls and women will be eventually released, how are we working together to best prepare each individual for success?*

Fortunately, much of the work discussed and cited by the authors throughout this edited volume appears to be richly interdisciplinary. These articles and research endeavors appear from not only criminology and criminal justice, but also many areas of psychology, mental health and counseling. In addition, these works appear in public health, women's studies, sexuality and reproductive journals, and nursing as well. This is to show that many researchers and practitioners alike are coming together to discuss the important topic of incarcerated girls and women.

The authors represent this variety in disciplinary backgrounds and are practitioners, educators, and academics in many areas.

J. Hector (✉)
University of Louisiana at Lafayette, Lafayette, LA, USA

© Springer Nature Switzerland AG 2020
J. Hector (ed.), *Women and Prison*,
https://doi.org/10.1007/978-3-030-46172-0_11

Jodi Lane, Ph.D., is Professor of criminology in the Department of Sociology and Criminology and Law at the University of Florida. She is interested in reactions to crime from both an individual and policy perspective. Her primary research areas include the causes and consequences of fear of crime and juvenile justice and corrections policy. She and her colleagues recently authored Fear of Crime in the United States: Causes, Consequences and Contradictions (2014) and Encountering Correctional Populations: A Practical Guide for Researchers (2018). Dr. Lane has received many accolades over the years, including being cited by several independent peer-reviewed studies as a top elite and prolific scholar in criminology and criminal justice.

Karen Smith is a U.S. Navy veteran and a retired detective from the Jacksonville Sheriff's Office in Florida. She served as both a major case detective for nearly 11 years and as the training coordinator for 3 years, developing curriculums and instructing 26 detectives in the Crime Scene Unit and for attorneys in the Fourth Judicial Circuit. She conducted 500 death investigations and worked on 20,000 other cases ranging from burglaries to multiple shootings and police-involved homicides. She moved to Knoxville, TN after being hired as the Training Consultant for the National Forensic Academy at the University of Tennessee. While at UT, she had the distinct privilege of working with Dr. Bill Bass, Dr. Arpad Vass, Dr. Murray Marks, Drs. Richard and Lee Jantz, Dr. Darinka Mileusnic, and many more distinguished field experts at the Anthropological Research Facility (The Body Farm). Karen has appeared on NBC's Dateline 20/20, CNN's Inside Man with Morgan Spurlock, the PBS documentary How Sherlock Changed the World, HLN's Lies, Crimes and Video, CNN's Special Investigation into the Missy Bevers case, and ID Discovery's Murder Board. She currently appears regularly on Crime Stories with Nancy Grace on her Sirius XM radio show that also airs on Fox Nation. She hosts the podcast "Shattered Souls: A Forensic Detective's Diary" (available in May 2020) and has been hired as a forensic expert for two new unscripted television shows, filming hundreds of hours of forensic and reconstruction footage.

Dr. Michelle Jeanis is a criminology, criminal justice, and sociological researcher. Her research interests range from missing persons, juvenile justice, media and crime, and gender and crime. Much of Dr. Jeanis' research focuses on the missing persons phenomenon. In this research process she works with law enforcement agencies to identify best practices for the recovery of missing persons and runaway youth. In addition, Dr. Jeanis has published peer-reviewed articles that examine the social forces that shape exposure of missing persons cases and related victim recovery. She also maintains the largest missing persons and media attention data base in the nation, which she uses to examine the missing persons phenomenon from a multifaceted approach, as well as train students in social science research methods. Dr. Jeanis earned her doctorate in criminology from the University of South Florida in 2017 and since then, has worked with several Florida and Louisiana law enforcement agencies in order to help bridge the gap between practitioner and researcher.

Sarah Smith graduated in Fall 2019 from the University of Louisiana at Lafayette with a B.S. in Psychology and a minor in Criminal Justice. She will be going on to graduate school for Clinical Psychology. She plans to use this degree to work with incarcerated and troubled adolescents in a rehabilitative setting, as well as forensic mental health assessment in a legal setting.

Kathleen Murphy is graduate of North Carolina State University with a B.A. in Political Science, 1985. She attended Campbell University Law School and received her Juris Doctorate, 1988. Ms. Murphy has been a family law attorney for over 30 years and has limited her practice solely to family law since 1988. Ms. Murphy is a member of the North Carolina State Bar, North Carolina Bar Association, NCBA Family Law Section Member, is a trained Family Financial Mediator and a trained Child's Advocate. Ms. Murphy is a contributor to an International podcast. Crime Stories with Nancy Grace is broadcasted daily and you can hear Ms. Murphy's comments on cases involving victims of family crimes and the impact of family court.

Haley R. Zettler is an Assistant Professor at the University of North Texas. Her primary research interests focus on corrections, substance abuse, mental health, and recidivism. She is a former Adult Probation Officer. Recent publications can be found in Youth Violence and Juvenile Justice, International Journal of Offender Therapy and Comparative Criminology, Criminal Justice Policy Review, and Aggression and Violent Behavior.

Jada Hector an accomplished mental health clinician with an array of experience from treating severe mental illness, substance use and abuse, juvenile violence and delinquency, persistent trauma, vicarious trauma, among other non-justice related topics such as relationships and sexual health. Ms. Hector specializes in forging systemic change for lasting success of mental health and substance abuse programming through education and technical assistance. In addition, she has co-authored scholarly work related to justice-involved persons and crime and mental health. She has experience monitoring and evaluating several federally funded grant programs (OVC/VOCA, SAMHSA, and FEMA). She is a graduate of the Louisiana State University with a master's degree in counseling and is a Licensed Professional Counselor in the state of Louisiana. She also attended B.I. Moody III College of Business Administration at the University of Louisiana at Lafayette where she earned an undergraduate degree in business with a concentration in marketing.

Kristy Fusilier, Ph.D., is the Assistant Director of the Counseling and Testing Center at the University of Louisiana at Lafayette. She is a talented Licensed Professional Counselor who not only works to aid in the help of students, but also mentors professionals working in the community. She serves as the coordinator for S.L.I.D.D.E., Student Leaders Involved in Drinking and Drug Education in addition to being an Instructor in the Counselor Education program.

Frances P. Abderhalden is a doctoral candidate in the Department of Criminal Justice at the University of Central Florida. Her anticipated graduation date is in May of 2020. Frances received her undergraduate and master's degrees from the University of West Florida in Criminology and Criminal Justice with a minor in Public Administration. Her past research work includes institutional corrections, life course theory, and siblings and crime. She has partnered and led projects with multiple jails and their stakeholders to work to improve jail conditions. Her current ongoing research interests include institutional corrections, primarily involving people incarcerated in jails, suicidality and mental health of inmates, reentry mapping between jails and communities, and correctional policy. Upon graduation she will begin her work as a faculty member at California State University, Los Angeles.

Rebecca Hayes is Associate Professor of Sociology in the Department of Sociology, Anthropology and Social Work at Central Michigan University. She received her Ph.D. in Criminology, Law, and Society from the University of Florida. Her research currently focuses on social justice, violence against women, and media impacts on the justice system. Further, her work has appeared in popular criminology and criminal justice journals, such as Feminist Criminology, Critical Criminology, Violence Against Women, and the American Journal of Criminal Justice. She is the author of a text, #crime, that features a one-of-a-kind look at the intersectionality of social media, our relationships online, and criminal behavior.

Katherine Lorenz, Ph.D., is an Assistant Professor of Criminology and Justice Studies at California State University, Northridge. She received her Ph.D. in Criminology, Law, and Justice from University of Illinois at Chicago in 2017. Dr. Lorenz is a sexual violence researcher focusing on the post-assault experiences of survivors including: help-seeking, reporting and disclosure, coping, and recovery in relation to social reactions and social support provided from various informal and formal/institutional sources. She engages the community through activism and advocacy in the areas of sexual assault, sexual harassment, domestic violence, and criminal justice reform.

Rashaan A. DeShay is an Assistant Professor in the Department of Criminology and Criminal Justice at the University of Texas at Arlington. She received her Ph.D. in Criminology from the University of Texas at Dallas, and her J.D. from Paul M. Hebert Law Center at Louisiana State University. Her research interests include offender decision-making, institutional corrections, prisoner reentry, wrongful convictions, and qualitative methodology.

Catherine Fontenot has been dedicated to changing deviant behavior and increasing public safety for over half of her life. She has worked with inmates, their families, crime victims, and their families and has toured and audited many jails and prisons both in-state (Louisiana) as well as local, state, and federal facilities in other states. She currently serves as the deputy warden (rank of major, of corrections) of East Baton Rouge Parish Prison for the East Baton Rouge Parish Sheriff's Office serving the Baton Rouge, Louisiana community. Major Fontenot has a wealth of knowledge from firsthand experiences with those incarcerated as well as knowledge gained through working with the public, press, and other agencies who seek assistance. Her specialties include bridging victim-offender dialogue, working with the media (including on documentaries and major motion pictures), coordinating major public events and symposiums, and expertise in the conditions of confinement (as a vetted expert witness). Further, Major Fontenot excels in advocating for resources and programming for incarcerated women and those returning back to their communities and families.

Additionally, there were other women contacted to contribute, but were overwhelmed and overburdening with participating in the true efforts to improve the issues surrounding women and prison. Thanks to all for current and continued efforts to help women. Special thanks to all future women working to research and inform on these topics.

Index

© Springer Nature Switzerland AG 2020
J. Hector (ed.), *Women and Prison*,
https://doi.org/10.1007/978-3-030-46172-0

Printed by Printforce, the Netherlands